Black Indians and Freedmen

Black Indians and Freedmen

The African Methodist Episcopal Church and Indigenous Americans, 1816–1916

CHRISTINA DICKERSON-COUSIN

1 2 3 4 5 C P 5 4 3 2 1
∞ This book is printed on acid-free paper.

Library of Congress Cataloging-in-Publication Data
Names: Dickerson, Christina, author.
Title: Black Indians and freedmen: the African Methodist Episcopal church and indigenous Americans, 1816–1916 / Christina Dickerson-Cousin.
Description: Urbana, Chicago: University of Illinois Press, [2021] | Includes bibliographical references and index.
Identifiers: LCCN 2021031554 (print) | LCCN 2021031555 (ebook) | ISBN 9780252044212 (hardback : acid-free paper) | ISBN 9780252086250 (paperback) | ISBN 9780252053177 (ebook)
Subjects: LCSH: African Methodist Episcopal Church—Missions—History. | Church membership—History. | Indians of North America.
Classification: LCC BV2551 .D53 2021 (print) | LCC BV2551 (ebook) | DDC 287/.83—dc23
LC record available at https://lccn.loc.gov/2021031554
LC ebook record available at https://lccn.loc.gov/2021031555

To my husband, Steven,
and to my sons, Steven and Samuel

Contents

Preface

This project began in 2004, shortly after I graduated from Spelman College in Atlanta, Georgia, with a BA in history. That summer, I began working as a research assistant in the Department of Research and Scholarship of the African Methodist Episcopal (AME) Church. While examining microfilm of the *Christian Recorder*, the official newspaper of the AME Church, I noticed numerous references to the Indian Mission Annual Conference in Indian Territory. I studied Indigenous history at Spelman, but I was unaware that the historically Black denomination to which I belonged had close ties to Native people. In 2007, I published a short article about my initial findings in the *A.M.E. Church Review*, the denomination's scholarly periodical. Over the ensuing years, I continued to gather more information. In 2015, I traveled to Oklahoma City, Oklahoma, where I did extensive interviews with Dr. Lonnie Johnson Sr., a retired presiding elder in the AME Church whose ancestors were pioneers in the Indian Mission Annual Conference. He and his family took me to Boggy Depot, Atoka, and other locations relevant to the subject.

It has taken from 2004 until today, 2021, to complete this work. In that time, I earned a PhD in history from Vanderbilt University in Nashville, Tennessee, I married my beloved husband, Rev. Steven Anthony Cousin Jr., and I had two beautiful sons, Steven Anthony Cousin III and Samuel Philip Allen Cousin. This book shaped a very special period of my life. I present it now, hoping that it both illuminates an unappreciated aspect of AME history and raises more exciting questions.

Portions of chapter 2 are adapted from my article "I Call You Cousins." I want to thank Duke University Press for allowing me to use this material. "'I

Call You Cousins': Kinship, Religion, and Black-Indian Relations in Nineteenth-Century Michigan" was originally published in *Ethnohistory* 61, no. 1 (2014): 79–98.

Portions of chapter 5 are adapted from my article "Triangular Integration in a Black Denomination." I want to thank the General Commission on Archives and History of the United Methodist Church for allowing me to use this material. "Triangular Integration in a Black Denomination: James Sisson, African Methodism, and the Indian Mission Annual Conference" was originally published in *Methodist History* 53, no. 3 (2015): 133–51.

Acknowledgments

Many people have supported this project. The late Dr. Lonnie Johnson Sr., the late Gracie M. Johnson, Lonnie Johnson Jr., and Donna Renee Johnson Rhodes welcomed me into their home in Oklahoma City in 2015. They provided me with information that I could not have gained elsewhere. Professor Kenneth M. Hamilton of Southern Methodist University, Professor Reginald F. Hildebrand of the University of North Carolina (retired), Professor Bernard E. Powers Jr. of the College of Charleston, and Professor Brandi C. Brimmer of the University of North Carolina have served as significant mentors whose guidance has proven invaluable.

James Engelhardt was the first acquisitions editor with whom I worked at the University of Illinois Press. He believed in the project from its earliest stages and guided it through the revision and peer-review process. Alison Syring Bassford, my current editor at the University of Illinois Press, has expertly guided the project through the final stages of the publication process.

Rev. Alfred T. Day III, the former general secretary of the General Commission on Archives and History (GCAH) for the United Methodist Church, offered crucial support for this project. During his tenure as general secretary, the GCAH provided me with a Racial/Ethnic History Research Grant that funded my trip to Oklahoma City in 2015. The American Historical Association awarded me an Albert J. Beveridge Grant that funded my trip to the National Archives in Washington, DC, that same year. I also want to acknowledge the staff at the Oklahoma Historical Society and the National Archives for their assistance. Additionally, I owe a debt of gratitude to Sean G. Smith at the Boston University School of Theology Library for digging into the archives and retrieving a rare document by John T. Jenifer that proved vital to my research.

Most of all, I want to thank my family for their unyielding love and support. My husband, Rev. Steven Anthony Cousin Jr., has never wavered in his belief in me, and our sons, Steven Anthony Cousin III and Samuel Philip Allen Cousin, have provided me additional motivation to persevere through this process. My father, Dennis C. Dickerson, PhD, encouraged me to pursue this project, read numerous drafts, and offered valuable feedback. My mother, Mrs. Mary Anne Eubanks Dickerson, has supported me every step of the way. So too have my siblings, Nicole Dickerson Kinnard, Valerie Dickerson Cordero, and Dennis C. Dickerson Jr.

A Note on Terminology

All terms are imprecise, but they are necessary for the sake of clarity. I use the terms *Indigenous, Native*, and *Indian* to describe the descendants of the first inhabitants of North America. Throughout the book, these terms refer specifically to Wyandotte, Seneca, Oneida, Ojibwe, and Pottawatomi people as well as members of the so-called Five Civilized Tribes (Cherokee, Creek, Choctaw, Chickasaw, Seminole).

I use the term *Black Indian* to describe people of African heritage who were enslaved by the Five Civilized Tribes. This term also refers to their descendants. Black Indians were immersed in Native cultures and sometimes had blended Indigenous and African ancestry. After the Civil War, the Five Civilized Tribes were forced to emancipate their enslaved population of roughly ten thousand people and adopt them into their tribes (the Cherokee technically freed their enslaved population in 1863, two years before the war ended). Thereafter, Black Indians also became known as freedmen, a term that was also a legal designation. I use the term *freedmen* to refer to Black Indians after emancipation. African Methodists began to evangelize the freedmen in the late 1860s and quickly recognized their hybrid culture and heritage. They referred to them as their "Indian-raised brethren."

Black Indians and Freedmen

Introduction
The Drums of Nonnemontubbi

Emma Thompson Hampton was born in Indian Territory in 1880. Her parents, Pink and Lucy Thompson, were formerly enslaved by the Choctaw Henry Folsom and the Chickasaw Pameetchie, respectively.[1] After emancipation arrived, Pink and Lucy married and began raising their children near Doaksville in the Choctaw Nation.[2] While living there, they were neighbors to Captain Nonnemontubbi, a Choctaw who likely earned his title during the Civil War. Captain Nonnemontubbi was friendly with the Thompsons and frequently visited their home. The Thompson children picked flowers and wild strawberries for him, and he taught them words in the Choctaw language. Most memorably, Captain Nonnemontubbi beat his drum every morning and every evening. Emma spoke about this ritual years later, recalling that "when he would first begin it seemed like we could not hear it so plainly but as he would keep on beating the sound seemed to just roll to us." She and her siblings heard the drumming "all of our lives" and, therefore, took it for granted until they left for school. When they returned home for school vacations they, "would be listening for the sound of that drum beating up at Captain Nonnemontubbi's."[3] The sound of these drums meant that they were home.

Emma's family members, who were interwoven into the complex cultural fabric of Indian Territory, also belonged to the African Methodist Episcopal (AME) Church. This historically Black denomination began its work in Indian Territory in the late 1860s and established the Indian Mission Annual Conference (IMAC) in 1879. By the early 1900s, this jurisdiction included roughly seventy congregations and 2,379 members. The Thompson clan, with its close ties to the Choctaw, helped pioneer African Methodism in Indian

Territory. The Thompsons attended and financially supported the AME church in Fort Towson in the Choctaw Nation. Pink also served on the board of trustees for Flipper-Key-Davis University, an AME school near Muskogee. Pink's sisters, Mary and Minerva, also belonged to the Fort Towson church. Mary married Alfred Gross, an AME minister who officiated Emma's wedding to Wilburn Hampton in 1900. Additionally, Minerva's daughters, Lillie Harris and Rosa Jackson Brunner, attended the AME churches in Fort Towson and Pecan Creek, respectively.[4]

The Thompsons were one of many Black Indian families who inhabited Indian Territory. The ancestors of these Black Indians were Africans and African Americans who were enslaved by the so-called Five Civilized Tribes of the Southeast. The Five Civilized Tribes included the Cherokee, Creek, Choctaw, Chickasaw, and Seminole Nations, and these tribes began enslaving Black people in the late eighteenth century. During their enslavement, Black people learned Indigenous languages and cultures. They also had sexual encounters with Indigenous people, creating mixed-race offspring. In the 1830s, the federal government forced the Five Civilized Tribes to relocate to Indian Territory, making their fertile homelands available for settlement by white Americans. The tribes brought their enslaved population on this forced march to the West, often called the Trail of Tears.[5] While in Indian Territory from the 1830s to the 1860s, enslaved Black people continued to have prolonged engagement with the language and culture of the Five Civilized Tribes. They also continued to have children with Indigenous people, children like Emma Thompson Hampton's mixed-race mother.[6] By the time of emancipation, the enslaved population among the Five Civilized Tribes had become a hybrid people with both African/African American and Indigenous language, culture, and ancestry. After emancipation, these Black Indians attempted to build lives for themselves in Indian Territory. They also sought to validate their Indigenous heritage by gaining formal citizenship within the Five Civilized Tribes. The tribes sometimes resisted such inclusion and denied that they had cultural or blood ties to those they had formerly enslaved.[7]

While living within this complex cultural milieu, Black Indians welcomed the AME Church into their communities. They appreciated this denomination's legacy of self-government and resistance to white hegemony. They also recognized that the AME Church, notwithstanding its predominantly African American membership, welcomed people of all cultures. Emma Thompson Hampton, who grew up in Indian Territory listening to the drums of Nonnemontubbi, also grew up listening to AME hymns and knew that the AME Church embraced her, too.

The Foundations of African Methodism

Erroneously, the AME Church is often viewed as a racially monolithic organization. Certainly, the vast majority of its members have been African Americans. Richard Allen, the denomination's founder, however, intended for African Methodism to be racially and ethnically diverse. He believed that promoting such openness would maintain the egalitarian roots of Methodism.

Richard Allen was born enslaved in Philadelphia in 1760. Allen's master, the Quaker lawyer Benjamin Chew, later sold him and his family to the Delaware farmer Stokeley Sturgis. Sturgis, whom Allen generously described as a decent man, nevertheless sold Allen's mother and other family members. While coping with this loss, Allen began attending Methodist revivals and was converted. With his master's permission, Allen invited Methodist preachers like Freeborn Garrettson to Sturgis's farm. Garrettson's impassioned words convinced Sturgis that slavery was evil. Thereafter, Sturgis agreed to let Allen and his brother John purchase their freedom at the cost of $2,000 in Continental money. Allen attained this objective in 1783, earning some of his funds by hauling salt between Pennsylvania and Delaware during the Revolutionary War.[8]

After he was manumitted, Allen traveled extensively. He had received his preaching license in 1782 and was free to become an itinerant minister. He spent several years journeying through Pennsylvania, Delaware, New Jersey, New York, Virginia, Maryland, North Carolina, and South Carolina, preaching mainly to white audiences. He also "spent about two Months in visiting the Indian Natives."[9] Extant evidence reveals nothing about which tribes Allen visited, perhaps the Lenni Lenape (Delaware) or the Haudenosaunee (Iroquois). Allen's efforts demonstrate that from the beginning of his ministry, he considered Native people as potential Methodists. In this way, Allen followed in the footsteps of John Wesley, the Anglican priest who founded Methodism. In 1736, Wesley attempted his first evangelizing efforts in the Americas among Indigenous people in Savannah, Georgia. He was largely unsuccessful, and—as was typical among British missionaries—he characterized Native people as noble savages. Still, Allen took seriously that Wesley desired to include Indigenous people within the Methodist movement.[10]

During his travels, Allen observed that the few Black people to whom he preached had been largely neglected. So, he eagerly accepted, in February 1786, an invitation to preach to Black Methodists at St. George's Methodist Episcopal Church in Philadelphia. In 1787, he and Absalom Jones also established the Free African Society (FAS), a mutual aid organization that assisted needy Black people.[11] Over time, Allen developed a significant following. As the number of Black Methodists at St. George's grew, white Methodists became uncomfortable with his evangelical success. As Allen explained, "when the colored people began to get numerous . . . they moved us from the seats we usually sat on, and placed us around the wall." One Sunday morning in November 1787, Allen, Absalom Jones, and a few others sat in their normal places. During prayer, white church trustees tried to physically remove Jones from his knees and force all of them to sit in a segregated section. After prayer ended, Allen and his friends, "went out of the church in a body, and they were no more plagued with us."[12]

Allen was profoundly disappointed and disgusted with the white Methodists' behavior at St. George's. These feelings were deeply rooted in his Wesleyan beliefs. Allen had converted to Methodism because of its egalitarian ethos. Early Methodists preached to Indigenous, enslaved Black, and poor white people without discrimination. They made clear that Methodism was for everyone regardless of race or social status. Allen had adopted this outlook, believing that it reflected white Methodists' "authentic Christianity" and "genuine religiosity."[13] He had begun to detect a change in his white brethren at the Christmas Conference of 1784, the meeting that officially created the Methodist Episcopal Church (MEC). He noted that "many of the ministers were set apart in holy orders at this conference, and were said to be entitled to the gown." Because of this push toward formalism, he lamented that "religion has been declining in the church ever since."[14] So when the white Methodists at St. George's displayed racial prejudice, Allen viewed it as evidence that Methodism was losing its way. It was this realization that ultimately compelled him to break with the MEC.[15]

After the 1787 incident, Allen and Black Methodists from the FAS banded together. In 1791, Allen purchased a plot of land at Sixth and Lombard Streets in Philadelphia. In 1794, he directed a pack of mules to transport a blacksmith's shop, which he had converted into a church, to the lot. Bishop Francis Asbury of the MEC named the church, Bethel, and dedicated it on July 29, 1794. For the next two decades, Allen and his allies struggled against white Methodists who argued that Bethel was subject to the MEC's jurisdiction. In January 1816, the Pennsylvania Supreme Court ruled against the MEC and granted Bethel its autonomy. On April 9 of that year, sixteen Black Methodists, disaffected by their treatment from white Methodists, met at Bethel.[16] These delegates hailed from churches in Pennsylvania, Maryland, New Jersey, and Delaware. They, ultimately, decided to merge their various unincorporated congregations into the African Methodist Episcopal Church.

Allen was elected and consecrated as the first bishop of this independent denomination.[17]

In creating the AME Church, Allen intended to "re-establish authentic Wesleyanism in America."[18] To do so, Allen instituted in his denomination the racial and ethnic inclusivity that he had witnessed in early Methodism. The AME Church primarily attracted African Americans, but Allen encouraged ministers to include an assortment of diverse and vulnerable peoples. As a result, AME ministers evangelized in Africa, Canada, the Caribbean, and Mexico throughout the nineteenth century.[19]

Spreading Methodism to Native people also interested Allen. He had begun this work in the 1780s, and the ministers of his denomination continued his vision. During the 1820s and 1830s, Jarena Lee evangelized among the Seneca in New York and among the Wyandotte around Sandusky, Ohio.[20] The AME Church also expanded among Native communities in the Midwest. The conduit for this expansion was John Hall, an Ojibwe from Michigan who became an ordained AME minister in the 1890s. Hall felt kinship with Black people because, like Indigenous people, they had endured white oppression. Also, he felt bonded to them because of the similarities that he saw in Black and Native worship practices. During his years as a designated "Indian missionary," Hall evangelized among various Native groups in the Midwest and brought them into the AME Church. Hall repeatedly used kinship language to describe his relationship with African Methodists. In his speeches before AME audiences, he called them "cousins" and "brother-cousins." No Native person described the essence of African Methodist and Indigenous interactions as poignantly as he did.[21]

AME work in Indian Territory became the denomination's most ambitious evangelization effort toward Indigenous people. African Methodists from the Arkansas Annual Conference spread to Indian Territory in the late 1860s and early 1870s. This initiative brought African Methodists into contact with the Five Civilized Tribes and the ethnically diverse Black people who lived among the tribes. African Methodists' interactions in Indian Territory compelled them to concretize the intercultural openness already inherent in their denomination. Toward that end, they established the Indian Mission Annual Conference in 1879. Whenever the AME Church created a new conference, the denomination constructed a complex infrastructure to support it. This included the appointment of a bishop, who would oversee the conference and appoint presiding elders and pastors. Meanwhile, as the IMAC developed in the 1880s and 1890s, Black migration to Oklahoma Territory steadily increased. The AME Church responded by creating the Oklahoma

Annual Conference in 1896. After Oklahoma gained statehood in 1907, the denomination divided the state into three conferences: Central Oklahoma (formerly Indian Mission), Northeast Oklahoma, and Oklahoma. The name Indian Mission Annual Conference fell out of usage.[22]

AME Perceptions of Indigenous People

African Methodists interacted with various Indigenous groups throughout the nineteenth and twentieth centuries. They recognized the plight of Native people and viewed them as fellow victims of white hegemony. They contended that Indigenous people would benefit from Christianization and American-style education as offered by a historically Black denomination.[23]

African Methodists expressed their concern for Native people in their denomination's newspaper, the *Christian Recorder*.[24] In October 1873, T. M. Malcolm wrote to the newspaper about the Modoc War, a conflict that occurred between the Modoc and the US Army from 1872 to 1873 in California and Oregon. The war ended with the Modoc people's defeat.[25] In his letter to the *Christian Recorder*, Malcolm pondered the tribe's future and offered a solution: "Could not the African M.E. Church, or some other body of Christian[s] make an arrangement for the removal of the Modoc Indians to the Indian territory on this side of the Rocky Mountains, and then train them in the arts of peace, open schools for the children, and preach the gospel to the adults?" He suggested that "one of the Bishops of the African M.E. church should confer with the excellent Commissioner of Indian Affairs, Rev. E.P. Smith, whose appointment marks a new era of hope for the election of the Indians."[26] Malcolm's suggestions reflected his genuine interest in Native people and his belief that it should be African Methodists who brought them religion and education.

In public speeches, other African Methodists expressed their sympathy for Indigenous people and connected their struggle to that of Black people. On July 13, 1876, Henry McNeal Turner and Benjamin Tucker Tanner, both future AME bishops, spoke about the Battle of the Little Bighorn during Sabbath services at "Mother" Bethel Church in Philadelphia. This battle occurred on June 25, 1876, and resulted in Colonel George Armstrong Custer's defeat by Lakota (Sioux/Oceti Sakowin) warriors including Crazy Horse. Turner spoke first and criticized those who pitied Custer yet ignored the suffering of African Americans. He contended, "I am sorry for the General, as I would be for any other man, but I could not forget that the General has been an apologist, and a defender of those who have been murdering Republicans in the South, and that hundreds of black men greater than General Custer ever was are sleeping in bloody graves, with the sanction and approval of this same picayune General."[27]

Tanner's remarks highlighted the hypocrisy of those who would mourn Custer while ignoring the relentless victimization faced by Indigenous and Black people. Tanner described Custer as a man who delighted in violence and who hated all people of color, including "red nagurs [Native people]." He contended that "have we tears to shed—and we have—we shed them for the scores and hundreds of our people who die violently every day in the South. Have we a heart to bleed, it is rather for our brothers cowardly assaulted and more cowardly riddled with Southern bullets." Furthermore, he argued that those who battled Custer and the Seventh Cavalry were simply protecting their lands, lands guaranteed to them by government treaties: "by the sacred obligations of treaty, no white man had any right or business to the Black Hill country. It belongs to the Sioux, and is guaranteed him by the nation. As well might the President allow men to come and put me out of my own house, as allow settlers to possess themselves of that region. If, therefore, the Sioux make war for his rights he does no more than the common law sanctions and the thing to do is not to fight him, but to secure him his right."[28] Tanner's remarks revealed his interest in and affinity for Native people. He saw a commonality between Black and Indigenous people in terms of the oppression they faced.

Still other African Methodists shared Turner and Tanner's concern for Native people. In 1884, presiding elder J. W. Malone, who was serving in Iowa, corresponded with J. M. Townsend, the missionary secretary.[29] In this correspondence, Malone contended that "we ought to educate at Wilberforce two young men of the Indian race so as to have their assistance in working among the Indians." He went further, stating that, "we ought to have an intelligent, young and active preacher to come out and learn the Sioux language or dialect so as to the [*sic*] able to teach and preach among the Indians." He hoped that Townsend would agree because of his "broad and expansive love for humanity, irrespective of nationality, race or color."[30] Eventually, African Methodists began evangelizing in South Dakota, though it remains unclear whether they reached out to its Native inhabitants.[31]

African Methodists clearly had an affinity for Indigenous communities. They recognized that Native people had diverse religious backgrounds but encouraged them to embrace Christianity just as Black people—who themselves had emerged from diverse African religious traditions—had done.[32] Notwithstanding the problematic history of the Christian encounter with

Native people, it is worth noting that these African Methodists believed that they were offering authentic racial egalitarianism. They viewed themselves as sharing with Indigenous people the same liberation experience that Christianity had provided to them during the dark days of slavery. They believed that theirs was the church for the marginalized and oppressed and that those Indigenous people who became Christians would fare far better with their similarly subjugated Black cousins rather than with their white oppressors. The Ojibwe AME minister John Hall certainly drew this conclusion, and he praised the AME Church for offering Native people a venue in which to engage in worship practices that were forbidden in white denominations.[33]

The African Methodist Migration

During the late nineteenth century, AME ministers sought to fulfill their denomination's egalitarian and emancipationist ethos. Toward that end, they had prolonged and substantial interactions with diverse Indigenous people within the Five Civilized Tribes of Indian Territory. The ministers first went to the region at the direct invitation of Black Indians including Annie Keel, and they received property and other assistance from Native leaders including Chief Allen Wright and Chief Green McCurtain.[34] The ministers' efforts led to the formal establishment of the IMAC in 1879 and the steady expansion of that conference in the ensuing decades. Throughout the existence of the IMAC, AME ministers from throughout the United States filled the pulpits of churches in Indian Territory. They were primarily men, and most were born in the South, whether enslaved or freeborn. Some married and had children with Black Indian women, becoming fully incorporated into their wives' communities. Integration, then, defined the AME denomination's relationship with Native people in Indian Territory.[35]

The ministers working in Indian Territory were part of a larger phenomenon that I call the African Methodist Migration (AMM). Beginning in the 1830s, AME ministers and evangelists traveled throughout the West. They sought out communities of African American migrants and later Black Indians and established churches and schools for them. Through the AMM, hundreds of Black religious leaders relocated to places like California, Montana, New Mexico, and Indian Territory. Some stayed for a few years, while others settled permanently. Their presence assured potential Black migrants that they could re-create their religious communities in the West. This assurance gave those who might have otherwise been too fearful to migrate an additional incentive to relocate to new and distant places. Those African Methodists who participated in the migration played crucial roles in their new communities, helping ensure their success. They were particularly fruitful in Oklahoma, where they participated in the all-Black town movement.[36]

Between 1865 and 1920, Black Indians and African Americans established about fifty all-Black towns in what would become the state of Oklahoma. Kenneth Marvin Hamilton's *Black Towns and Profit* correctly focuses on these municipalities as examples of Black economic enterprise. A deeper probe reveals that AME involvement aided the spread of all-Black towns and aligned them to the expansion of African Methodism. By 1907, African Methodists had built churches in Boley, Rentiesville, Red Bird, Clearview, Tatums, and Grayson. Numerous other churches would follow in the ensuing decades. These churches contributed to the social and cultural life of all-Black towns. AME ministers moved to these sites to pastor the churches, thus continuing the AMM. In 1911, a group of migrants even named their town, Vernon, after William Tecumseh Vernon, who was a prominent AME minister and a future bishop.[37]

The African Methodist Migration helped facilitate the movement of hundreds of Black ministers west of the Mississippi River, and these ministers aided the growth and development of Black migrant communities throughout the West. The AMM was concurrent with and reinforced other Black migration movements, like the Exoduster movement of 1879. It was unique, however, because of its duration and its association with a Black religious institution. Scholars have recognized both racial and economic reasons for Black migration yet have not fully recognized religious motivations. This book corrects this oversight.[38]

Argument and Chapter Outline

Black Indians and Freedmen argues that the AME Church pursued evangelism within diverse Native communities throughout the nineteenth and early twentieth centuries. In doing so, the denomination fulfilled Richard Allen's vision of creating a racially and ethnically inclusive Methodist institution. The outreach of African Methodists toward Indigenous people started at the denomination's inception in the North and reached its apex in Indian Territory, where African Methodists engaged with the Five Civilized Tribes. This book spans the period from 1816, the year that the AME Church was officially created, to 1916, the year that the denomination established Flipper-Key-Davis University, its flagship school in Oklahoma.

This book contributes to AME Church history by exploring the little-known narrative of the denomination's presence within a diverse population of Indigenous people. It shows that the AME Church never functioned as an ethnically monolithic institution. Scholars have recognized the denomination's appeal throughout the African Diaspora. James T. Campbell's *Songs of Zion* details the denomination's work in South Africa. Dennis C. Dickerson, who served as historiographer of the AME Church, has continually written about the denomination's efforts throughout the Atlantic World. Generally, though, scholars have minimized the AME Church's ethnic diversity and ignored its impact within Native communities. *Black Indians and Freedmen* is the first comprehensive study to correct this oversight. This book also sheds new light on well-known African Methodists like Jarena Lee and uncovers figures like James Fitz Allan Sisson and Cornelius King.[39]

This book also contributes to Methodist history in general. Scholars have become increasingly interested in intercultural interactions within Methodist denominations. This scholarship has neglected to fully explore the AME Church. *Capture These Indians for the Lord*, Tash Smith's otherwise thorough book on Methodism in Indian Territory, makes only a passing reference to the AME Church's efforts there.[40] *Black Indians and Freedmen* adds African Methodists to this important historical narrative.

This book also brings a new perspective to the exciting scholarship being done on Black and Native interactions. Scholars including Theda Perdue, Tiya Miles, Celia Naylor, Claudio Saunt, Barbara Krauthamer, and Gary Zellar have explored slavery among the Five Civilized Tribes. They have also examined the thorny issues of tribal citizenship and cultural belonging that Black Indians faced after emancipation. This history is crucial to understanding Black and Indigenous relations in the nineteenth and twentieth centuries.[41] *Black Indians and Freedmen* builds on this important scholarship and is the first study to comprehensively examine Native peoples' interactions with a historically Black institution like the AME Church. Taking this perspective reveals that Native people in the North and the West were receptive to a predominately Black church with a tradition of self-government and resistance to white hegemony. This book, therefore, displays a richness of interaction between Black and Native people that existing scholarship has not fully recognized.[42] In *Cherokee Women: Gender and Culture Change*, Perdue highlights the difficulty of reclaiming Native voices from non-Native historical sources.[43] As much as possible, this book emphasizes the perspectives of diverse Indigenous people, including Thomas Sunrise, John Hall, Allen Wright, Green McCurtain, Annie Keel, Robert Grayson, and John A. Broadnax.

Additionally, this book contributes to studies on Black migration to the West. Scholars such as Nell Irvin Painter and Kenneth Marvin Hamilton have demonstrated that Black migrants moved to the West to escape racial violence and to take advantage of unfettered economic opportunity. *Black Indians and Freedmen* argues that religious objectives provided another significant reason for Black migration. Through the African Methodist Migration, AME ministers moved to distant locales throughout the West seeking to spread African Methodism. This religious motivation must be recognized in order to gain a full understanding of Black migration.[44]

Chapter 1 establishes that African Methodists pursued outreach to Indigenous people from the inception of their denomination and that Indigenous people were receptive to their message. Chapter 2 builds on that narrative, showing that from the 1850s to the 1890s, Native people became credentialed members of the AME clergy and evangelized among diverse populations. While both chapters 1 and 2 focus on the North, chapter 3 shifts the focus to the West, specifically Indian Territory, where African Methodists began evangelizing in the 1860s and 1870s. It places AME efforts in Indian Territory within the context of the African Methodist Migration. Chapter 4 discusses the early years of the Indian Mission Annual Conference, while chapter 5 explores the diverse ministers who participated in the AMM and spread African Methodism among the Five Civilized Tribes in Indian Territory. Chapter 6 explains the complex infrastructure that African Methodists established in Indian Territory that allowed them to become incorporated into Black Indian communities. Finally, chapter 7 shows how the AME Church, because of the efforts discussed in the previous four chapters, was able to assist Black Indians in their fight for tribal citizenship through the Dawes Commission.

1

Richard Allen, John Stewart, and Jarena Lee

Writing Indigenous Outreach into the DNA of the AME Church, 1816–1830

Though usually described as a Black religious body, the African Methodist Episcopal (AME) Church, during its foundational development in the late eighteenth and early nineteenth centuries, identified with Native people. Perhaps, a fluid understanding of racial identity led early African Methodists to view Indigenous people, if not as brothers and sisters, then certainly as "cousins." The disparate activities of Richard Allen, John Stewart, and Jarena Lee established a precedent for Native interactions, and these interactions affirmed an ethos of ethnic diversity within African Methodism. While an infrastructure for Indigenous evangelization and Atlantic expansion had not been developed, the individual initiatives of Allen, Stewart, and Lee set an important example for future African Methodists. Their efforts reveal an aspect of early AME history that scholars have underappreciated. Allen and his contemporaries viewed their denomination as one open not only to Black people but to all marginalized people of color. They displayed this intercultural openness by reaching out to Indigenous communities from the inception of the AME Church.

This discussion commences with Richard Allen, the founder and first elected and consecrated bishop of the AME Church. Though his general biography is well known, scholars have minimized the intercultural openness that characterized his early ministry. This openness had a profound effect on the development of the AME Church, making it into a religious venue that welcomed Indigenous people. Allen began his ministry in 1783, after purchasing his freedom from slave master Stokeley Sturgis. Even before his manumission, Allen, already an active Methodist, had attained a preaching license.[1] From 1783 until 1785, Allen sojourned throughout the

Middle Atlantic, the Chesapeake, and the Carolinas. During this time, he spent two months evangelizing among Native groups. Extant evidence reveals nothing about which groups he worked among.[2] Nevertheless, Allen's actions demonstrate that he viewed Native people as potential Methodists from the beginning of his ministerial career. He poured this perspective into the African Methodist Episcopal Church both before and after its formal founding in 1816.

Due to Allen's foundational influence, AME ministers pursued outreach to Native communities during the 1820s and 1830s. In 1822, African Methodists sought out John Stewart, a Black man who had established the Methodist Episcopal Church's (MEC) first permanent mission to Indigenous people. Stewart defected from the white denomination to join the AME Church because he recognized the institution as one that would embrace his work with Native people. Jarena Lee, the AME Church's first authorized female preacher, emulated Allen and Stewart through her evangelization of Indigenous people in the 1820s and 1830s. Her efforts proved short lived because of an undeveloped denominational infrastructure. At the same time, African Methodists were also beginning their efforts in Haiti and Sierra Leone. All this work occurred during what Llewellyn Longfellow Berry, a historian of AME overseas expansion, called the "unorganized" period. During this time, which lasted from 1820 to 1864, motivated individuals carried out domestic and foreign missionary endeavors without consistent institutional support. It was not until 1864 that the AME Church established and funded a missionary department and elected a secretary of missions to oversee that department. Notwithstanding an absence of regularized operations for evangelistic outreach, an ethos of ethnic diversity informed AME identity.[3]

This chapter argues that Richard Allen, John Stewart, and Jarena Lee wrote Indigenous outreach into the very DNA of the AME Church. For their part, Native communities in the North welcomed Black religious personnel into their midst, interested to hear the Christian message espoused by other marginalized people. Scholars have not adequately acknowledged these experiences and have, therefore, underappreciated the extent to which Black and Native people built intercultural networks during the early republic period. These interactions between the AME Church and Indigenous communities occurred during the Second Great Awakening (C. 1795–1835), a religious movement that swept the nation and empowered Black evangelists, particularly from Methodist and Baptist denominations, to travel widely while preaching the Gospel. This chapter contributes to the historiography of the Second Great Awakening by illuminating unacknowledged examples of Black evangelists laboring among Native people.[4]

Richard Allen

Because of formative experiences during his early ministry, Richard Allen deliberately developed the AME Church into a sacred venue that welcomed Indigenous people. These formative experiences included his interactions with Native populations during the Revolutionary War, his friendship with Methodist evangelist Benjamin Abbott, and his two-month-long missionary project among Indigenous communities in the 1780s. Historians have failed to fully appreciate the role that these experiences played in Allen's life and on the development of the AME Church. Charles H. Wesley's landmark biography of Allen in 1935, *Richard Allen, Apostle of Freedom*, did not mention his interactions with Native people. In the 2008 book *Freedom's Prophet*, another major Allen biography, Richard S. Newman discussed some of Allen's experiences with Native people but did not analyze how these experiences shaped his perspective on African Methodism.[5]

Years before becoming a founder of the AME Church, Allen was an enslaved man living in Delaware with his master, Stokeley Sturgis. In 1777, while still enslaved, Allen became a Methodist. He was attracted to the young Methodist movement in large part because of its racial egalitarianism and the way that it reflected his understanding of the scripture. He recalled that the "Methodists were the first people that brought glad tidings to the colored people."[6] Methodist ministers genuinely sought out converts regardless of race or class, including Native people. In 1736, John Wesley himself performed his first evangelizing efforts in the Americas among Indigenous groups including the Yamacraw in Georgia. Wesley's brief but consequential experiences allowed him to conceive of a Christianity that was accessible to everyone and devoid of Anglican pretentions.[7]

Allen's early years as a Methodist coincided with the Revolutionary War, and during this time his labors brought him into contact with Native people. Allen recalled that he was "employed in driving of wagon in time of the Continental war, in drawing salt from Rehoboth, Sussex County, in Delaware."[8] He delivered the salt to various locations throughout Pennsylvania, including General George Washington's army encampment at Valley Forge. The Continental Army remained at Valley Forge from December 1777 until June 1778, and Allen's salt deliveries were critical for preserving the soldiers' meat rations. During his visits to Valley Forge, Allen was exposed to Native people from the Haudenosaunee (Iroquois) Confederacy.[9] He might have met the Mohawk leader Atiatoharongwen. Also called Louis Cook, Atiatoharongwen had an Abenaki mother and an African father, but was adopted by the Mohawk at the Jesuit mission of Kahnawake. During the Revolutionary War, Atiatoharongwen fought alongside the Continental Army and was present at Valley Forge during the winter of 1777–78. Allen also might have interacted with any of the roughly fifty Oneida warriors who arrived at Valley Forge in May 1778. Allen regularly preached on the route to and from his salt deliveries. His exposure to Native people at Valley Forge compelled him to contemplate their role in his ministry.[10]

After the Revolutionary War, Allen obtained his freedom and became an itinerant preacher. He soon developed a friendship with Benjamin Abbott, a prolific Methodist minister. His relationship with Abbott, coupled with his experiences at Valley Forge, pushed Allen to view Native people as potential Methodists. Abbott was born in 1732, became a Methodist in 1772, and evangelized in New Jersey, Maryland, and other locations until his death in 1796.[11] Allen first met Abbott in New Jersey during the spring of 1784. Allen spent significant time with the patriarchal preacher and attended several of his evangelistic engagements. He marveled that, "[Abbott] seldom preached but what there were souls added to his labor." Allen concluded that Abbott was "one of the greatest men that ever I was acquainted with" and described him as "a friend and father to me."[12] Abbott is the only religious figure whom Allen described with such effusive language and with whom he formed a fictive kinship bond. Historians have not sufficiently examined the significance of Allen and Abbott's relationship. This relationship was crucial, however, in demonstrating to Allen that racial egalitarianism was central to the Methodist movement and that Native people must be included within it.[13]

Abbott regularly preached to racially diverse audiences that included Indigenous people. While in New Jersey he accepted an invitation to visit a mixed Black and Native Congregationalist meeting.[14] The worshippers responded enthusiastically to Abbott's preaching: "many fell to the floor; some cried aloud for mercy, and others clapped their hands for joy, shouting, Glory to God! so that the noise might have been heard afar off."[15] This experience led Abbott to conclude, as the apostle Peter had in the Book of Acts, that "God is no respecter of persons; but all those who fear him and work righteousness, of every nation are accepted of him."[16] The members of the interracial congregation were so impressed by Abbott that many of them followed him to his next preaching appointment. On another occasion, Abbott recalled a meeting during which "three Indian women [professed] justification in Christ Jesus." He also encountered an "old Indian woman" who sought his interpretation of a religious experience she had undergone. Abbott assured her that she was saved and that "God would do greater things for her yet."[17]

Abbott's commitment to creating a multiracial Christian community that included Native people inspired Allen's reverence for him.

Abbott refused to tolerate the bigotry that he saw some Methodists display toward Indigenous individuals. Near Cape May, New Jersey, he met with a Methodist congregation that was attempting to expel a mixed-race Native man. Abbott explained that "some of them, having more pride than religion, could not stoop to sit in class with him; and to cloke [*sic*] the matter a little. They had raised several objections against him, and without supporting anything, insisted on my expelling him." Abbott, after observing the man's good character, refused to oblige the discontented white Methodists. Two of them were so offended that they quit the congregation. Abbott accepted their departure and crossed their names off the list of church members. In his view, their racial intolerance was incompatible with Methodism, and he preferred to lose their membership rather than compromise his beliefs.[18]

Allen probably remained in contact with Abbott throughout the 1780s and the 1790s, each man reinforcing the other's belief in the racially inclusive message of Methodism. Given their close familial relationship, Allen was surely aware of Abbott's continued efforts among Native populations. These efforts encouraged Allen to view Indigenous people as potential converts. Moreover, Allen's relationship with Abbott made the segregationist and exclusionary behavior of other white Methodists that he encountered all the more jarring.[19]

After Allen's experiences at Valley Forge and the development of his relationship with Abbott, sometime between 1783 and 1785 he devoted two months to evangelizing among Native communities himself.[20] Extant evidence gives no indication of which people he visited, but perhaps they were Haudenosaunee like those who had encamped at Valley Forge. Whatever groups he met would have had similar stories of war and land loss. The 1783 Peace of Paris, the treaties that ended the Revolutionary War, brought catastrophe for Indigenous nations regardless of which side they had supported. As Ethan A. Schmidt explains in *Native Americans in the American Revolution*, "whether they sided with the British, the Americans, or attempted to maintain neutrality, the Peace of Paris left them to the mercy of land-hungry settlers who moved quickly to appropriate native land and disrupt their cultural, political, and economic systems."[21] Allen's visits in the 1780s would have exposed him to communities struggling to maintain their sovereignty and their territory. To them, he might have preached that the same God who had seen him through his "bitter" days of slavery would sustain them through their painful and perilous experiences.[22]

Allen's interactions with Native people did not end after his two-month sojourn. In the late 1780s, Allen had sustained contact with an Indigenous man, Israel Tolman (Tallman), whom he hired as an indentured servant. Newman first brought attention to this relationship in *Freedom's Prophet*.[23] Tolman was born in Allentown, Pennsylvania, around 1773 and was the son of a white man and an Indigenous woman. Allen employed him in his chimney sweeping business in Philadelphia, probably as a part of his general effort to hire people of color and teach them marketable trades. It is possible that Tolman shared aspects of his Indigenous culture with Allen. It is also possible that Allen, drawing on his previous experiences with Native people, attempted to convert Tolman. Around August 1788, Tolman ran away from Allen, breaking his indenture contract. Newman surmised that Tolman fled to escape "the drudgery of chimney sweeping" and Allen's "fearsome work ethic."[24] Allen ran two advertisements in the *Pennsylvania Gazette*, offering a four-dollar reward for the return of Tolman. These advertisements were evidently unsuccessful.[25]

By 1787, Allen's accumulated experiences had shown him that the Methodist movement embraced all people, whether they were Black, white, or Indigenous. His view changed after an ugly and transformative incident in St. George's Methodist Episcopal Church in Philadelphia. He had been preaching to Black congregants at the church for over a year when white Methodists became discomfited by their growing presence. One Sunday morning in November 1787, church trustees physically accosted Absalom Jones and tried to force him, Allen, and others to sit in a racially segregated section. A disappointed and disgusted Allen left the church convinced that white Methodists at St. George's had abandoned the egalitarian ethos of authentic Wesleyanism. Afterward, Allen and Black Methodists from the Free African Society (FAS) banded together and established Bethel Church in Philadelphia. They dedicated the edifice on July 29, 1794. For the next two decades, Allen and his allies struggled against white Methodists who argued that Bethel was subject to the jurisdiction of the newly formed MEC. In January 1816, the Pennsylvania Supreme Court ruled against the MEC and granted Bethel its autonomy.[26]

In April 1816, Allen and over a dozen Black Methodists from Pennsylvania, Maryland, New Jersey, and Delaware met at Bethel Church and discussed their common grievances. They, ultimately, created their own independent denomination, the African Methodist Episcopal Church. For Allen, the "African" in African Methodist Episcopal was an inclusive term that encompassed a range of ethnicities. By serving as a sacred venue for marginalized people of color, some with and some without African heritage, Allen's denomination would represent the authentic Wesleyanism that the MEC seemingly had abandoned. The denomination maintained the same structure and theology as the MEC, as reflected in *The Discipline of the African Methodist Episcopal Church*, which Allen and Jacob Tapsico first published in 1817.[27] For Allen, what set his denomination apart was its commitment to racial egalitarianism. His denomination would serve as a corrective to what had gone wrong in the MEC. Allen was elected and consecrated as the first bishop of the AME Church. In this role, he encouraged his ministers to bring in members regardless of race or ethnicity.[28]

AME historian Dennis C. Dickerson was the first to recognize that Allen's disenchantment with white Methodists and his decision to create the AME Church were rooted in his Wesleyan identity, not just his racial identity. When white Methodists at St. George's pulled Jones from his knees during prayer, Allen was offended not only as a Black man, but more critically as an authentic Wesleyan. Allen believed that what initially set Wesley's followers apart from others was their commitment to a racially inclusive Christian community. To Allen, this proved that they truly believed, as Abbott did, that "God is no respecter of persons." When Allen had the chance to create his own denomination, he determined that it would serve as a course correction for the Methodist movement. That is why it was so important to him to make the AME Church racially inclusive. If the denomination only included Black Americans, it would be no better than the MEC. Previous scholars like James H. Cone have, understandably, placed Allen's creation of the AME Church within the context of the Black liberationist struggle. Dickerson, however, recognized that it was Allen's Wesleyan identity that compelled him to create a denomination that would truly reflect the racial inclusivity inherent in the early Methodist movement.[29]

Upon the creation of their denomination, Allen and the African Methodists immediately sought out members of diverse ethnicities. As a result, "ministers and members, Negro and white, and Indian were early admitted" to the denomination, and "missionaries were sent almost immediately to foreign countries."[30] Included among the Native people who were "early admitted" to the AME Church were the Montaukett, an Algonquian people living on Long Island in New York.

Throughout the nineteenth century, the Montaukett migrated to free African American settlements on Long Island like North Amityville, Eastville, and Freetown. They intermarried with Black people and created a vibrant interracial community. In 1815, Daniel Squires and Delancy H. Miller established a church in North Amityville for this mixed-race community, and it soon became incorporated within the AME denomination. Among the earliest members of Bethel AME Church in North Amityville were Elias Hunter and his wife, Fanny Hunter (née Cuffee). According to historian and genealogist Sandi Brewster-Walker, the "Hunter and Cuffee families are related to every original North Amityville family, and can be found among the Montaukett, Shinnecock and Unkechaug people."[31] In 1839, the Hunters donated the land on Albany Avenue on which Bethel's congregants erected an edifice in 1850. The church remained at this location until 1962, when the congregation moved to a larger space on Simmons Street in Copiague.[32] The original Amityville church burned down in 1989, but the Babylon Historic Commission erected a marker at the site to inform all visitors of its unique history: THE ORIGINAL SITE OF THE BETHEL AME CHURCH, ORGANIZED IN 1815 BY BLACKS AND NATIVE AMERICANS OF AMITYVILLE.[33] This church, established during Allen's lifetime, represented the very intercultural openness that he desired.[34]

Around the same time that Black and Native people were establishing Bethel AME Church in North Amityville, a Black preacher, John Stewart, was beginning his missionary enterprise among Indigenous communities in Ohio. Although Stewart began his pioneering work under the auspices of the MEC, he later defected in favor of the AME Church. African Methodists embraced his work, confident that it would fit perfectly into their ethnically inclusive denomination.

John Stewart

In summer 1822, shortly after the formal creation of the AME Church, a group of African Methodist ministers sought out John Stewart. Stewart was a freeborn Black man who had established the MEC's first permanent mission for Indigenous people. It was located among the Wyandotte in Upper Sandusky, Ohio. The AME ministers, evidently, hoped that Stewart would help them establish a similar enterprise in their denomination. Their timing was ideal, for Stewart had grown disenchanted with the MEC. He began attending AME meetings and decided to join the denomination.[35] He contended that "he could be more useful among his own people than among the whites; and that he had to make no sacrifice of principle in doing so, for they held fast to the Methodist doctrine, and, with but little alteration, to the Discipline."[36] Scholarly accounts of Stewart's life have largely ignored African Methodists' successful efforts to woo him. This event, though, is crucial to understanding

Stewart's life and African Methodists' early interest in Indigenous outreach. Historians have also failed to recognize Stewart's impact on Jarena Lee, a pioneering female evangelist in the AME Church.[37]

John Stewart's unlikely path to establishing a missionary enterprise among Native people began in Virginia, where he was born to free parents in 1786. His parents claimed Indigenous ancestry, but they were unsure of their specific tribal origins. Stewart later moved to Marietta, Ohio. Formerly a part of the Northwest Territory, Ohio achieved statehood in 1803. By that time, roughly forty-five thousand settlers lived there. The state prohibited slavery, but it passed Black Laws in 1804 and 1807 to limit Black settlement. Nevertheless, by 1810, Ohio had a Black population of roughly two thousand.[38]

While living in Ohio, Stewart joined the MEC. By this time, the MEC had been working in the region for several years and had established the Ohio Annual Conference, which included the Ohio, Erie, Shenango, Grand River/Mahoning, and Chautauqua districts. The denomination had made little progress among Native communities.[39] Around 1814, Stewart secured an exhorter's license and began his efforts to spread Methodism among Indigenous people. His first stop was in Goshen, Ohio, at a Delaware mission established by Moravians. During his stay, the Delaware informed him about their Wyandotte relatives who lived in Pipetown, a reservation in Upper Sandusky. Stewart began his pioneering work in the Wyandotte village in autumn 1816, declaring that, "he was sent by the Great Spirit to tell [the Wyandotte] the true and good way."[40]

The Wyandotte are descendants of the Huron Confederacy. They speak a Northern Iroquoian language and, historically, lived in the Saint Lawrence River Valley and in the Upper Great Lakes region. In the seventeenth century, French Jesuits began a missionary enterprise among them. Gradually, the Wyandotte incorporated elements of Catholicism into their traditional religious practices. Like most tribes, the Wyandotte suffered societal upheaval and land loss as they interacted with Europeans and Americans. When Stewart arrived, they were still recovering from the War of 1812. Some had supported King George III during this conflict and were facing repercussions from backing the losing side. In 1817, shortly after Stewart arrived, the Wyandotte signed the Treaty of Fort Meigs, which established their Grand Reserve in Upper Sandusky.[41]

Although Stewart was an enthusiastic missionary when he first arrived in the Wyandotte village, he lacked the language and cultural fluency that he needed to achieve success. He sought out another Black man, Jonathan Pointer, to assist him. Pointer was born into slavery around 1780 in Point

Pleasant, Virginia (now West Virginia). When he was young, a Wyandotte war party attacked and killed his master. The warriors took him to Ohio, where the revered Wyandotte chief Tarhe adopted him. Pointer remained loyal to Tarhe until the chief's death in 1818, even fighting alongside him during the War of 1812. His fluency in both English and the Wyandotte language enabled him to work as an interpreter throughout his life.[42] Pointer was not the only person of African descent whom the Wyandotte adopted. Samuel Wells, who was born in 1770, was captured by the Wyandotte around 1782, grew up among them, and also became fluent in their language.[43]

Pointer was initially reluctant to assist Stewart, in part because he found Stewart's naivete and attitude regarding missionary work in Native communities problematic. Pointer knew that Catholic missionaries had made inroads in part because some employed *il modo soave* (the gentle way) among the Wyandotte. This was a Jesuit policy of "tolerance of cultural difference that did not directly violate the basic principles and tenets of Christianity." As a result, the Wyandotte had developed syncretized religious practices that incorporated elements both from their traditions and from Catholicism.[44] The Wyandotte participated in their customary religious practices but also prayed to the Virgin Mary and used rosary beads. Unlike the Jesuits, the Protestant Stewart expected the Wyandotte to abandon central aspects of their culture, like the Green Corn ceremony, as well as Catholic practices.[45] Just as Pointer foresaw, Stewart faced understandable resistance to his approach. Between-the-Logs, one of Stewart's first and most ardent converts, recalled that "we treated him ill, and gave him but little to eat, and trampled on him, and were jealous of him for a whole year." Watching Stewart's perseverance through this treatment convinced Between-the-Logs and others of his sincerity and divine calling. So, they "adopted him, and gave him mother and children."[46]

Like other Methodist ministers, Stewart deployed hymnody to attract converts. Charles Wesley, who was John Wesley's brother, and numerous other composers created hymns that were poetic, aurally appealing, and imbued with Methodist theology. Stewart recognized the ability of hymnody to disseminate Methodism among populations with primarily oral cultures.[47] According to his colleague and biographer James Bradley Finley, Stewart possessed tremendous vocal talent. To draw a crowd during his religious meetings, he always "mixed his prayers and exhortations with songs." Probably, he sang hymns that had already been translated into the Wyandotte language like "Hail the Blest Morn" and "Come, Thou Fount of Every Blessing."[48]

During his ministry among the Wyandotte, Stewart remained connected to Ohio's African American community. He had sustained contact with the residents of Negrotown, a nearby free Black settlement that had been in existence since at least 1812.[49] Negrotown was "notorious—or celebrated, depending on one's point of view—for being a free black community that was also a haven for escaped slaves."[50] The free Black residents of Negrotown intermarried with local Indigenous people and often served as interpreters. Jonathan Pointer, for example, lived on fifteen acres in Negrotown, married a Delaware woman, and interpreted for the Wyandotte. Negrotown became an important meeting site for the Methodists. Stewart held his first religious meetings at Pointer's cabin, and throughout the 1820s, the Methodists held several other significant meetings at the settlement. Stewart's connections with local African Americans became crucial as he grew increasingly disenchanted with his white religious colleagues.[51]

In winter 1819, Stewart faced a challenge from local missionaries who questioned his ministerial authority. He admitted to them that although he only possessed an exhorter's license, he had solemnized marriages and performed baptisms of children and adults. He argued that necessity had justified him in performing these services, although he was not technically authorized to do so. These missionaries disagreed and called him a fraud. To regain his standing in the community, Stewart resolved to bolster his credentials. In March 1819, he attended the MEC quarterly conference in Urbana, seeking to become properly licensed as a local preacher. Several Wyandotte whom Stewart had converted spoke on his behalf. The conference unanimously and enthusiastically voted to grant him his license. Moses Crume, the minister in charge of the meeting, later effused that licensing Stewart, and thereby validating his efforts among Native people, was the highlight of his ministerial career.[52] This event occurred as the MEC was just beginning to accept the ordination of Black clergy. Richard Allen, in 1799, had been the first African American to become an ordained deacon in the denomination. The MEC added only a handful of others to these ranks in the next couple of decades. This reticence to validate Black clergy contributed to the rise of Black denominations like the Union Church of Africans in 1813, the AME Church in 1816, and the AME Zion Church in 1821.[53]

Stewart's appearance at the quarterly conference brought greater attention to his ministry in Upper Sandusky. On August 7, 1819, the Ohio Annual Conference, which was meeting in Cincinnati, formally recognized Stewart's Wyandotte mission and placed it within the Lebanon district. The Ohio Annual Conference also appointed a presiding elder to oversee the mission and sent missionaries to assist Stewart. James Bradley Finley became the first presiding elder over the Wyandotte mission. In this capacity, he led the mission's first quarterly conference and marveled at the multicultural experience. Finley remained presiding elder for two years and spent another six years serving as a missionary in Upper Sandusky.[54]

Stewart continued his labors among the Wyandotte, but now he did so within the jurisdiction of the Ohio Annual Conference. These labors included teaching a small school for twelve Native children at Big Spring in the winter. Then, around 1820, local white residents convinced some Wyandotte that they should reject him on racial grounds. These white people claimed that "as he was a colored man, the whites would not have him preach for *them*, although they considered him good enough to teach *Indians*; and that it was a degradation to the nation to have a colored man for their preacher."[55] This argument convinced some Wyandotte to reject Stewart and "discharge him in form." Finley admonished them for rejecting their "first teacher." He also assured them that he was now overseeing the mission and that "John Stewart had been appointed to help me." This pronouncement quelled the chatter, but it must have been a bitter pill for Stewart. He likely resented being Finley's "helper" at the mission he himself had established. Others noticed Stewart's apparent demotion and charged that "[Finley and others] had come and entered into Stewart's labors, and had thrown him off without any support."[56] Finley vehemently denied the accusation, but Stewart's later defection from the MEC implies that he saw validity in the charge.[57]

Amid the difficulties in his professional life, Stewart made significant steps in his personal life. In either 1818 or 1820, he married Polly Carter, a woman of mixed race living in Negrotown who was both literate and a committed Christian.[58] The couple lived on a sixty-acre plot of land on the Grand Reserve. Bishop William McKendree of the MEC purchased this land for Stewart with money that he had raised at various camp meetings and conferences. Finley cited McKendree's actions as proof that the MEC always supported Stewart. Stewart built a log cabin on the land and lived there with Polly, though it does not appear that they had any surviving children.[59] As Sakina M. Hughes has noted, many free Black people seeking to establish new lives attempted to "procure and settle lands taken from Indigenous people." Stewart's willingness to accept this Wyandotte land coupled with his Christian evangelism made him a part of the American "settlement process" in the West.[60]

While Stewart was developing his ministry among the Wyandotte, African Methodists were evangelizing among the Black community in Ohio. This community had grown steadily, despite racist efforts to prevent it. In 1810, there were 2,000 Black residents in Ohio. This number increased to 9,568 in 1830 and 17,342 in 1840.[61] African Methodists labored assiduously among this population. By 1824, they had established six churches in Ohio. In 1830, they formally created the Ohio Annual Conference, which included all territory west of the Allegheny Mountains. By 1833, this conference had fifteen ministers including Lewis Woodson and William Paul Quinn, who was a future AME bishop. This conference also possessed almost 1,200 members in locations including Zanesville, Chillicothe, Columbus, and Urbana.[62]

African Methodists in Ohio recognized that in order to fulfill the true purpose of their young denomination and follow the example of Bishop Allen, they needed to evangelize beyond the Black community. They heard about the MEC's Wyandotte mission and likely marveled that its founder was a Black man. In summer 1822, they sought out Stewart, evidently hoping that he would help them establish a Native mission for the AME Church. Finley explained that "[Stewart] was visited by some of the colored preachers belonging to the Allenites, which separated from the Methodist Episcopal Church. He attended their conference, and joined with them at that time."[63] Stewart was confident that by joining with the African Methodists, he could continue his pioneering work without experiencing the humiliations that he had endured in the MEC. So, like Richard Allen, Daniel Coker, Dandridge Davis, Daniel Alexander Payne, and a host of other Black Methodists, Stewart left a white religious organization in favor of the AME Church.[64]

Extant records reveal little regarding Stewart's ministry in the AME Church. Perhaps he gave his African Methodist colleagues valuable advice about how to create their own mission among Indigenous people. Perhaps he introduced the African Methodists to his Wyandotte converts in an attempt to compete with the MEC. Perhaps he sought out a different tribe altogether. Scholars can only speculate. It does appear that he evangelized among the Black population in the Detroit area and that his efforts led to the founding of Bethel AME Church there. He likely also worked among the free Black population in the Negrotown settlement, located near the Wyandotte mission. He died from pneumonia in 1823, only a year after joining the AME Church, and was buried on his land. The African Methodists who first sought out Stewart, apparently, abandoned their hopes of establishing a Native mission without him. A different AME preacher would continue Stewart's Indigenous outreach efforts within the AME Church.[65]

Jarena Lee

After Stewart's death, Jarena Lee paralleled his outreach to Native communities. Her work occurred during a period in which the AME Church could not offer sustained institutional support. This fact, as well as her lack of cultural fluency and linguistic training, prevented her from establishing a permanent Native mission. She was effective, however, in exposing Indigenous people to the AME Church and making them aware that it was a viable alternative to white denominations.

Lee was born on February 11, 1783, in Cape May, New Jersey, the daughter of free Black parents. Lee's spiritual awakening began in 1804, when she heard the preaching of a Presbyterian minister. Later, while living in Philadelphia, she attended a meeting led by Richard Allen, who was still years away from founding the AME Church. Set afire by his words, Lee realized that "this is the people to which my heart unites." She was converted and became a member of the Methodist Society.[66]

Over time, Lee became convinced that God had called her into the ministry. She discussed the matter with Allen, who said that the Methodist Discipline "did not call for women preachers."[67] In 1811, she married a Methodist minister, Joseph Lee. Over the next six years, she lost several children as well as her husband. Around 1819, she attended a service at "Mother" Bethel AME Church in Philadelphia. Allen, who by this time had become the first bishop of the newly established AME Church, sat in the audience as well. Richard Williams gave the sermon that day from the Book of Jonah. While preaching, he suddenly "lost the Spirit." Lee rose from her seat and began exhorting in his stead: "I told them I was like Jonah; for it had been then nearly eight years since the Lord had called me to preach his gospel to the fallen sons and daughters of Adam's race, but that I had lingered like him, and delayed to go at the bidding of the Lord, and warn those who are as deeply guilty as were the people of Ninevah." Lee's impromptu sermon convinced Allen, and he authorized her right to preach, though he did not formally ordain her. And so, Jarena Lee, a widow with two small children, began her itinerant ministry in the AME Church.[68]

Over the next several decades, Jarena Lee traveled throughout the Middle Atlantic states, preaching the Gospel on behalf of the AME Church. Although Bishop Allen had validated her ministry, she still faced opposition. During a visit to Salem, New Jersey, in 1821, she "met with many troubles." These troubles appeared in the form of a contentious elder, "who like many others, was averse to a woman's preaching."[69] Lee persevered despite this hostility.

John Stewart's legacy inspired Lee to reach out to Native communities, a fact that she highlighted in her memoir, *The Religious Experiences and Journal of Mrs. Jarena Lee*.[70] This autobiographical work has been available since the nineteenth century, but scholars have not examined what she said about Stewart's influence on her ministry. Instead, they have focused on her rhetorical significance and her unique role as a female preacher.[71] Lee learned about Stewart's Wyandotte mission in fall 1827 while visiting and preaching in Albany, New York. During her stay, she met Rev. Mitchell, a "good old" Methodist minister who carried with him and sold a book that she remembered as *The Essence of John Steward*. The book greatly affected Albany's residents and compelled them to "hold a fast." Lee was particularly impressed by Stewart's story and described him as "a Colored man" who had experienced a "miraculous call to the ministry" and became "the first one who succeeded in Christianizing the Methodist Indians in Sandusky and that province."[72] Lee felt an affinity with Stewart, who, like her, had pioneered a unique missionary enterprise. She was the first woman preacher to evangelize on behalf of the AME Church, while he was the first Methodist to successfully evangelize among Native people.

In March 1828, Lee made her first attempt to follow in Stewart's footsteps by evangelizing among the Seneca living at the Buffalo Creek Reservation near Buffalo, New York. Unlike Stewart, she did not intend to live among the Seneca and create a permanent mission. Her purpose was to expose this Native community to African Methodism and, perhaps, pave the way for future efforts.[73] The Seneca were the westernmost tribe in the Haudenosaunee (Iroquois) Confederacy and were thus designated as the "Keepers of the Western Door." They had been living at the Buffalo Creek Reservation since the 1790s.[74]

By the time that Jarena Lee arrived, the Seneca had already experienced a religious revival, this one spearheaded by Handsome Lake, the Seneca prophet. In 1799 Handsome Lake, deeply affected by the land losses and cultural assaults that the Seneca had endured, created the "Longhouse religion." This religion fused traditional Haudenosaunee beliefs with Christianity. By creating this religion, Handsome Lake demonstrated a way to adapt to outside cultural influences while also retaining Indigenous traditions.[75] Handsome Lake's religion became particularly popular after his death in 1815. By then, "many Iroquois accepted rejection of alcohol, and his concepts of social relationships, as well as concepts of good and evil that closely resemble Quakerism, which Handsome Lake studied. Handsome Lake also borrowed heavily from the Iroquois Great Law of Peace, emphasizing its values of reciprocity and mutuality."[76] So, by the time that Jarena Lee arrived in 1828, some Seneca had already embraced certain aspects of Christianity, but they had never seen a Christian messenger like her.

Black female preachers were a rarity during the first half of the nineteenth century. Lee's small cadre of contemporaries included Zilpha Elaw, Julia Foote, and Sojourner Truth, all of whom came from the Wesleyan tradition. Lee met Elaw in western Pennsylvania in 1839, and the two women formed a "temporary preaching team."[77] The next year, Lee followed her abolitionist inclinations and joined the American Anti-Slavery Society. She lectured at the organization's 1853 convention in Philadelphia, where she likely met Truth. Although all these Black women shared similar religious backgrounds, only Lee attempted evangelization among Native communities.[78]

In March 1828, two Christian Seneca sought out Lee. Probably, they had attended one of her preaching engagements in western New York. During their initial meeting, Lee asked the two men to pray, and they obliged her. They spoke in their own language, forcing Lee to face a communication barrier just as Stewart had with the Wyandotte. Despite her inability to comprehend their words, she claimed that she "felt the power of God in my own heart."[79] Afterward, the two Seneca privately conversed. Having developed a positive impression of her character and abilities, they invited her to visit the Buffalo Creek Reservation.

Lee and her two Seneca companions traveled together to Buffalo Creek, which was located roughly three miles from Buffalo, New York. When they arrived, fifty of the village's children were still attending school. When class dismissed, the village convened for its worship service. As they were gathering, Lee noticed an old man who "stood and prayed very devoutly, tears running down his cheeks." The prayers of this man convinced her of the genuine religiosity of the villagers, an assumption that made her eager to preach to them rather than simply attend the worship service. She conveyed this desire, and a Seneca council met to discuss the matter. The council members, ultimately, agreed to let her preach.[80]

Like other missionaries of her time period, Lee believed that Native people should embrace "civilization" efforts. She praised the Buffalo Creek schoolteachers for instructing the children in the English language and dressing them in "English style." She outright stated that Native people, "can be civilized and Christianized. We might call them heathens, but they are endowed with a Christian spirit."[81] By her words and actions, Lee seemed to endorse the same harmful cultural imperialism that white missionaries had been espousing for centuries. It is important to note, however, that she was a woman from an oppressed minority who viewed Christianity through the lens of African Methodism. To her, being "Christianized" was as much about fighting against the inequities in American society as it was about attaining salvation and spiritual fulfillment. She wanted to equip Native people with the knowledge that Christianity, as expressed by Richard Allen and herself, was a religion for the oppressed, not the oppressor.

Word spread that Lee would be preaching at Buffalo Creek. This news motivated Native people from eight miles away to sojourn there, even in difficult weather. Lee marveled that her presence elicited this reaction, saying, "it was in the month of March—it rained and snowed yet, they walked in their moccasins, and some bare headed. They made a large congregation."[82] The Seneca and their neighbors filled the church and waited to hear the Christian message as interpreted by a Black woman. It is possible that the Seneca were receptive to hearing from Lee because they practiced matrilineal descent and were accustomed to seeing women in positions of authority.[83]

The missionary who usually resided with the Seneca was visiting another tribe, so Lee conducted the worship service according to her own preferences. Aided by an interpreter, she instructed the congregation to sing the traditional Wesleyan hymn "O for a Thousand Tongues to Sing," which they performed "beautifully." She noted that "two long benches of them sang by note," reading from hymn books that were in their own language. Again supported by an interpreter, Lee then preached a "plain and deliberate and very pointed" sermon. Unlike the Seneca people's regular missionary, who "only taught them very plainly, and read out of pamphlets the experiences of others," Lee drew from her own rich personal testimony.[84] Her exact words remain unknown, but she might have expressed that God's grace had sustained her throughout her familial losses and the daily dangers and indignities that she faced because of her race and gender. It is unclear whether she made a direct appeal for her audience to join the AME Church, but at the very least she exposed them to the notion of a truly inclusive denomination in which people of color served as bishops and in other positions of authority. Her words deeply affected her audience, eliciting shouts of "Amen" and considerable tears. Sometime afterward, the missionary returned and asked her to preach again that evening. She declined, citing a prior commitment, and departed feeling "happy in my visit."[85]

Jarena Lee's next experience in Indigenous outreach occurred in summer 1830, when she visited John Stewart's Wyandotte mission. Some of Stewart's earliest converts, like Between-the-Logs, had died, but Wyandotte ministers including Squire Grey Eyes and Matthew Peacock had replaced them. The Wyandotte Mission Church had been erected in 1824, and its members remained devoted Methodists. The mission school remained open and continued to educate future ministers, traders, and lawyers.[86]

In 1827, three years before Lee's arrival, the Wyandotte had agreed to divide their lands on the Grand Reserve into plots for individuals and family units. This undertaking undermined the Wyandotte people's traditional form of communal land ownership. The Wyandotte enacted this plan with support from Methodist leaders and government officials, and as a result, "houses now went up in almost all directions; and it was done without any altercation. Villages were evacuated, and industry generally promoted."[87] By embracing Methodism and American-style farming and land ownership, the Wyandotte could credibly argue that they were as "civilized" as their white neighbors.[88]

The Wyandotte people's level of "civilization" did not save them from the horrific policy of Indian Removal that the US government pursued in the 1830s and 1840s. On May 28, 1830, President Andrew Jackson signed the Indian Removal Act into law. This legislation empowered him to grant unsettled land in the West to tribes living east of the Mississippi River. Jackson knew that by forcing these tribes to relocate, he would make their fertile lands available for white settlement. One by one, tribes made the long and arduous march to the West. The journey of the Cherokee is called the Trail of Tears and remains the best-known example of this process. Scholars are now examining how removal unfolded among tribes in the North. Mary Stockwell's *The Other Trail of Tears: The Removal of the Ohio Indians* narrates the experiences of tribes like the Wyandotte. She notes that after the division of their lands in 1827, the Wyandotte became prosperous farmers, even renting out land to neighboring white people. White settlements increasingly surrounded them, and settlers looked jealously at their economic success. Following the passage of the Indian Removal Act, the Wyandotte still hoped to remain in Ohio. In 1843, after over a decade of negotiations, they were forced to relocate to Kansas. Lee met the Wyandotte at the beginning of the tribe's decade-long removal process.[89]

During the summer of 1830, Lee traveled to Urbana, Ohio, for an AME quarterly conference meeting. Afterward, she rested in the area for several weeks and became acquainted with Polly Stewart, John Stewart's widow.[90] A likely scenario is that Polly remained an African Methodist after her husband's death, she met Lee at the Urbana conference, and the two women bonded over their mutual experiences as widowed pastors' wives and their connections with Native communities. Polly might have offered to take Lee to Upper Sandusky, knowing of Lee's admiration for her late husband's work.[91]

Polly had maintained close ties with the Wyandotte, so she, Lee, and an unnamed minister were welcomed at the Wyandotte Mission Church. Lee recalled that "we heard them preach in their own language, but I could not understand when he said Jesus Christ or God, and the interpreter had gone to the conference." When Lee addressed the congregation she spoke in English, probably telling them that she had been an admirer of John Stewart and that she represented the denomination that he had joined not long before his death. Afterward, she was "entertained in an Indian family, and they were very kind."[92] During her stay, which lasted for an unspecified amount of time, Lee must have examined as much of the mission as she could, soliciting information about Stewart's ministry from those Wyandotte who had known him. She certainly felt great satisfaction at physically walking in his footsteps.[93]

The presence of Jarena Lee and Polly Stewart at the Upper Sandusky mission must have caused the Wyandotte to reflect on John Stewart's ministry. Since his appearance in 1816, they had embraced Methodism, allowed ministers to establish a school, and adopted American-style farming and land ownership. They must have wondered whether those developments would protect them in the removal era. They could not know then that in thirteen years, they would be forced to relocate to Kansas. Just before they left, they reinterred Stewart at the Wyandotte Mission Church cemetery and fashioned a gravestone.[94]

Extant evidence does not reveal whether Lee remained in contact with the Seneca, the Wyandotte, or Polly Stewart. Although Lee certainly informed other African Methodists about her efforts, the AME Church did not build on her work with the tribes. During the 1820s and 1830s, the AME Church was in the so-called unorganized period of its missionary development. At this time, the denomination relied on motivated individuals to finance and perform mission work with minimal institutional support. Had the AME Church granted Lee substantial and sustained financial assistance, she might have been able to develop an AME mission to rival what Stewart had created among the Wyandotte.[95]

Lee publicized her outreach to Native communities within the 1849 version of her memoir. Her account showed readers that she, as one of the earliest itinerant AME ministers, had pursued Indigenous converts and that they had appeared genuinely interested to hear the Christian message expressed by a Black woman. Lee, like Stewart and Allen before her, sought to show that intercultural cooperation between Black and Native people was both possible and desirable.[96]

AME Outreach in Africa and the Caribbean

The early efforts of African Methodists toward Native people must be understood within the context of the AME Church's broader missionary endeavors. Around the same time that African Methodists were reaching out to Indigenous communities in America, they were also evangelizing in West Africa and Haiti. These efforts exemplified the AME ethos of ethnic inclusion. During this period of AME outreach, zealous individuals carried out their work without institutional support. This led to ambitious but unsustainable efforts.[97]

In 1820, Daniel Coker, one of the founders of the AME Church, arrived in Sierra Leone, in West Africa, aboard the *Elizabeth*. Coker was born in Maryland in 1780, possibly to a white mother and an enslaved father. He achieved freedom by the efforts of a Quaker abolitionist and then, in 1807, opened a school for Black children in Baltimore. Coker became a devoted member of the Baltimore African Church and represented that church at Richard Allen's 1816 meeting at Bethel. He spearheaded the incorporation of his Baltimore church into the new AME denomination. Due to his prominence, Coker was elected the first bishop of the AME Church, but he resigned the following day in favor of Richard Allen. A few years later, guided by the AME ethos of intercultural inclusion, he set sail for West Africa. He was among the first group of Black Americans to do so through the American Colonization Society. Coker gathered eighty-nine of the colonists, and with them he established a derivative body of the AME Church in Sierra Leone. He continued in this work until his death in 1846.[98]

During Coker's life, the AME Church did not financially support his enterprise in Sierra Leone. Coker was solely responsible for maintaining the church, or perhaps churches, that he built. The lack of institutional support remained the status quo for decades after his death. Finally, in 1891, Bishop Henry McNeal Turner traveled to Sierra Leone and established the Sierra Leone Annual Conference, the first AME annual conference created in Africa.[99]

At the same time that Coker was working in Sierra Leone, other African Methodists were immigrating to Haiti. Haitians had thrown off the yoke of slavery and achieved independence from France in 1804. They formed the first Black republic in the western hemisphere, and it served as a beacon of hope for enslaved populations throughout the Atlantic World.[100] In 1824, Haiti's president, Jean-Pierre Boyer, offered land to African Americans who immigrated to the island. He hoped that this diplomatic move would encourage the United States to formally recognize Haiti's government. Between 1824 and 1826, eight thousand free Black people accepted this offer. Richard Allen helped facilitate this process, and African Methodists were among these first immigrants. John Allen, Richard Allen's son, immigrated to Haiti and was hosted by secretary general Joseph Balthazar Inginac. Another AME immigrant was John Sommersett, a cigar maker and member of "Mother" Bethel Church in Philadelphia.[101]

The African Methodists who immigrated to Haiti soon called on the AME Church to send ministers to the island. In 1827, Scipio Beanes of the Baltimore Annual Conference became the first AME minister to answer this call. He established a church in Port-au-Prince that grew from seventy-two members in 1828 to 182 members in 1829; it became known as St. Peter's AME Church. During his ministry, he even performed the wedding ceremony of the French ambassador. He died on the island in 1835. Other AME missionaries labored in Samaná, on the Spanish side of the island. Over the next several decades, AME outreach to Haiti remained sporadic and insufficient in terms of funds and qualified personnel.[102]

The episcopal leadership of the AME Church recognized that the denomination's support for international outreach was lacking, but they doubted that the institution had the means to sustain both domestic and foreign efforts. Bishops Daniel Alexander Payne, William Paul Quinn, and Willis Nazrey reflected on this reality at the 1856 General Conference. In their Quadrennial Address, they contended that "one thing, however, is certain, for it is a fact of history that we have made two attempts to occupy foreign fields, but have never maintained ourselves in them. More than thirty years ago, in Africa and Haiti, we unfurled the bloodstained banner of the cross. Did many rally beneath it? If so, where are they now? If there were fruits to the labors of those venerable pioneers . . . where are those fruits?"[103] They could have added outreach efforts to Native communities to their list of underfunded AME enterprises. They believed that foreign work was important, but they argued that if the denomination could not do such work properly, it should refrain from doing such work at all.

In 1864, the AME Church began providing full support to the Home and Foreign Missionary Department and elected a secretary of missions to head it. The department had been created in 1844, but it remained unorganized until the first secretary, John M. Brown, was elected. The missionary department gradually grew in strength, and by the end of the nineteenth century, two women's auxiliaries existed that supported its work. Had such structure and financial backing been available to Jarena Lee, the denomination might have seen its own permanent Indigenous mission in the 1820s or 1830s.[104]

Conclusion

Outreach to Native people has been a part of the AME Church since its inception. The founder of the denomination, Richard Allen, performed some of his earliest evangelism among Indigenous communities. After witnessing the racially intolerant behavior of white Methodists in Philadelphia, behavior that was at odds with his experience with Benjamin Abbott, Allen created a genuinely inclusive denomination. This denomination, the AME Church, particularly embraced marginalized people of color. John Stewart appreciated the ethos of African Methodism and defected from the MEC to join the AME Church. He brought with him all the knowledge and connections he had gained as the founder of the MEC's first permanent Native mission. Inspired by Allen and Stewart, Jarena Lee evangelized among at least two Indigenous communities. The actions of Stewart and Lee occurred within the first fifteen years of the AME Church's existence, solidifying Native outreach as a legitimate aspect of early AME history.[105]

Native communities from New York to Ohio welcomed Black evangelists into their midst and listened to their version of the Christian message. These are significant examples of intercultural interaction that scholars have not adequately acknowledged. They demonstrate that when given the opportunity, Black and Native people in the North embraced each other as members of marginalized communities. To understand these communities during the nineteenth century, scholars must acknowledge the ministries of Allen, Stewart, and Lee. If not, they will be hard pressed to explain what happened next.

2

Seeking Their Cousins

The AME Ministries of Thomas Sunrise and John Hall, 1850–1896

During the latter half of the nineteenth century, two Indigenous ministers, Thomas Sunrise and John Hall, became credentialed clergy in the African Methodist Episcopal (AME) Church. Sunrise, an Oneida from New York, pastored AME churches in New England and Ohio, while Hall, an Ojibwe from Michigan, established small but significant missions among Native communities in Michigan and Wisconsin. The ministries of Sunrise and Hall represent a continuation of the Indigenous outreach efforts that Richard Allen, John Stewart, and Jarena Lee spearheaded decades before. These ministries were also concurrent with the establishment of the AME Church's Indian Mission Annual Conference in Indian Territory, demonstrating the appeal of African Methodism among Native people in geographically diverse regions. Sunrise preceded Hall in discovering the world of independent Black churches. He embedded himself within the AME denomination and, like many of his African American contemporaries, endured the vicissitudes of pastoral rivalries and eclectic denomination affiliations. Hall, for his part, seems to have encountered more amicable relationships than did Sunrise. Like his predecessor, however, he sought out the AME Church and concluded that Native experiences and aspirations closely aligned with those of African Americans.

Sunrise and Hall became African Methodists at a time when Indigenous communities faced relentless pressure. From the 1850s to the 1890s, Native people engaged in armed conflicts with US military forces to protect their land and sovereignty. They also fought to preserve their language and culture against aggressive "civilization" efforts from white people.[1] Sunrise viewed the struggles of Indigenous and Black people as painfully similar and inextricably linked. He embraced the AME Church as a venue through which he could express his affinity for Black people and fight slavery. Hall embraced the AME Church as a denomination that respected Native spirituality and opened worship space for its expression. Using kinship language, he described the historical connection between Black and Native people as a relationship between cousins.

The previous chapter argued that outreach to Native communities was a foundational aspect of the AME Church and that Native people were receptive to African Methodism. By examining Sunrise and Hall, this chapter takes that argument a step further, showing that by the latter half of the nineteenth century, Indigenous people had progressed from being receptive to the AME Church to becoming credentialed ministers in the denomination. This reality indicates that Native people in the North viewed Black people as fellow sufferers of white hegemony and as valuable allies against it. African Methodism provided them with a means to express their strong affinities for Black people and to fight against racist oppression. Scholarship on Black and Native interactions has focused on exploitation and slavery within the Five Civilized Tribes, an important topic that subsequent chapters will explore. This emphasis, however, has overshadowed stories like those of Sunrise and Hall. This chapter contributes to a more complex discussion of how Black and Native people interacted during this period. It also demonstrates that although the AME Church was a historically Black denomination, individuals like Sunrise and Hall ensured that it was not an exclusively Black denomination.[2]

Thomas Sunrise, Early Life and Ministry

Thomas Sunrise was the first Native minister ordained within the AME Church and, probably, the first Native minister ordained in any historically Black religious body. This position made him unique among Indigenous clergy, who typically worked through predominantly white organizations. Samson Occom, a Mohegan who lived from 1723 to 1798, was affiliated with the Presbyterian Church in the United States of America, an organization that was established in 1789. William Apess, a Pequot who lived from 1798 to 1839, belonged to the Methodist Episcopal Church (MEC) and then the Methodist Protestant Church.[3] Sunrise chose a different path. He chose a historically Black denomination that took seriously its commitment to cultural inclusivity and equality. He viewed the AME Church as the best venue for his ministerial talents and interests and remained loyal to African Methodism throughout his ministerial career.

Thomas Sunrise, or To-wis-car-ga, was born on June 1, 1829, near Utica, New York, the traditional territory of the Oneida.[4] In his youth, the US policy of Indian Removal caused painful upheavals within his community. By the 1830s, about half of the tribe had migrated to Wisconsin. In the ensuing years, other Oneida moved to Ontario, Canada, and to the Onondaga Reservation near Syracuse. Some remained near Utica.[5]

During Sunrise's youth in Oneida County, New York, he was surrounded by free Black people and abolitionists. By 1820, nearly all the 377 Black people living in the county were free. From the 1830s through the 1850s, residents of the county worked hard for the cause of abolition, submitting dozens of antislavery petitions. Perhaps the most impressive was their petition to repeal the Fugitive Slave Act, which 1,041 people signed. The presence of this antislavery fervor in Oneida County heightened Sunrise's awareness of the struggles of Black people and the abolitionist movement.[6]

Sunrise converted to Christianity as a youth, and the experience shaped the rest of his life. His conversion occurred on September 23, 1836, when he was only seven years old. He was in the midst of a deep depression, probably caused by the upheavals that the Oneida faced during this period.[7] Decades later, he recalled the exact circumstances surrounding his conversion experience: "One day, in a strange fit of fascination, he dressed himself up in bright colored clothes and ran into the woods, hoping a wolf or some other animal would find him appetizing and thus end his wretchedness. The night of the same day found him still alive, and he prepared to sleep in a hollow tree. It was here that he received a divine visitation and was told to pray and to take off his gay clothes."[8] Sunrise also recalled experiencing "a loud voice from heaven" and a "great ball of fire" that "burst over his head."[9] Sunrise's mother, who was already a Christian, motivated his conversion as well. Of Christianity's appeal, he would later explain that "he had found the gospel easy to understand" and easily "adapted to its wants."[10] He eagerly shared his experiences with his community, but was met with skepticism. He continued in his Christian religious development, learning the Lord's Prayer in the Oneida language.[11]

In the 1850s, Sunrise began his itinerant ministry, preaching throughout the Northeast and Mid-Atlantic.[12] During his travels, he learned that Black Christians had established a network of independent churches dating back to the late eighteenth century. This network was particularly strong in Philadelphia, a city that was then home to eighteen venerable congregations including Richard Allen's Bethel AME Church and First African Presbyterian Church. First African, established in 1807, was the oldest Black Presbyterian church and among the earliest independent Black congregations in America. The founder of the church was John Gloucester, who was a contemporary of Richard Allen and who, like Allen, had been formerly enslaved. Between 1848 and 1855, First African was without a pastor. A series of clergymen—Griffin Owen, Dr. Cuyler, and Dr. Joseph H. Jones, all of whom pastored their own churches—took charge of First African's affairs. They began to open the pulpit to guest preachers, and Sunrise took advantage of this opportunity.[13]

In April 1852, Sunrise preached at First African Presbyterian Church, formally acknowledging his respect for and interest in independent Black churches.[14] While the text of Sunrise's sermon has not survived, it is likely that he referenced the mutual suffering of Native people and African Americans and noted the latter's peril due to the 1850 Fugitive Slave Act. Having experienced the horrors of Indian Removal, Sunrise was particularly sensitive to the relentless intrusion of white authorities into people's lives. He might have preached a defiant message to his Black audience, assuring them that God would deliver them from the evils of bigotry and oppression. Sunrise's sermon was likely viewed as an audition for the position of the church's pastor. At this point in his life, though, his desire to travel outweighed his desire to pastor. Indeed, the next month he was lecturing in Maryland.[15] Although it did not turn into a permanent position, Sunrise's preaching engagement at First African was a significant milestone. It introduced him to the world of independent Black churches, a world that included African Methodists, who welcomed him as a beloved cousin.[16]

After his experience at First African Presbyterian Church, Sunrise continued to engage with Black Christians. Around 1852 in Maryland, he met Robert A. Johnson, a recently converted African Methodist minister. The two men began traveling and evangelizing together.[17] In 1882, Alexander Wayman noted the relationship in his *Cyclopaedia of African Methodism*, describing it as formative for Johnson's ministerial development.[18] Sunrise's relationship with Johnson was probably his first sustained contact with an African Methodist. The experience convinced him that the AME Church embraced Indigenous people. If he was aware of the connection between the denomination and the Montaukett on Long Island, that would have only bolstered his affinity for his AME cousins.[19]

Around 1853, Sunrise moved to New Bedford, Massachusetts, and began his pastoral career. He was ordained at the predominately white Middle Street Church. Then, around 1854 he at last accepted his first pastorate at the predominately Black Third Christian Church in New Bedford. Third Christian Church, organized in 1826, was known as African Christian until 1840. Its members originated in the predominately white North Christian Church, but they exited to form their own congregation. That Sunrise's first pastoral assignment was Third Christian Church demonstrates his continued affinity for Black people and his eagerness to participate in the world of independent Black churches. He filled his forty-member congregation with the belief that there were "better and brighter days" ahead.[20] His pastoral experience there prepared him for his future in the AME denomination.[21]

While pastoring Third Christian Church, Sunrise was certainly aware of the other Black churches in New Bedford. Among them was the AME church, which had been established in 1842.[22] James D. S. Hall served as the pastor from 1854 to 1855. During this period, Sunrise left Third Christian to affiliate with Hall's AME church. After establishing his good standing there, Sunrise attended the church's quarterly conference, which was a meeting of all the clergy and officers held every three months.[23] At this gathering, Hall granted Sunrise a preaching license, the first step toward his becoming an ordained minister within the AME Church.[24]

Sunrise displayed his serious commitment to African Methodism by seeking formal ordination as an itinerant minister. Toward that end, he attended the 1855 New England Annual Conference meeting in Providence, Rhode Island. The presiding prelate was Bishop Willis Nazrey, a broad-minded leader who, on the heels of the Fugitive Slave Act, had established a residence in Canada. On June 18, James D. S. Hall "presented the petition and certificate of Rev. Thomas Sunrise, to be admitted into the itenerancy [*sic*]."[25] The next day, the conference engaged in a lengthy discussion about the manner in which preachers like Sunrise could legally become itinerant ministers. Nazrey was eager to include Sunrise within the ranks of the AME clergy, so he consulted the AME Discipline for guidance. He determined that potential ministers would first face an examination to judge their sincerity for spreading the Gospel and their knowledge of the rules and regulations of the AME denomination. If the examiners were satisfied with their answers, the ministers would then take their ordination vows and be placed on probation for two years.[26] Sunrise faced this process, and, after a protracted discussion about his affiliation with Third Christian Church, the examiners passed him. The next day, the conference voted to admit Sunrise to the itinerancy, and he took his ordination vows. Nazrey, who needed as many qualified ministers as possible to fill the pulpits in New England, was pleased with this result. He considered the ordination of an Oneida preacher as perfectly in line with African Methodism and appointed Sunrise to the Maine Mission in Portland.[27]

Sunrise departed for Portland after the Providence conference and spent a year at the church, then located on Franklin Street.[28] He attended the 1856 New England Annual Conference meeting, at which Bishop Nazrey again presided. During this meeting, which was held in June in Boston, Sunrise reported on the progress of his church. He noted that his congregation was of a modest size, yet it still raised $2.50 for Nazrey's salary and travel expenses. Unlike at the previous year's conference, Sunrise was this time in a position to evaluate other ministers. As a member of the Committee on Orders, he helped examine and pass George A. Rue for his deacon's orders. Nazrey, for reasons that remain unclear, declined to send Sunrise back to the church in Portland. Instead, he appointed him to work for the bishop's general agent in Boston.[29]

Sunrise's growing cachet in the AME Church placed him in a position to affect important decisions within the denomination. In September 1856, Sunrise traveled to Chatham, Ontario, to participate in the Canada Annual Conference meeting. He might have been familiar with the area, given that Chatham was in the same region where some Oneida had settled. At the General Conference that past May, the members of the Canadian churches had successfully petitioned to separate from the AME Church and form the British Methodist Episcopal (BME) Church. They believed, particularly after the passage of the 1850 Fugitive Slave Act, that their futures would be more secure under the jurisdiction of the British. During the meeting in Chatham, AME leaders like Sunrise managed the logistics of the Canadian separation. In this way, Sunrise personally witnessed the impact of the Fugitive Slave Act, a law that resulted in forced migrations to Canada just as the Indian Removal Act resulted in forced migration to the West.[30]

One issue under discussion was which AME bishop would take jurisdiction over the BME Church. Sunrise, Bishop Daniel Alexander Payne, Elisha Weaver, and Richard Warren formed the committee that made this consequential decision. They wrote: "having duly considered the important question submitted to us, we have concluded . . . that the Rev. Willis Nazrey, of the Bishops of the A.M.E. Church, shall serve in Canada, in accordance with the wishes of the Canadian Church."[31] Nazrey was a natural choice. Along with Payne, he had been elected an AME bishop in 1852. Shortly thereafter, he began living in Canada and gained the favor of the Canadian churches. Sunrise had known Nazrey since at least 1855, and he recognized the bishop as the ideal leader for the BME Church. During his tenure in this religious body, which lasted until his death in 1875, Nazrey also remained a credentialed AME bishop. The BME churches returned to the AME denomination in 1884, a choice that reaffirmed the AME Church as an institution not bound by national boundaries, but open to those throughout the African Diaspora.[32]

After attending the Canadian meeting, Sunrise traveled to Ohio, where he joined the Ohio Annual Conference. Beginning in 1856, he pastored Bethel AME Church on Bolivar Street in Cleveland. As the Oneida pastor of a predominantly Black congregation, Sunrise became well known in the Cleveland community. He sought out new members by advertising his church services. From January to September 1857, the *Cleveland Leader* ran ads for his 2:30 p.m. and 7:00 p.m. worship services. As a result, Cleveland residents were informed about Sunrise and his work in the AME Church. Sunrise continued to pastor in Cleveland until 1859. Interestingly, in the 1860s, Sunrise's friend Robert A. Johnson also began pastoring in Ohio. In 1867, he established a congregation of forty members in Sandusky. Perhaps his earlier association with Sunrise influenced him to establish a congregation in an area where John Stewart had earlier carried on his evangelism among Indigenous people.[33]

Sunrise remained in the Ohio Annual Conference until 1859, when conflicts with AME ministers temporarily derailed his ministry. The year before, he had secretly joined the United Brethren Church while maintaining his AME membership. M. T. Newsom, an AME minister, discovered this fact after reading an unflattering article about Sunrise in the United Brethren's *Christian Telescope*. In the article, an elder accused Sunrise of "drunkenness and disorderly conduct."[34] The merits of this accusation are difficult to verify, but it is possible that this elder was playing into negative stereotypes about Indigenous people to undermine Sunrise.[35] Newsom evidently believed the accusations, and he informed AME leaders. In a letter, Sunrise defended his decision to join the United Brethren, complaining that AME ministers like M. T. Newsom and J. P. Underwood had been interfering with his work. For that reason, "he intended to go to his tribe" and "withdraw from the AME Church."[36] At the 1859 Ohio Annual Conference meeting in Cleveland, Sunrise was temporarily suspended.[37] He eventually returned to the AME Church, showing that this conflict did not destroy his affinity for the denomination.

Sunrise bounced around between several other denominations in the 1860s and 1870s. In the 1870s, he belonged to the New York Annual Conference of the AME Zion Church, in which he was appointed "a missionary to he [*sic*] Indians of Canada."[38] He also affiliated with the MEC. During this period, he hoped to evangelize in Europe. His passport application from 1872 requested authorization to travel to "Canada, England, France and other foreign countries." This application also described him as five feet five in height, with dark brown eyes, a Grecian nose, straight black hair, a copper complexion, and a full, round face.[39] It remains unclear whether his overseas evangelism ever came to fruition, but this application indicates his international ambitions.[40]

Throughout the 1870s and 1880s, Sunrise gave lectures across the country, defending Indigenous culture and advocating temperance.[41] In these ways, he was an important precursor to Progressive Era lecturers like Charles Eastman.[42] As he had for years, Sunrise often appeared at his lectures wearing traditional Oneida regalia, a shrewd marketing strategy that played on his audiences' desire to hear from an "authentic" Indigenous person.[43] John Hall would do the same when he appeared at AME meetings in the 1890s, and Eastman would later employ this tactic to great effect on his lecture tours in the twentieth century.[44] Sunrise's lectures placed him in the company of important government officials. Among them was Roscoe Conkling, a US senator from New York. Conkling, a Radical Republican who advocated on behalf of Black people during Reconstruction, once complimented Sunrise on his "mission and his zeal."[45] Sunrise also had the support of Edward P. Smith, the commissioner of Indian Affairs from 1873 to 1875. Endorsements from such as Conkling and Smith helped Sunrise secure future engagements.[46]

Sunrise resumed his ministry in the AME Church in the 1880s. His first appointment was a congregation in Providence, Rhode Island.[47] Then, in 1888, newspapers from around the country reported with astonishment that "Rev. Thomas Sunrise, a full-blooded Indian and once medicine-man of the Oneida tribe . . . has volunteered to become pastor of a colored Methodist Church at Putnam, Conn."[48] His decision to pastor this church should not have been a surprise to anyone following his career. Determined to help the struggling congregation in Putnam, Sunrise took no salary, content to "depend upon the generosity of his flock for maintenance."[49] Sunrise remained in New England during the 1890s, spending several years in Worcester, Massachusetts. Presumably, he continued to pastor, preach, and lecture until his death, sometime after 1891.[50]

This section has explored Sunrise's life and ministry and shown his commitment to serving as a credentialed clergyman in the AME denomination. His work validated the evangelization efforts of Allen, Stewart, and Lee and served as a logical next step for the racially open denomination. Sunrise was unique among Indigenous ministers, most of whom worked through predominantly white organizations. It is likely, however, that his affinity toward Black people was shared among other Native people in the North.

Thomas Sunrise, an Oneida AME Abolitionist

Having already examined Sunrise's life and ministry, I turn in this section to the way that he used the AME Church as a vehicle to undermine the system of slavery. As an abolitionist, Sunrise was, yet again, unique among his Indigenous peers.[51] He joined the AME Church in the 1850s, a time in which the US government's actions diminished the hopes of enslaved persons and abolitionists. In 1850, Congress passed the controversial Fugitive Slave Act. This law strengthened the 1793 Fugitive Slave Act and empowered federal officials to relentlessly pursue those who escaped from bondage and return them to slaveholders. The 1850 law enacted harsh punishments for those who refused to assist slave catchers. Freedom seekers and free Black people lived in constant terror. In 1854, Congress passed the Kansas-Nebraska Act, a law that created two new territories and allowed their residents to decide whether to permit slavery within them. The period known as Bleeding Kansas, marked by a series of violent confrontations between proslavery and antislavery advocates, ensued. In 1857, the Supreme Court dashed the hopes of antislavery advocates when it ruled against Dred Scott, a Black man suing for his freedom based on the fact that he had lived with his master in Illinois, a free state. The court concluded that Scott, as a Black man, was not a citizen and, therefore, had no right to sue. The tumultuous decade ended with John Brown's unsuccessful attempt to foment a slave rebellion in Harper's Ferry, Virginia, in 1859.[52]

The events of the 1850s struck a chord with Sunrise. As a child of the removal era, he had experienced firsthand how the US government intruded into the lives of Native people, forcing them to relocate. The Fugitive Slave Act reenacted this dynamic by empowering federal authorities to interrupt the lives of Black people and force them to flee to Canada or face slavery in the South. He personally witnessed how the Fugitive Slave Act compelled African Methodists to sanction the establishment of the BME Church in Canada. The particular struggles of Indigenous people and Black people were different, but Sunrise saw similarities in their treatment by the government. After recognizing an affinity with his Black cousins, Sunrise became an abolitionist. His association with the AME Church strengthened his abolitionist inclinations and gave him a platform from which to support antislavery efforts.[53]

Sunrise became an ordained minister in the AME Church in 1855, drawn to the unequivocal abolitionist stance of the denomination and its members. The very first AME Discipline, printed in 1817, addressed how the denomination would contribute to the "extermination" of slavery: "We will not receive any person into our society, as a member, who is a slave-holder; and any who are now members, that have slaves, and refuse to emancipate them after notification being given by the preacher having the charge, shall be excluded."[54] African Methodists also participated in direct action to undermine slavery. In 1822, Denmark Vesey, a member and class leader at Emanuel AME Church in Charleston, South Carolina, organized an unsuccessful slave revolt. As a result, the church was burned down, and its pastor, Morris Brown, fled to Philadelphia.[55] Sarah Allen, the second wife of Richard Allen, was well known for assisting runaway slaves. Her 1849 obituary declared that "the poor, flying slave, trembling and panting in his flight, has lost a friend not easily replaced; her purse to such . . . was ever open, and the fire of those eyes . . . kindled with peculiar brightness as she would bid them God speed to the land of liberty, where the slave is free from his master, and the voice of the oppressor is no longer heard."[56] Numerous AME churches served as sites on the Underground Railroad. Among those were Israel AME Church in Albany, New York; Brooklyn AME Church in Brooklyn, Illinois; Allen Temple in Cincinnati, Ohio; St. Paul AME Church in Bellefonte, Pennsylvania; Bethel Church in Wilkes-Barre, Pennsylvania; and Bethel Church in Gettysburg, Pennsylvania.[57]

Sunrise was unique in attaining ordination in a historically Black denomination and working as an abolitionist. He was not, however, the first Native minister to sympathize with Black people and to recognize an affinity with them. During the colonial era, Samson Occom developed a friendship with the legendary Black poet and antislavery advocate Phillis Wheatley.[58] In 1773 or 1774, Occom wrote to her about the onerous position of enslaved Black people. His letter has not survived, but Wheatley's response has. In it she declared that she was, "greatly satisfied with your Reasons respecting the Negroes, and think highly reasonable what you offer in Vindication of their natural Rights."[59] Decades later, William Apess preached throughout New England and acknowledged the connection between Black and Native people as fellow "people of color." In his 1833 speech "An Indian's Looking-Glass for the White Man," Apess defended the humanity and divine purpose of both races saying, "If black or red skins, or any other skin of color is disgraceful to God, it appears that he has disgraced himself a great deal—for he has made fifteen colored people to one white, and placed them here upon this earth."[60] Apess also cited the same scripture as had eighteenth-century Methodist evangelist Benjamin Abbott, declaring that "God is no respecter of persons."[61] By joining the AME Church and laboring as an abolitionist, Sunrise built on the ideology of Indigenous preachers like Occom and Apess.

Sunrise expressed his commitment to abolitionism at the 1855 and 1856 New England Annual Conference meetings. At both gatherings, assembled AME clergy affirmed John Wesley's antislavery beliefs. They pledged to "do all we can to arrest [slavery's] progress" and agreed not to "permit any slaveholder in our pulpits; nor any slaveholder in principle, we knowing him to be such, either white or black." They contended that anyone violating those rules would be "censurable by this Annual Conference."[62] At the 1856 conference in Boston, the African Methodists also condemned the violent actions of Representative Preston Brooks of South Carolina. That May, Brooks had nearly killed Senator Charles Sumner of Massachusetts, an antislavery advocate, by beating him with a cane on the floor of the Senate. The African Methodists condemned Brooks for this "attempt to murder" a champion of the antislavery movement.[63]

As was explored in the previous section, Sunrise accepted his first pastoral appointment in the AME Church in 1855. It was the Maine Mission in Portland, Maine. As the leader of a prominent Black church in Portland, Sunrise was in a position to support the abolitionist cause. Sunrise's members were a part of Portland's small but vibrant Black community. Some may have belonged to the Portland Anti-Slavery Society, established in 1841. The proximity of Portland to Canada made the city an attractive destination for freedom seekers, and Black residents willingly assisted them. Black stevedores and mariners aided those who arrived in Portland having stowed away on ships coming from the South. Black barbers helped freedom seekers disguise their appearances with wigs and fake facial hair. Antislavery advocates booked them passage on boats bound for New Brunswick, sometimes twenty at a time, or on trains to Montreal. The passage of the Fugitive Slave Act in 1850 only increased the traffic in Portland. Brown Thurston, a Portland abolitionist, testified to this reality and recalled once having care of thirty freedom seekers at one time. Given his clear abolitionist inclinations, Sunrise would have been compelled to utilize his church and encourage his members to aid desperate souls fleeing from slavery.

That the prominent abolitionist Reuben Ruby joined Sunrise's church is suggestive of the church's antislavery activism. Ruby had owned a cab (hack) stand since 1834 and was a prolific conductor on the Underground Railroad. Ruby used his home and probably his horse-drawn cab to assist freedom seekers. A friend of William Lloyd Garrison, Ruby cofounded the Maine Anti-Slavery Society in 1834. Ruby had helped establish the Abyssinian Church in Portland and used it as a station on the Underground Railroad. But like many others during the 1850s and 1860s, he defected from the Abyssinian congregation and joined Portland's AME church. The staunch abolitionist would not have taken this step unless he was sure that the African Methodists would support his antislavery activities. It is reasonable to posit that Sunrise assisted Ruby in his efforts.[64]

Sunrise continued his abolitionist work when he transferred to the Ohio Annual Conference. In July 1856, he appeared at Greenwood Hall in Cincinnati and gave his familiar lecture on Indigenous culture, politics, and religion. Ahead of the lecture, the *Cincinnati Commercial Tribune* announced that the proceeds would go toward "liberating an aged [woman] and [a] young mother and her three children."[65] Sunrise must have informed the newspaper about these plans. In doing so, he revealed to Cincinnati residents his abolitionist sympathies, and he signaled to others fleeing slavery to seek him out. Scholars have conclusively documented that freedom seekers in Kentucky frequently crossed the Ohio River into Cincinnati, where they achieved freedom.[66] The women whom Sunrise supported through his lecture might have been following this course. These women must have been fleeing dire circumstances since they were willing to face the added danger of traveling with small children. That Sunrise used his Indigenous heritage to draw in a crowd and then used that crowd's money to help freedom seekers is a remarkable action that undoubtedly earned him great respect among other African Methodists.

On August 1, 1859, Sunrise participated in a celebratory event that marked the end of slavery in the British Caribbean, twenty-five years earlier. Black people in the United States regularly commemorated this 1834 occasion, hoping that their nation would follow Britain's example. The 1859 event that Sunrise attended was organized by the Social Band Association of Allegheny and held in Breed's Grove near Allegheny, Pennsylvania. Omnibuses ran every hour to pick up celebrants and bring them to the site. During the festivities, the Social Band Association marched in joyous procession with local Sabbath schools and the Hannibal Guards, a Black militia unit formed in Pittsburgh in 1855. Sunrise, who attended while wearing "Indian costume," was one of the featured speakers at the event. His attendance at and participation in this event demonstrated his continued commitment to the cause of Black freedom.[67]

Even after emancipation in the United States, Sunrise continued as an advocate for Black people. Sunrise, then a pastor to AME churches in New England, lectured in Worcester in 1888 at a Quaker meetinghouse. He reminded his Christian audience that Jesus called on his followers to "extend the blessings of their purer religion to these less enlightened brethren who have suffered so much and been so wronged in the past." To Sunrise, these brethren included the "unfortunate Indian, as well as the poor African," who "should be remembered as equally entitled to the prayers and sympathies and aid of those who have been more blessed with this world's opportunities and means."[68]

A week after his speech at the Quaker meetinghouse, Sunrise lectured in Trinity Church in Worcester. Again, he highlighted the struggles of Black people. This time, he averred that the "prejudice of the white race against the Indians and colored people was the greatest stumbling block in the way of the conversion of the masses of the Indian race to Christianity." According to Sunrise, Native people were observing white people's treatment not only of them but of Black people as well. After witnessing slavery and the collapse of Reconstruction, Native people concluded that white people were insincere Christians with whom they wanted no affinity. He went on to explain his own understanding of Christianity, which was remarkably similar to that of both Benjamin Abbott and Richard Allen. He declared that "Christ's doctrine . . . was one of peace and love and good will, recognizing the common blood of humanity; it placed all human beings on a level, regardless of race or color, in the sight of God, according to the condition of the heart and soul." He contended that "the light of God enlighteneth every person that cometh into the world, and if we live up to that light we shall be saved."[69]

Sunrise's two speeches in 1888 culminated a lifetime spent identifying with Black people and, through the AME Church, fighting for their rights. He learned of their struggles intimately, forged consequential associations with AME leaders, and concluded that their fight against white hegemony was linked to that of Native people. By his reckoning, other Indigenous people saw this connection as well. As the first ordained Native minister in the AME Church, Sunrise was a trailblazer whose work validated the earlier efforts of Allen, Stewart, and Lee. The exact date of Sunrise's death remains unknown, but it was sometime after 1891. In the 1890s, another Native minister would follow in his footsteps.

John Hall's Early Life and Ministry

Unlike Thomas Sunrise, who pastored predominately Black AME congregations, John Hall pastored predominately Indigenous AME congregations. Hall's congregations were small, but his outreach efforts touched a significant number of Ojibwe, Pottawatomi, and other Native people in Michigan and Wisconsin. Hall showed them that they could eschew white denominations and join with their "brother-cousins," who would respect and accept them as they were. This was an attractive message to a population facing both cultural and physical assault.

John Hall was born into the Ojibwe (Chippewa) community of Saginaw, Michigan, around 1830. The Ojibwe are Algonquin-speaking Anishinaabe people; so too are the Pottawatomi. The Ojibwe resided, and continue to reside, in Michigan, Minnesota, and western Canada. Hall maintained a strong connection with Saginaw and appeared in *Saginaw News* on several occasions. Possibly, he had relatives in Mackinac as well.[70] In the 1890s, an observer described Hall as "a keen-eyed, wiry built man of medium size" who, despite his age, still had "raven black" hair that was cut in "American fashion." He was healthy looking, and "only the countless wrinkles and seams on his face [told] of the winters and summers through which he [had] passed." When Hall attended AME meetings, he wore "tribal dress" and the "insignia of his office as chief of the Chippewas [Ojibwe]."[71]

During John Hall's lifetime, the roughly nine thousand Native people in Michigan battled cultural imperialism and loss of land.[72] The US government was trying to "civilize" them through legislation like the 1887 Dawes Act. The government divided their reservations into individual allotments, which undermined the system of communal landholding familiar to them. The government also implemented a rigid educational system on Michigan's Native communities. In 1893, the Department of the Interior completed the Mount Pleasant Indian Industrial Boarding School in Isabella County. By 1894, Mount Pleasant had 145 students, most of whom were Ojibwe. At this institution, which was modeled after Carlisle Indian Industrial School in Pennsylvania, students were forced to abandon their traditional upbringing, speak English, and learn "gender appropriate" skills.[73]

Meanwhile, white Christians from various denominations pursued outreach to Michigan's Indigenous communities.[74] Initially, John Hall became associated with the Wesleyan Methodist Church and served as an interpreter for this denomination in Canada.[75] He also hosted camp meetings throughout Michigan in the 1880s, presumably under the auspices of that white denomination.[76] The tradition of camp meetings originated among Protestant denominations in the United States in the early nineteenth century. Large groups of religious seekers would gather in an open area, often in the woods, and "camp out" for several days. During these meetings, they listened to various preachers, prayed, and sang. Many converted to Christianity or renewed their commitment to the faith. These services often became emotional, and participants might be "struck down" by the "power of God."[77] Native ministers like Peter Jones regularly participated in camp meetings. In 1827, Jones attended a gathering with sixty Indigenous people, most of whom were from Lake Simcoe. He reported that "I spoke to them the words of eternal life; they paid great attention and were much affected."[78] By Hall's time, camp meetings were a regular feature of Protestant evangelism.

After spending several years evangelizing through the Wesleyan Methodist Church, Hall became disenchanted with the organization. It remains unclear whether a specific incident caused him to defect. More likely, a series of events and slights over time compelled him to conclude, as Sunrise had, that the AME Church was a better alternative for him.

John Hall Joins His AME Cousins

Hall's introduction to African Methodism began in the 1880s, at the same time that Sunrise was pastoring AME churches in New England and defending Black people in his lectures. In 1887, Hall attended the Michigan Annual Conference meeting of the AME Church, which was held in Battle Creek. He evidently liked what he saw, and he joined the denomination. In this way, he was similar to John Stewart, who also defected from a white Methodist organization in favor of the AME Church.[79] Hall later explained that, "[Native people] have the same feelings [Black people] have. We are not afraid or ashamed to shout when the Great Spirit comes into our hearts. We cannot do that among the whites. When tears come into our eyes and we want to shout, they say, 'take them outdoors.'"[80] Hall appreciated the similarities that he saw between Black and Native worship practices. During this time when Indigenous cultures were under attack, Hall chose to join with people who would respect these cultures.

After he joined the AME Church in 1887, Hall spent the next several years evangelizing among Native communities in Michigan. In 1890, he attended the Michigan Annual Conference meeting in East Saginaw. During this event, he made a significant speech and explained his vision for the AME Church's Indigenous outreach efforts. He began his remarks by informing his audience that "it has been handed down from one generation to another that you are my dear cousins; that such is the relation between the Indian and colored man. It has been handed down from the old Indians a long time ago, before we saw each other."[81] After affirming this historical connection, Hall stated his true purpose: "Now I want to ask you, brother-cousins, if I could get protection in your conference. I want a home and I want a father, and I want to get a man who would go and organize a church; or if you will give me permission to organize a church." He claimed that "[Native people] are not capable of organizing a church as well as our brother-cousins. I wish you would please give us your attention and send your missionaries to us."[82] Hall respected the structure and the longevity of the AME Church, and he believed that this denomination could accomplish substantial work among Indigenous communities in Michigan.

Hall's speech made a "good impression" on the assembled African Methodists. Bishop John Mifflin Brown directed presiding elder Robinson Jeffries to place Hall "in such relationship as would enable the conference to utilize his services."[83] The result was that Hall was formally appointed the conference's "Indian Missionary." In this role, Hall traveled throughout Michigan promoting African Methodism among Native people. The members of the Michigan Annual Conference had been wanting to do outreach among the Ojibwe for awhile. Presiding elder James M. Henderson explained that "there is a large settlement of this tribe in the northeast section of the state, in which we have been interested for the past two years." Hall enabled the African Methodists to perform their desired outreach.[84]

Hall's appointment in the AME Church drew the attention of local newspapers. The *Detroit Free Press* reported that "among the more important steps taken yesterday [at the annual conference] was the engagement of John Hall, an Indian of the Chippewa tribe, to do mission work among the noble red men of Michigan's forests. John appeared before the conference and asked that something be done for his people."[85] *Saginaw News* cited Hall as the "Indian Missionary." The *Plaindealer*, a Black newspaper in Detroit, referred to him as the "Missionary to Chippewa Indians," and explained that "John Hall, the Indian, was received into church membership and appointed missionary with instructions to report to the presiding elder every quarter."[86] These articles in the *Detroit Free Press*, *Saginaw News*, and *Plaindealer* publicized Hall's name and made his association with the AME Church known throughout Michigan.[87]

Hall's first efforts as the AME Church's Indian missionary delighted his presiding elder, James M. Henderson. In November 1891, Henderson related that "we are pleased with the work of our missionary among the Indians. Rev. John Hall . . . has in his own veins a large percent of Indian blood." He noted that the Native communities that Hall visited were "highly pleased with the service of our church."[88] During his visits, Hall might have emphasized that unlike white people, African Methodists embraced enthusiastic worship and sympathized with Native people, who had similarly suffered under hegemonic oppression.

John Hall envisaged his relationship with Black people and particularly African Methodists in kinship terms, repeatedly referring to them as "brothers" and "cousins." As he once explained, "old Indians used to call colored men cousins, so I call you cousins."[89] Kinship was a core concept in Anishinaabe culture. It referred to the connection formed between people based on blood, marriage, and adoption. As early as the seventeenth century, the Anishinaabe organized their communities around the kinship network, or *nindoodemag*.[90] Whenever John Hall spoke to AME audiences, he used the terms "brother" and "cousin" synonymously. To him, both indicated a close familial relationship in which duty and affection were affirmed. These words were so closely connected to him that he merged them to create a new term, "brother-cousin."[91] In the Ojibwe language, *niikaanis* could refer to both a brother and a male parallel cousin. Perhaps "brother-cousin" was Hall's interpretation of this word.[92] In Hall's view, the common struggle that Black and Native people faced created a brotherly connection and a mutual understanding. This is a sharp contrast to the more formal and distant "father-child" relationship that Indigenous communities had established with Europeans and Euro-Americans.[93] Hall used kinship language to establish a connection between himself and the African Methodists. He hoped that by appealing to their sense of familial responsibility and by acknowledging their common struggle, he would encourage their continued support of their Indigenous kin.[94]

At the 1890 Michigan Annual Conference meeting, John Hall went beyond merely using kinship language to express his familial affection toward AMEs. After his speech, which was laden with kinship terms, he had a warm encounter with Rev. David A. Graham, the conference's secretary. At that meeting, Bishop Brown transferred Graham from Michigan to Iowa. Clergy and laypeople extended their best wishes to Graham. Hall showed his affection and appreciation for his "cousin" Graham by kissing him and making a joyful exclamation. As the conference scribe explained, "the last to take leave of [Rev. Graham] was Mr. Hall, the Indian, who kissed him with a loud report as he exclaimed 'Bazhoo!'"[95] *Bazhoo* or *boozhoo* means "hello" in the Ojibwe language.[96] By saying hello rather than good-bye, Hall expressed his belief that although Graham was leaving, he would remain among his friends in spirit.[97]

Hall's attitude toward Black people was informed by his place and time. Growing up in Michigan, Hall lived among a small but expanding Black population. In the 1830s, during Hall's youth, this population was roughly two hundred. Since slavery was prohibited in Michigan, most of this population was composed of free people. The state even became a crucial site for the Underground Railroad.[98] By 1880, the number of Black people in Michigan had risen to 15,100, and Black institutions like the AME Church had spread throughout the state.[99] Meaningful interactions between Black and Native communities were limited, but, as John Hall's example shows, they certainly occurred. Because of Michigan's demographic makeup and the relative absence of slavery throughout the state's history, Hall would have had minimal interaction with enslaved persons. Hence, he was not exposed to the kinds of prejudices that some Native people in Indian Territory held toward Black people.[100]

While engaging in his Indigenous outreach efforts, Hall solidified his position within the AME clergy by becoming an ordained itinerant deacon. Hall probably obtained ministerial credentials in the Wesleyan Methodist Church, which would have made this transition easier. As a deacon in the AME Church he would be required to "attend the General Superintendent [Bishop] and the Presiding Elder whenever they are present in his charge, and, shall give them by letter, all necessary information concerning the condition of his work."[101] In the absence of an elder, he would be empowered to perform baptisms and solemnize marriages. Also, he would have to "take an exact account of the number of members in the Society on his circuit, or in his station, and present it to the Annual Conference to be printed in the minutes."[102] Hall was dutiful in fulfilling these obligations throughout his tenure in the AME Church.

Hall applied for the diaconate at the 1892 Michigan Annual Conference meeting in Jackson. On September 3, he and two other ministers went before a three-person committee to undergo examination and demonstrate their qualifications for deacon's orders.[103] To prepare for this examination, Hall and his companions would have progressed through a rigorous two-year course of study as prescribed in the AME Discipline. During his examination in 1892, the committee members would have tested Hall and the others on their knowledge of scripture, theology, and the history and structure of the AME Church.[104] Following the evaluation, the committee members stated that "after carefully and prayerfully examining them, we find they are qualified to exercise the office of a Deacon in the Church of God. Therefore, we recommend them to be ordained Deacon under the missionary rule."[105] Hall was ordained a deacon on September 4 at the AME church in Jackson. Bishop Henry McNeal Turner preached the ordination sermon and presided during the ordination service. As a part of the ritual, Turner laid hands on Hall's head, an ordination practice that imparts spiritual power from the Holy Spirit. Turner probably viewed the ordination of this Ojibwe minister as a fitting continuation of his work among the Five Civilized Tribes, a subject that subsequent chapters will examine.[106] It was also a fitting continuation of the ministries of Allen, Stewart, Lee, and Sunrise.

John Hall's Indigenous Outreach

From 1890 to 1896, John Hall spread African Methodism among Native people in Michigan and Wisconsin. While not all those who heard him preach formally joined the AME Church, they still were exposed to the idea that the denomination was a viable alternative to the white institutions in which they had felt so stifled. During this time, when Native cultures were under attack, Hall preached that crying aloud "when the Great Spirit comes into our hearts" was acceptable among African Methodists. This was an appealing message for those Native people who wanted to maintain their traditional worship practices while also adjusting to the "civilization" program. Those who did join the AME Church became part of an institution in which Black people had enjoyed complete autonomy for nearly a century. It was gratifying for these Native people to view their Black "brother-cousins" successfully resisting white authority and domination.[107]

Hall reported on his progress at the 1892 Michigan Annual Conference in Jackson. He declared that the "Indians are getting along first-rate, but we want something more besides getting along."[108] He listed the following as the sites of his outreach efforts: the Isabella settlement, Seaton Station, Oscoda, Kakalling, Saginaw, Swan Creek, Aug-gans-te-gang, and De-wah-ne-gang. Between all these locations, Hall reported that fourteen Native people had become official members of the AME Church. This was certainly a small number, but it was larger than the membership at AME churches in Bay City and West Detroit. Also, regardless of whether they officially joined, Indigenous people at these sites heard Hall's message. Prior to his efforts, they might have never known that an institution like the AME Church existed. Hall showed them that they could worship among their "brother-cousins" and eschew affiliation with white religious groups. During the 1892 meeting, Hall also made an appeal for books so that he could encourage English literacy among Native youths.[109]

The Isabella settlement, which was created by treaty in 1855, was one of several sites of John Hall's outreach efforts. In the treaty, representatives from the Saginaw, Swan Creek, and Black River bands of Ojibwe agreed to accept a permanent reservation in Isabella County and relinquish all other lands in Michigan. Their reservation was eventually divided into allotments, destroying the system of communal ownership familiar to them. To survive, the Indigenous community in Isabella ascribed to aspects of "civilization" like living in fixed dwellings, speaking English, and attending the Mount Pleasant school. They converted to Christianity, and by 1891, roughly two hundred belonged to the four churches of the Isabella Mission. They also maintained traditional aspects of their culture such as speaking their native language and living together in small settlements instead of residing among white people.[110]

When John Hall visited the "Isabell settlement," he met with 162 of the area's Indigenous people.[111] He described forty-two of these as being Christians, meaning, "those that have got the burning in the heart."[112] The exact identities of these Isabella residents remain unknown, but Hall would have met people like Peter Jackson, an Ojibwe born in Michigan in the 1850s. By 1900, Jackson owned an allotment of land on which he had a farm. He acquired citizenship with allotment and could speak English, though he was illiterate. He lived with his wife and three sons, all of whom attended school, presumably Mount Pleasant. The older two boys spoke English and were literate; the youngest spoke English and was probably studying to become literate. Hall's message resonated with Isabella residents like Jackson who were trying to preserve their culture while also adapting to white societal norms.[113]

Hall spread African Methodism to other Native communities. He visited four families living in Swan Creek as well as fifty-five people residing at Aug-gans-te-gang. Moreover, he went to Kakalling (Kaukana) in Outagamie County, Wisconsin, where a community of ninety Native people resided.[114] He also visited a small Indigenous community in Oscoda, Michigan, where he was asked to organize a congregation. Community members claimed that they already had a preacher, but "he drinks whisky sometimes, and Indians don't like that. They want to get good. We know the ruination of whisky."[115] As a member of the Michigan Conference's Temperance Committee, Hall was sympathetic to their plight. At the 1895 Michigan Annual Conference, Hall and his fellow committee members submitted a "Temperance Report." In this report, the committee contended that "the subject of temperance [was] one of the most grave questions of the hour."[116] The committee also expressed support for the Women's Christian Temperance Union and its efforts to curb alcohol consumption.[117]

Presiding elder Robinson Jeffries visited Hall's mission sites at Saginaw and De-wah-ne-gang. The Saginaw residents had requested Jeffries's presence, evidently eager to learn more about the AME Church and its ministers. Hall reported that the "Indians met him at the station; when he got to the Indian village they used him like a brother. He had duck and fish to eat. We are glad to see all."[118] Jeffries probably enjoyed a similar scene at De-wah-ne-gang. The reception that "Brother Jeffries" experienced demonstrated the warm relationship between the Ojibwe and their "brother-cousins." They had grown weary of white religious personnel and instead desired attention from their Black "cousins." As Hall explained, "we can understand our cousins better. We do not want any proud man. . . . We would like to receive our cousins as missionaries. We want them."[119]

Some Indigenous people whom Hall met on his travels saw potential in him, but perhaps not in the way that he expected. He came across the Native residents of Seaton Station while he was "berry-hunting." He introduced himself and explained his affiliation with the AME Church. They responded with interest. The chief of this community claimed that the people were "living like a dog, and they wished [that the] conference would send [Hall] there." The chief explained that the community, which was already Christian, had been trying to build a church. They had raised $150 for the endeavor, and the women were committed to raising more "by selling baskets and things." What they needed was "a preacher who can speak a little English to make the white people understand what it is they want the money for." The white people whom they had approached for financial support had evidently rejected them, suspicious of their intentions. The community at Seaton Station wanted Hall not so much to guide them spiritually, but to become their emissary. Hall reported no hesitancy among this community about working within a Black organization like the AME Church. Their primary interest lay in furthering their goals, not quibbling over the race of those who would help them.[120]

In 1893, Hall spent three months evangelizing in Canada, this time under the auspices of the AME Church rather than the Wesleyan Methodist Church. When he returned to Michigan, he visited the offices of *Saginaw News* and informed the editors about his progress. He told them that he had labored in London, Ontario, and was headed back to Isabella County. He reported that he had "made thirty-two converts among the Indians recently and wished to express his thanks to the people of Saginaw who have rendered him financial assistance in his good work."[121] Probably, Hall had been visiting communities of the Mississauga Ojibwe, many of whom had become Methodists because of Peter Jones. The AME Church had a presence in Ontario at this time, and Hall built on it.[122]

Hall went beyond sharing his message with Indigenous communities as an itinerant visitor. By 1893, he had established a permanent mission in Athens, Calhoun County, Michigan.[123] The *Democratic Expounder* reported that "John Hall, of Saginaw, a full blooded Indian evangelist, has been doing missionary work among the Pottawatomie Indians of Athens. Seven braves have resolved to be good."[124] He reported on the progress of the Athens Mission at the 1894 Michigan Annual Conference. The conference scribe called this report "very interesting" but did not elaborate on its contents.[125] According to the statistical records of the conference, the Athens Mission had five members, residents of the nearby Pottawatomi village. The mission did not have a building, so services were likely held in a private residence. Despite these challenges, the mission raised seventy-three dollars that year, an impressive sum given the size of the congregation. As evidenced by the twenty-eight dollars in travel money that he received from the conference that year, Hall continued to evangelize in other locations.[126] By 1895, the Athens Mission showed some development. The membership had grown to fourteen, and there were twenty-five pupils and five teachers for the Sunday school.[127]

Neither John Hall nor his mission work is mentioned in extant AME records after 1896. Probably, Hall died or was for some reason unable to continue his work.[128] Like Thomas Sunrise, Hall represented the fulfillment of the AME Church's goal of Indigenous inclusion. Sunrise and Hall embraced African Methodism and took different paths in their ministries. Sunrise pastored predominately Black AME churches and became an ardent abolitionist. Hall created small AME congregations among Native communities. He informed them that they could eschew white denominations and join with their "brother-cousins," who would accept them as they were. As Indigenous ministers, Sunrise and Hall found in the AME Church religious allies whose affinities as fictive kin united them in defense against white hegemony. Whether it meant abolitionist advocacy, opposition to African American forced migration, or respect and protection for Indigenous spirituality, the denomination became a venue in which to advance the well-being of both Black and Native people.

Conclusion

This chapter has built on the previous one, showing that by the latter half of the nineteenth century, Native people had progressed from being merely receptive to the AME Church to becoming both members of and credentialed ministers in the denomination. These realities force a more nuanced vision of the AME Church and its too-simplistic designation as a "Black church." Certainly, the majority of the members have been of African descent. Yet, from the institution's inception, AME ministers have sought to include Indigenous people. At the beginning of his ministerial career, Richard Allen evangelized among Native communities. In 1815, a mixed congregation of Black and Native people established a church in New York that soon affiliated with the AME denomination. A few years later, AME ministers sought out John Stewart, the founder of the first permanent Indigenous mission in the MEC, and he joined the denomination. In the 1820s and 1830s, Jarena Lee preached to Native people in New York and Ohio. In 1855, Thomas Sunrise became an ordained clergyman in the AME Church and ministered through the denomination. In the 1890s, Hall became an ordained AME minister and performed Indigenous outreach in the Midwest. Cumulatively, these events paint a picture of a denomination that appealed to and embraced Native people from the Montaukett, Seneca, and Oneida to the Wyandotte, Ojibwe, and Pottawatomi. Scholars must acknowledge this reality and view the AME Church as a historically Black denomination that was truly open to marginalized people of color from non-Black communities.

AME interactions with Native people occurred in different chronological and geographic spheres. Chapters 1 and 2 have focused on these interactions in the nineteenth-century North. The remaining chapters will focus on the nineteenth- and twentieth-century West. Beginning in the late 1860s, African Methodists reached out to the Five Civilized Tribes in Indian Territory. This effort reflected the AME denomination's increased migratory ambitions after the Civil War. It was complicated by the fact that these diverse people, unlike those in the North, included former slaveholders like Allen Wright and Green McCurtain, who welcomed the AME Church into Indian Territory but displayed no interest in joining an autonomous Black organization alongside those who had formerly been enslaved. Even so, the formerly enslaved people of Indian Territory eagerly embraced membership in the AME Church and ensured the rapid development of the denomination in Indian Territory. Before we can turn to the full story of AME outreach in Indian Territory, however, it is first necessary to place it within the context of the larger movement of the African Methodist Migration. This is the subject of the next chapter.[129]

3

The African Methodist Migration and the All-Black Town Movement

The African Methodist Migration (AMM) was a movement that African Methodist Episcopal (AME) ministers initiated and that helped facilitate Black settlement in the West. The AMM began in the 1830s, continued into the early 1900s, and occurred in two stages. During the first stage of migration, an AME minister moved to a particular area in the West and organized churches and schools for diverse communities of color. When there was sufficient development, an AME bishop would visit the area and formally organize it into an annual conference. The presiding bishop over that annual conference was then required to send ministers each year to pastor the newly established congregations. Because of the AME denomination's rigorous credentialing process and its itinerant structure, the bishop would often import qualified pastors into the West. This led to the second stage of the AMM, when AME ministers from different regions of the country migrated to the West to serve at new churches in new annual conferences.[1] In 1876, for example, Bishop Thomas Myers Decatur Ward sent Dennis Barrows, a Georgia-born minister, to serve at the Fort Gibson Mission in the Cherokee Nation.[2] In 1880, Bishop Turner sent the South Carolina pastor A. J. Miller to serve at churches in the Choctaw Nation.[3] AME ministers like Barrows and Miller remained in the West for years and played significant roles in building up communities of color. Their presence encouraged other African Methodists to follow them west. Because of the AMM, the AME Church grew rapidly. By the 1890s, there were AME annual conferences in virtually every western state. By 1916, over 1,300 AME churches had been established in the West, with close to 100,000 members (see tables 1, 2, and 3).

Table 1. AME Churches in the West, 1890

Location	Number of Churches*	Members/Communicants
Arkansas	333	27,936
California	15	772
Colorado	6	788
Indian Territory	22	489
Iowa	29	1,820
Kansas	58	4,678
Minnesota	6	489
Missouri	126	9,589
Montana	2	32
Nebraska	4	399
New Mexico	3	62
Oregon	0	16
Texas	208	23,392
Utah	0	7
Washington	1	66
Wyoming	1	139
Total from the West	814	70, 674
Entire United States	4,124	452,725

Source: Henry K. Carroll, *Report on Statistics of Churches in the United States at the Eleventh Census: 1890* (Washington, DC: Government Printing Office, 1894), 543–44.

*This column represents the number of church buildings. Members in places that did not have formal churches presumably met in a private home or some other location.

Table 2. AME Churches in the West, 1916

Location	Number of Churches	Members/Communicants
Arizona	4	234
Arkansas	435	30,457
California	24	2,422
Colorado	15	1,849
Iowa	21	2,248
Kansas	69	4,975
Minnesota	5	1,426
Missouri	127	13,616
Montana	5	199
Nebraska	9	723
New Mexico	5	140
Oklahoma	152	7,250
Oregon	3	205
Texas	464	30,857
Washington	7	503
Wyoming	3	97
Idaho, Nevada, South Dakota, and Utah	6	136
Total from the West	1,354	97,337
Entire United States	6,633	548,355

Source: T. F. Murphy, *Census of Religious Bodies, 1936: Congregational and Christian Churches: Statistics, Denominational History, Doctrine, and Organization* (Washington, DC: Government Printing Office, 1940), 98.

Table 3. AME Annual Conferences Founded in the West, 1840-1892

Conference	Date Established	Presiding Bishop
Indiana	October 2, 1840	Morris Brown
Missouri	September 13, 1855	Daniel A. Payne
California	April 6, 1865	Jabez P. Campbell
Texas	October 22, 1868	James A. Shorter
Arkansas	November 19, 1868	Jabez P. Campbell
Illinois	August 1, 1872	Alexander W. Wayman
West Texas	December 2, 1875	John M. Brown
Kansas	October 4, 1876	James A. Shorter
South Arkansas	October 26, 1876	Thomas M. D. Ward
Indian Territory	October 25, 1879	Thomas M. D. Ward
Northeast Texas	November 27, 1879	Thomas M. D. Ward
Iowa	August 15, 1883	Thomas M. D. Ward
South Kansas	September 20, 1883	Thomas M. D. Ward
Central Texas	December 17, 1883	unknown
North Missouri	September 19, 1884	Thomas M. D. Ward
Colorado*	September 24, 1887	Jabez P. Campbell
Puget Sound**	1892	unknown

Sources: Richard R. Wright Jr., *The Encyclopedia of the African Methodist Episcopal Church*, (Philadelphia: AME Church, 1947), 357, 360, 361, 395; Richard R. Wright Jr., *The Centennial Encyclopedia of the African Methodist Episcopal Church* (Philadelphia: Book Concern of the AME Church, 1916), 15, 290; Charles Spencer Smith, *A History of the African Methodist Episcopal Church* (Philadelphia: Book Concern of the AME Church, 1922), 170; "Proceedings of the First Session of the Kansas Conference of the African M.E. Church," *Christian Recorder*, October 26, 1876; Charles Simpson Butcher, *The Ecumenical Budget of the African Methodist Episcopal Church: Giving the Status of the African Methodist Episcopal Church, Numerically, Financially, Educationally, and a List of the Delegates to the Ecumenical Conference, London, September 4th, 1901* (Philadelphia, 1901), historical table.

* The Colorado Annual Conference included Colorado, Utah, Wyoming, Montana, Arizona, and New Mexico.

** The Puget Sound Annual Conference included Oregon, Washington, Idaho, Alaska, and British Columbia.

The AMM was concurrent with and reinforced the general westward migration of African Americans both before and after the Civil War. The itinerancy, an intrinsic element of AME polity, enabled the denomination to respond readily to a "mobile laity" anxious to escape the violence and economic repression accompanying the end of Reconstruction in the former Confederacy.[4] AME migrants and their church's ministerial itinerancy constitute an overlooked facet of studies on Black westward migration. Nell Irvin Painter's *Exodusters: Black Migration to Kansas after Reconstruction* (1976) chronicles the high tide of the Black movement to Kansas in 1879. Kenneth Marvin Hamilton's *Black Towns and Profit: Promotion and Development in the Trans-Appalachian West, 1877–1915* (1991) focuses on land speculation and the way that town promoters persuaded Black migrants to settle and invest in all-Black towns. Both of these important books acknowledge an AME presence within their migration narratives, but they do not emphasize the denomination's role within this movement. This chapter presents a different perspective on Black westward migration, placing the AME Church at the center of the narrative.

This chapter argues that AME outreach in Indian Territory was part of a larger migration movement, the AMM. This movement helped energize Black migration to the West in two ways. First, it compelled hundreds of AME clergymen to move west to establish and serve AME churches. Second, it gave African Methodists the assurance that they could re-create their religious communities in the West, giving those who might have been reluctant to migrate to new and distant places a powerful incentive to do so. Those AME ministers who participated in the AMM played crucial roles in their new communities. These new communities included all-Black towns that Black Indians and African Americans established in Indian Territory. Although other Black migration movements including the Exoduster movement took place in this era, the AMM was unique because of its duration and its association with a Black religious institution. Scholars have recognized both racial and economic reasons for Black migration but have not adequately recognized religious motivations such as those seen through the AMM.[5]

The African Methodist Migration

Throughout the nineteenth century, African Americans migrated to the West seeking personal freedom, economic opportunity, and a respite from racial violence. African Methodists participated in this general movement as well as in a more specific movement, the African Methodist Migration. This phenomenon began in the 1830s when William Paul Quinn established the first AME churches in the West. In the ensuing decades, hundreds of ministers followed in Quinn's footsteps, traveling to increasingly distant locales and building AME churches among the Black communities developing in the West. It was within this context that the AME Church created the Indian Mission Annual Conference in Indian Territory in 1879, a process that will be discussed in full in the next chapter. The AMM continued into the twentieth century and, as this section argues, helped facilitate Black settlement in the West in two ways: it compelled hundreds of AME clergymen to establish and pastor western AME churches, and it encouraged African Methodists, who might otherwise have been hesitant to leave their homes and church communities, to relocate. The African Methodist Migration existed alongside and sometimes in tandem with other Black migration movements such as the Exoduster movement of 1879.[6]

William Paul Quinn, an AME minister from the British West Indies, considered it his duty as minister to follow Black people "into whatever clime they may go."[7] Included in his purview were free states like Illinois and Indiana, both of which were former French colonies where Black and Indigenous slavery had occurred.[8] Quinn also ventured into slave states like Missouri and Kentucky.[9] The populations among whom he worked were a mixture of freedom seekers and free Black people from the Upper South and Missouri. Some came from Methodist backgrounds, but few if any were already African Methodists.[10]

In the 1830s, Quinn organized Brooklyn AME Church, later named Quinn Chapel, in Brooklyn, Illinois. The origins of the church lay with two formerly enslaved individuals, Priscilla and John Baltimore. Priscilla, born in 1801, was the daughter of an enslaved woman from Kentucky and her white slaveholder. She purchased her freedom and became a prolific Methodist missionary, preaching to large gatherings of enslaved people. She married John, an enslaved man from Virginia, and eventually purchased his freedom. The couple settled in Missouri and started a family. In the early 1830s, they led eleven families of free people and freedom seekers across the Mississippi River from Missouri to St. Clair County, Illinois. This group included John and Matilda Anderson, Philip and Josephine Sullivan, James and Elizabeth Singleton, Daniel and Sarah Wilson, Russell Cox, Mrs. Wyatt, and Nicholas Carper. Together, these families established Freedom Village, later known as the town of Brooklyn, Illinois.[11]

Priscilla and John held religious meetings in their home. Quinn visited Brooklyn sometime between 1832 and 1837 and was pleased to find this small group of Black Methodist migrants. He organized them into an AME congregation. In this way, he embodied the pattern that David Hempton discusses in his *Methodism: Empire of the Spirit*: Quinn followed the "mobile laity" to Illinois and provided them with a denominational infrastructure.[12] He did the same in winter 1839 when he organized Lower Alton AME Church in the small Black community of Alton, Illinois. In 1841, John Baltimore purchased twenty-three plots of land in Brooklyn, one of which he gave to the congregation for their use. On this plot, they built an edifice for Brooklyn AME Church.

In 1840, the AME General Conference validated Quinn's western ministry by appointing him missionary to the states west of Ohio. Quinn spent the next four years organizing more churches in Illinois, Indiana, Missouri, and Kentucky. By 1841, Quinn had established St. Paul AME Church in Saint Louis. This church, located in a slave state, was often difficult to access. He depended on the support of his AME network in the West to help him maintain this charge. At night, Priscilla Baltimore often ferried Quinn and Ezekiel Pines, a member of St. Paul, across the Mississippi River into Saint Louis to visit the church. During one of these dangerous trips, Quinn was captured, probably by slave patrollers. They released him, but they warned him not to return.[13]

Quinn reported on his progress in the West at the 1844 General Conference meeting. Out of the population of eighteen thousand Black people in Illinois and Indiana, he had established forty-seven churches with two thousand members. He had also established numerous schools that serviced hundreds of students. He described the Black population of Illinois and Indiana as mostly farmers who were "rapidly improving themselves by cultivation of the ground, from which they make, under the providence of God, a good living for themselves and families, and sustain churches and schools in a manner truly surprising." He noted that this population was mostly composed of migrants like the Baltimores who had come to those states in the 1830s after they "broke away the fetters of slavery." He credited them with rising above all difficulties to become not only farmers but also mechanics, shoemakers, blacksmiths, and carpenters. Of his progress in the slave states, he noted that St. Paul in Saint Louis had 150 members, while the church in Louisville, Kentucky, was in a "flourishing condition." Quinn's remarkable work in the West compelled the 1844 General Conference to elect him as a bishop.[14]

In the decades that followed, Quinn and a host of other AME ministers fanned out ever farther into western lands, eager to plant the banner of African Methodism. These early participants in the AMM included Quinn's protégé, Jordan Winston Early. Early, born in Virginia in 1814, moved to Saint Louis with his family in 1826. He became an African Methodist and joined St. Paul. After entering the ministry, he spent the 1840s and 1850s laboring in Missouri and Louisiana. Once, in the mid-1840s, Bishop Daniel Alexander Payne visited St. Paul and was arrested for lacking the proper permit. Early secured a lawyer for Payne, and due to a technicality, the magistrate released him. Fearful of white violence against the bishop, Early spirited him away in his horse-drawn carriage. They found refuge in Brooklyn, Illinois, in the home of Priscilla Baltimore. Another early participant in the AMM was Willis R. Revels. Revels, both a minister and a physician, was the brother of Hiram R. Revels, US senator for Mississippi. Willis Revels pastored Quinn Chapel in Chicago from 1858 until 1861.[15]

In the 1850s, the AMM extended farther west as AME ministers migrated to California. These ministers, some of whom hoped to strike it rich in the Gold Rush, targeted Black migrant communities in places like San Francisco, Sacramento, and Los Angeles. Charles Stewart labored in San Francisco in 1852 and, with the assistance of other Black Methodists, saw the erection of an AME church in August of that year. In 1854, T. M. D. Ward, the first ordained AME minister to work in California, began his twelve-year tenure in the state. John Thomas Jenifer, a formerly enslaved man from Maryland, joined Ward in 1862 and eventually pastored in Sacramento, Placerville, and Coloma. In April 1865, after over a decade of AME evangelism in California, Bishop Jabez P. Campbell formally established the California Annual Conference.[16]

Afterward, the AMM continued throughout the West. In 1868, AME ministers established the Texas Annual Conference and the Arkansas Annual Conference; the latter included both Arkansas and Indian Territory. A decade later, there was enough activity in Indian Territory to justify the creation of a separate conference, the Indian Mission Annual Conference. In 1876, AME ministers established the Kansas Annual Conference, which included both Kansas and Nebraska. There were churches in Topeka, Kansas City, Fort Scott, Wyandotte, Lawrence, and Leavenworth by the time that the Exodusters arrived in 1879. The Iowa Annual Conference was established in 1883 and eventually included Iowa, Minnesota, North and South Dakota, and parts of Wisconsin and Canada. In 1887, African Methodists created the Colorado Annual Conference, which included Colorado, Utah, Wyoming, Montana, Arizona, and New Mexico. Finally, in 1892, African Methodists established their last major western conference. This was the Puget Sound Annual Conference, which included Oregon, Washington, Idaho, Alaska, and British Columbia.[17]

The AMM led to the establishment of hundreds of churches in the West. By 1890, there were 814 churches with 70,674 members. Missouri alone possessed 126 of these churches. Even states like Montana and Wyoming, locations not typically associated with Black communities, had AME churches. The AME presence in the West only increased in the ensuing decades. By 1916, there were 1,354 churches with 97,337 members in the West (see tables 1 and 2).

The AMM helped facilitate Black settlement in the West by assuring potential migrants that they could re-create their religious communities. This gave them a powerful incentive to relocate to new and distant places. The *Christian Recorder*, established in 1852 as the official newspaper of the AME Church, played a vital role in this process by publicizing western development.[18] After AME ministers arrived in the West, they and their members sent letters to the *Christian Recorder*, updating AME readers on their progress. In September 1878, James Dorsey, a member of an AME church in Sacramento, informed newspaper readers that "we held our first quarterly meeting in the 7th St. A.M.E. Church," during which they "had a very pleasant time throughout the day and also at our love feasts on Monday evenings."[19] In 1890, Rev. D. E. Johnson gave another update on the progress in California, writing that "about ten per cent of the Negro population on the coast are members of our church.[20] Such letters, which came from every corner of the West, allayed some of the fears of potential migrants, assuring them that the AME Church would be there to greet them wherever they went.

The AMM also helped facilitate Black migration by compelling hundreds of clergymen to move west to pastor AME churches. By 1890, more than eight hundred ministers were serving the various western churches. Among them was James Woods Sanders. Sanders was born near Nashville, Tennessee, in 1857, and his mother, Mary, was a devout African Methodist. He attended public schools and eventually earned his DD from Kittrell College, an AME institution in North Carolina. Afterward, he migrated to Colorado, where he joined the AME Church. He began his ministry in Pueblo, Colorado, in 1884 and spent years migrating throughout the West. He pastored in Colorado Springs, Colorado; Salina, Kansas; Helena, Montana; Salt Lake City, Utah; Albuquerque, New Mexico; Cheyenne, Wyoming; and Denver, Colorado. Additionally, he organized churches in Eddy and Roswell, New Mexico, and built a church in Salt Lake City worth $2,500. As was the case with most clergymen who participated in the AMM, Sanders began his ministry as a single man. He later married twice, first in 1891 and again in 1899.[21]

John Turner also joined the AMM, becoming known as the "pioneer minister of the AME Church west of the Mississippi River." Turner was born in Maryland in 1826, but he spent much of his youth in Illinois. He first learned of the AME Church while living in Terre Haute, Indiana, and he became a licensed preacher in the denomination in 1851. Beginning in 1859, he was the first minister to expand African Methodism in Missouri beyond Saint Louis, organizing churches in Carondelet, Kirkwood, and Jefferson City. He also established a congregation in Leavenworth, Kansas, and, during the Civil War, he helped recruit the "first and second Kansas colored volunteers" at that post. After the war, he organized churches in Atchison, Fort Scott, Wyandotte, and Quindaro, Kansas. In 1879, while he was the pastor of St. Paul in Saint Louis, he led efforts to assist the Exodusters, even serving as the chairman of that city's Colored Relief Board. By the 1880s, he was pastoring in the Colorado Conference. Turner became well known throughout the AME Church, serving as a delegate to every General Conference from 1856 until at least 1888. Because of his work, there were even calls for him to be elected as a bishop at the 1888 General Conference in Indianapolis.[22]

The AMM coincided with and reinforced other Black migration movements, including the Exoduster movement of 1879. Nell Irvin Painter's *Exodusters: Black Migration to Kansas after Reconstruction* was groundbreaking when it was released in 1976. It was the first book to comprehensively examine the Exoduster movement and, therefore, take seriously the efforts of the Black masses to resist the oppression of the post-Reconstruction South. Since *Exodusters*, scholars have paid greater attention to Black migration, but none have fully appreciated the role of the AME Church in this process. Painter made references to the denomination's efforts on behalf of the Exodusters, but neither she nor any other scholars have recognized that African Methodists facilitated their own migration efforts for decades. In fact, by the time that the Exoduster movement began, the AMM had been in effect for about forty years.[23]

In *Exodusters*, Painter explains that after the Civil War, freedmen and freedwomen in the South faced a host of new choices. One of the most significant choices was where they wanted to live. For the first time, they could decide to remain in place or move elsewhere. Some stayed on their former plantations but negotiated for wages and improved working conditions. Others remained within the vicinity of their former homes and farmed their own plots of land. Still others chose to leave the South altogether, opting for new lives in the West. In 1879, a significant group of them migrated to Kansas. They were known as the Exodusters.[24]

The Exodusters hailed from Louisiana, Mississippi, and Tennessee. They had been hopeful that their lives in the South would improve after the Civil War. The end of Reconstruction in 1877 and the reimposition of white supremacy through violence and economic disenfranchisement convinced them to migrate. So, thousands of them departed their homes for the "Promised Land" of Kansas. Black leaders like Benjamin Singleton and Henry Adams played crucial roles in organizing and promoting the migration of the Exodusters.[25]

The AME Church supported the Exodusters. According to Painter, in March 1879, thousands arrived in Saint Louis en route to Kansas. St. Paul AME Church, where John Turner was then the pastor, hosted a mass meeting to determine how best to aid the refugees. Out of this meeting came the creation of the Colored Relief Board, which offered multiple services and financially aided the Exodusters in reaching Kansas. St. Paul, along with other churches, housed the migrants and provided them with food and other necessities.[26]

In May 1880, African Methodists held their General Conference in Saint Louis, evidence of how deeply entrenched the denomination had become in the city since William Paul Quinn's time. During this meeting, they directly addressed the Exodusters' plight. Speaking to the conference, Rev. W. R. Carson acknowledged that "our people have been moving from the South in large numbers, and this exodus has been the most prominent public topic as to its cause and effect." He also recognized that a great deal of misinformation was circulating about this migration. As a result, he asked that "a committee of one from each annual conference be appointed to report upon the exodus."[27]

When the Exodusters finally arrived in Kansas, they faced significant difficulties. Those with money immediately purchased land and began farming. Those without money barely scraped by, but still considered their new lives preferable to their former ones in the South. In 1886, the Kansas Bureau of Labor reported that almost three quarters of the Exodusters owned their own homes. Black heads of household made an average of $262.75, while their white counterparts earned over $70 more. Some Black people could not find steady work at all and migrated to Nebraska and Oklahoma. Despite these challenges, "by 1900 Blacks in Kansas were generally, if not overwhelmingly, more prosperous than their counterparts in the South; politically they were enormously better off. . . . Kansas was no Canaan, but it was a far cry from Mississippi and Louisiana." Clearly, the decision to leave the South paid off for the Exodusters. They refused to accept the racial violence and political and economic disenfranchisement that white people were meting out in their former homes. They were determined to make the end of slavery mean the beginning of a better future for themselves and their posterity.[28]

As this section has demonstrated, the AMM helped facilitate Black migration in the West, often doing so alongside other Black migration movements. AME outreach in Indian Territory, which began in the 1870s, was part of this movement. As the next section argues, the AMM played an important role in the development and success of the region's all-Black towns.

The All-Black Town Movement

The previous section explained how the AMM operated on a macrolevel, helping facilitate Black settlement throughout the West. This section examines how the AMM functioned on the microlevel in Indian Territory. Between 1865 and 1920, Black Indians and African Americans established about fifty all-Black towns in what would become the state of Oklahoma. Many towns were located in Creek country, where Black Creek had been "fashioning an independent lifestyle on the frontier for generations."[29] Some were established on Black Creek land allotments, awarded to them by the Dawes Commission. Kenneth M. Hamilton's *Black Towns and Profit* correctly focuses on all-Black towns as examples of Black economic enterprise. A deeper probe also reveals that AME involvement contributed to the spread of these municipalities and aligned them to the expansion of African Methodism.

This section argues that African Methodists helped establish all-Black towns in Indian Territory and played crucial roles in the success of these settlements. AME ministers supported and bolstered these efforts. Thomas M. Haynes, an entrepreneur, was the driving force behind the creation of Boley, while Buck Colbert Franklin, father of the preeminent historian John Hope Franklin, served in various municipal roles in Rentiesville. African Methodists like Haynes, Franklin, and their families also established AME churches, drawing ministers to these new pulpits. Because of the combined efforts of AME laity and clergy, the AME Church was firmly planted in Indian Territory by the early twentieth century, not only in Boley and Rentiesville, but also in Red Bird, Clearview, Tatums, and Grayson. The sustained AME presence in Indian Territory even affected those who were not affiliated with the denomination. In 1911, a group of Black migrants, inspired by this venerable institution and its leaders, named their all-Black town Vernon, after the AME minister and future bishop William Tecumseh Vernon. At least two schools in all-Black Oklahoma towns were named for him as well. By helping facilitate migration and by aiding settlements in creating a cultural life and an identity, African Methodists and the AME Church played an integral part in the all-Black town movement.[30]

Indian Territory was contested land, and some in the Five Civilized Tribes seemed to resent the growth of all-Black towns. For Black Indians, however, the acquisition of this land was equitable recompense for generations of enslavement by the Five Civilized Tribes. For Black migrants to Indian Territory, these towns offered a sanctuary from deadly racial violence in the South and the chance to attain economic autonomy. These diverse Black communities were not consciously engaged in the colonial enterprise that the US government was carrying out in the West. Rather, they were an oppressed people seeking refuge and opportunity.[31]

Map 1. All-Black Towns in Indian Territory and Oklahoma Territory, 1907. The * indicates a town that had an AME church by 1970.

BOLEY

In spring 1905, Thomas M. Haynes and Henry C. Cavil appeared in the federal court in Sapulpa, where they filed paperwork to formally incorporate the all-Black town of Boley. Both men were African Methodists and belonged to Ward Chapel AME Church in Boley. Haynes was also one of the founders of the town and served as its manager. Together with Hilliard Taylor, Haynes and Cavil submitted a petition signed by two hundred Boley residents requesting the incorporation of their settlement. The court at Wewoka heard the petition and granted the request on May 10, 1905. Boley had come a long way since its establishment in 1903. With the support of African Methodists like Haynes and Cavil, it would become the premiere all-Black town in Indian Territory.[32]

In 1903, Haynes spearheaded the creation of what would become the town of Boley. He was an entrepreneur originally from Red River County, Texas, who joined forces with Lake Moore, a commissioner to the Five Civilized Tribes, and William Boley, an employee of the Fort Smith and Western Railroad Company. Together they formed the Fort Smith and Western Townsite Company. James Barnett, a Creek freedman, allowed this company to lease and then buy forty acres of his daughter Abigail's land allotment, which she had received from the Dawes Commission. This land became the foundation for the all-Black town of Boley, which was named for William Boley. The town was located in the Creek Nation and was surrounded by the allotments of Black Creek like the Barnetts, the Johnsons, and the Walkers. The Fort Smith and Western Townsite Company formally established the town of Boley in September 1904, and Haynes served as the town manager.[33] In this capacity, he held "big celebrations with free eats, which were advertised through circulars sent to friends throughout the United States." These events encouraged migrants to settle in the new town.[34]

Boley's proximity to the Fort Smith and Western Railroad energized its prosperity. One lifelong resident recalled that in 1905 and 1906, new residents arrived in Boley "by train loads." She explained that "in some instances eight and ten families would alight from the same train. Their luggage would fill the depot platform and would be piled six and seven feet high. Gangs like that started Boley off in a big way. Many persons from the town would meet the trains to welcome the new comers."[35] Some migrants were African Methodists, and they established Ward AME Church likely between 1905 and 1907. Boley became a municipal paradigm for other all-Black towns. Booker T. Washington visited in 1905 and called it, "the most enterprising and in many ways the most interesting of the Negro towns in the United States."[36] He noted that the town attracted farmers, doctors, and other professionals from Texas, Arkansas, and Mississippi.[37]

In those early years of settlement, Boley residents did not feel entirely safe. Some in the Five Civilized Tribes resented the Boleyites' presence on lands that they considered their own; they made their displeasure known. As Gary Zellar has noted, the land allotments that Boley and several other all-Black towns were built on had been granted by the Dawes Commission to people who had been enslaved by the Five Civilized Tribes, as well as their descendants.[38] Some tribal members opposed this policy, viewing it as yet another example of the federal government depriving them of their sovereignty and their lands.[39] Hallie S. Jones, who moved to Boley in 1905, recalled that several times a week, Native people on horseback rode through the Boley settlement shooting their guns. Jones and her neighbors extinguished all of the lights in their homes lest they provide an easy target. She remembered spending "many fearful nights sitting in the dark house for safety."[40] For African Americans who had fled racial violence in the South, these experiences in Indian Territory felt uncomfortably familiar. Over time, relations between the Boleyites and their neighbors warmed considerably. One resident recalled that in June or July every year, a powwow was held near the all-Black town of IXL. Boleyites were welcome to attend and regularly did. They enjoyed singing, dancing, eating, and attending a service out in the open under tents.[41]

By 1913, Boley had 3,500 residents, who were both Black Creek and African American migrants. The town had also developed a government structure including a mayor, five councilmen, and a justice of the peace. In terms of infrastructure, the town had municipal waterworks with a "65,000 gallon steel tank reservoir," a fire department with "modern equipment," an electric light plant constructed by a Tuskegee Institute graduate, a post office, six miles of cement sidewalks, and a bank with "over $75,000 deposits."[42] Additionally, the Creek and Seminole College and the Methodist Episcopal College provided educational opportunities for both Black and Native students.[43]

Churches played a crucial role in town life. Hallie S. Jones recalled that Boley's first residents shared worship services in a one-room schoolhouse and then fellowshipped together on Main Street. Violence sometimes interrupted these services, though the culprits of this violence remain unclear. Perhaps it was neighboring white people who were furious to see an all-Black town flourishing. The incidents left a deep impression on Jones. She recalled that evening programs and Christmas programs were "often broken up . . . by someone standing in the door . . . and firing a shot into the building." Since the door was the only exit, the terrified churchgoers were forced to escape through windows or any other crevices they could find. Mrs. Jones exclaimed that "I thank the Lord for not being pulled apart on one occasion when my husband jumped through a window and pulled me through behind him, with many others trying to make an escape through the same opening at the same time." These violent occurrences finally ended when T. R. Ringo, the Boley police officer, shot back at the offenders as they rode away on their horses. His expert aim ensured that it was "impossible for the intruder to sit any place."[44]

The Boley Townsite management team, eventually, gave each religious denomination its own site on which to build an edifice. The Colored Methodist Episcopal (CME) Church was the first to erect a building, doing so on the corner of Cedar Street.[45] The African Methodists initially worshipped under a brush arbor but later built Ward Chapel AME Church, which still stands at 123 North Pecan Street (figure 1). By the 1930s, there were "nine Protestant Churches and one Catholic Church erected in Boley."[46]

Figure 1. African Methodist Episcopal Church in Boley, Oklahoma (Oklahoma Historical Society).

The establishment of Ward Chapel AME Church necessitated the migration of ministers to serve in that pulpit. One of the first AME ministers to move to Boley to pastor Ward Chapel was K. W. Oliver.[47] G. B. Richardson, who was originally from Texas, followed him around 1907. During Richardson's tenure, the congregation had 145 members, a missionary society, and a Sunday school with eight teachers and fifty-seven students. The church edifice was worth $1,200 and could seat 450 people. The parsonage, where Richardson lived, was worth $150.[48] Hallie S. Jones credited AME clergymen like Richardson and their counterparts from other denominations with "bringing Christ to the unsaved and causing many youngsters to look onward and upward." She contended that "without this influence, Boley could not have progressed so fully."[49]

AME ministers sometimes served other congregations in addition to their own. In 1920, J. S. Dawson, who was originally from Texas, simultaneously pastored Ward Chapel as well as the CME, Methodist Episcopal, and Baptist churches in Boley.[50] This hard-working clergyman was so beloved that his parishioners published a laudatory letter about him in Oklahoma City's *Black*

Dispatch newspaper. In the letter, they celebrated that he had been appointed to Boley for another year. They effused that "we, the members of Ward Chapel AME Church, and the members of all the other churches of Boley, are indeed glad to have him with us. He is an able preacher, intelligently, morally and religiously, and is fully able to master and pastor any church in our AME domain." This letter was also complimentary of his wife.[51]

Ward Chapel attracted some of the best-educated ministers that the AME Church had to offer. P. W. DeLyles pastored Ward Chapel from 1929 to 1930. He was born in Mississippi, where he attended the public schools, and then earned a DD and an LLD from Shorter College, an AME institution in Arkansas. He began his ministerial career in the Arkansas Annual Conference but transferred to Oklahoma. An advocate for education, he served as a trustee at Flipper-Key-Davis University in Muskogee from 1922 to 1941 and as dean of that school's Theological Department from 1939 to 1941. By 1948, he was a presiding elder in the Northeast Oklahoma Conference.[52]

Ward Chapel also attracted several of Boley's most prominent residents. Thomas M. Haynes and his wife, Julia, were founding members of this congregation. Haynes even served as one of the first stewards of the church. His son Tommie married a young woman, Edna Still, whose family belonged to Ward Chapel. Attorney M. J. Jones and his wife, Hallie S. Jones, were prominent members as well. He served as one of the church's first trustees, while she organized and directed the choir and played the organ. She continued in these roles into the 1930s. In her detailed account of the history of Boley, she described her husband as "an ardent church worker" who was "never too busy to serve his church when he was needed." Other leading members of Ward Chapel included Henry C. Cavil and his wife, Willie, as well as Jeff Gooden. In addition to professionals, Ward Chapel had numerous members who were farmers. W. H. Jessie and his wife, Mary, both from Alabama, engaged in this profession. So too did Charles, Hannah, and Charlie Chiles, who were from Texas. Charles Chiles became one of many "substantial farmers who own their farms and serve as a backbone to Boley." Eventually, the Chilesville Cemetery in Boley was named for the Chiles family.[53]

The African Methodists at Ward Chapel played crucial roles in the development of Boley. In addition to working as town manager, Haynes also served on the first city council, as did Cavil, who established a successful general mercantile business, and M. J. Jones, who also became Boley's first city attorney.[54] Hallie S. Jones was the town's first postmaster. Eventually, both she and Willie Cavil worked in the Boley school system and supervised Okfuskee County schools. By 1934, Hallie was working as a vice principal, while Willie was teaching fourth and fifth grade.[55] Rev. Louis C. Taylor, an attorney who served as a steward and trustee at Ward Chapel, secured the charter for Boley's First National Bank.[56] Jeff Gooden and his wife opened Boley's first hotel, which was "a two-story frame building with about 12 rooms on the second floor, and on the first floor was the dining hall, office, reception room and a kitchen." The Goodens operated this hotel for "a long, long time," before selling it and moving farther west.[57]

George W. Perry, a World War I veteran who served in the American Expeditionary Forces, also belonged to Ward Chapel. He taught Sunday school and served as both a secretary and a steward at the church. Perry was a well-respected journalist and worked as the editor and manager of Boley's highly regarded newspaper, the *Boley Progress*. During his time at this newspaper, he was "the first man to expose the Chief Sam graft that ruined thousands of wealthy Negroes" in Oklahoma. In 1922, he was appointed the postmaster of Boley.[58]

Captain James S. Webb, who was born in Texas in 1904, attended another AME Church in Boley, Chiles Chapel. Presumably, the Chiles family broke away from Ward Chapel and established this congregation. Webb was converted at Chiles Chapel in 1913 and became an AME minister in 1927. He pastored at Camp Chapel AME Church in Clearview from 1937 to 1938 and at Salter Chapel in Langston from 1938 to 1941, among other appointments. He also served as the principal at the Clayton School in Boley from 1937 to 1939. He later matriculated at the Chaplain School at Harvard University and became a US Army chaplain. He served at posts in Mississippi, Texas, and the Aleutian Islands.[59]

Ward Chapel played an integral role in the social life of Boley. In 1908, this church hosted the final meeting for the Indian Mission Annual Conference.[60] In October 1917, the church hosted the yearly meeting for its new jurisdiction, the Northeast Oklahoma Annual Conference. During this meeting, the town was swarmed with ministers from the Muskogee, Tulsa, and Fort Gibson districts. Dignitaries like Bishop James M. Connor were also in attendance. No doubt the residents of Boley opened their homes to accommodate the visitors, and local businesses boomed with activity.[61] Bishop William H. Heard preached in Boley on February 23, 1921, accompanied by the ministers T. W. Kidd and A. E. Hubbard.[62] In April 1922, the *Black Dispatch* singled out the church for praise for its Easter services: "The program at the AME Church deserves special mention. Little Teressa Doss, the promising prima donna, was at her best. Little Marie Taylor won the prize for bringing in the largest number of eggs, 108; while Hallie Morgan brought in 84. Mrs. W. C. Gowdy presented the gift. Miss Hallie Taylor and Mrs. Alice Mariott conducted the program."[63]

Ward Chapel remained a bustling church from the 1930s to the 1950s. Rev. Homer Williams, who was born in 1935, recalled that the church regularly held Sunday school conventions and that visiting children roomed with local families. He also remembered that African Methodists and Baptists fellowshipped together every fifth Sunday of the month. Rev. Williams grew up in North Boley, a settlement located roughly six miles from Boley proper, where he attended Aaron Chapel AME Church. His father, Walter Williams, had moved to North Boley from Georgia in 1910. He became an AME minister in the 1930s and pastored Pleasant Hill AME Church in the all-Black town of IXL. Homer followed in his father's footsteps and also became an AME minister. He served as pastor at Tyre Chapel in Clearview and at Ward Chapel in Boley.[64]

African Methodists like Haynes, Cavil, and a host of others participated in the AMM. They came from various southern states and settled in the Creek Nation. They played crucial roles in the establishment and the success of Boley. Ministers flocked to the town to pastor Ward Chapel and, later, Chiles Chapel. Their efforts ensured that the AME Church was inextricably linked to Boley and that this all-Black town was a site for important meetings that attracted denominational dignitaries.

RENTIESVILLE

Like Boley, Rentiesville was an all-Black town that was established in Creek country and had close ties to the AME Church. In 1903, William Rentie and Phoebe McIntosh, both Creek freedmen, used the twenty acres of land between them to start the town. It was located roughly five miles from Checotah. Rentiesville maintained a post office, a school, and numerous businesses. William Rentie served as the town's police officer until he was murdered sometime after 1910.[65]

African Methodists had built Bethel AME Church in Rentiesville by 1907. That year, the church had forty-three members, among them Black Indians like Fannie Love. The church building was worth $300 and had a seating capacity of 150 people. The African Methodists also had a parsonage worth $75.[66] John Wesley Curry was one of the early pastors of Bethel. He was born in Arkansas in 1868 and began his career in the AME ministry in 1908. He pastored in Rentiesville from 1911 to 1912, Muskogee from 1912 to 1916, and Langston from 1916 to 1917. He later transferred to Missouri and Pennsylvania and wrote for publications like the *Christian Recorder*, the *AME Church Review*, and the *Crisis*.[67]

Buck Colbert Franklin was an early member of Bethel AME Church and played several municipal roles in Rentiesville. He was an enrolled Choctaw freedman through his grandfather David Franklin. He moved his family to Rentiesville in 1912, hoping that this all-Black oasis would provide "emotional security" for his wife and children.[68] Buck and his wife, Mollie Parker, were both alumni of Roger Williams University, a Baptist institution in Nashville, Tennessee. He became a lawyer, she a teacher. While in Rentiesville, Buck worked as "postmaster, justice of the peace, notary public, and president of the Rentiesville Trading Company."[69] In fact, the town's mail was distributed from the front room of the Franklin home. Mollie taught at the local school and cared for her growing family.[70]

Buck was a devout Methodist, so he and his family joined Bethel shortly after arriving in Rentiesville. Rev. Curry was then the pastor.[71] Buck's decision to join Bethel angered the members of First Baptist Church. They had assumed that the Franklins, because they had attended Roger Williams, were Baptists as well. The African Methodists and the Baptists had developed a poisonous rivalry in Rentiesville, and it manifested in destructive ways. The Baptists were more powerful, but Buck refused to bow to them. He and Mollie remained African Methodists, determined to "pursue lives of dignified self-determination, and to instill that same resolve in their children and their neighbors."[72] This loyalty to African Methodism cost them. In 1915, Mollie was pregnant with her fourth child. She asked the school board to grant her a leave of absence until she gave birth. The pastor of the Baptist church persuaded the school board not only to deny her entreaty, but also to ask for her resignation. Fortunately, the superintendent intervened and granted her request. Mollie returned home and, on January 2, 1915, gave birth to John Hope Franklin.[73]

John Hope Franklin, who would grow up to become one of the most revered historians in the United States, recalled a great deal about his childhood in Rentiesville. Among his most vivid memories was when Mary Blake, a Black evangelist, held a revival at Bethel in 1924. Blake was "eloquent and persuasive," and watching her conduct the revival gave him "an unusual example of female empowerment" that influenced him for the rest of his life.[74]

In February 1921, Buck Franklin moved to Tulsa seeking new opportunities. He intended for his family to follow him after the school term ended. Unfortunately, the Tulsa race massacre occurred only a few months later.

Buck lost his clothes, rented home, office, and most of his other belongings. As a result, it took until 1925 for Mollie and the children to relocate to Tulsa. They renewed their commitment to African Methodism by joining Vernon AME Church, which was named for Bishop William Tecumseh Vernon.[75]

African Methodists established churches in other all-Black towns. These included Red Bird, Clearview, Tatums, and Grayson. As was the case in Boley and Rentiesville, ministers migrated to these towns to fill these pulpits. Along with their devoted members, these clergymen played a significant role in developing not only their churches, but also these historically significant communities.[76]

VERNON

African Methodism provided inspiration and identity for all-Black towns. In 1911, a group of Black migrants that included Thomas M. Haynes named their town after William Tecumseh Vernon, a prominent AME minister and future bishop. Vernon's status as an AME leader as well as his other professional accomplishments impressed these sojourners. They wanted their town to represent Black excellence and self-determination. In their eyes, these qualities were synonymous with both the future bishop Vernon and with the AME Church. Haynes, undoubtedly, played a significant role in naming the new town after a fellow African Methodist.[77]

William Tecumseh Vernon was born on July 1, 1871, in Lebanon, Missouri (figure 2). His parents were AME minister Adam Vernon and Margaret Vernon. He attended Lincoln University in Missouri, where he graduated as valedictorian, and Wilberforce University. In 1896, he entered the AME ministry, joining the Missouri Annual Conference. He was appointed the president of Western University, an AME institution in Quindaro, Kansas. He served in this position for ten years and, through his efforts, significantly raised the profile of the school. Vernon was a staunch Republican and, in 1906, was appointed registrar of the treasury by President Theodore Roosevelt, which meant that all US currency printed bore Vernon's name. Vernon continued in this position throughout Roosevelt's term, giving him a powerful platform from which to assist other Black people.[78]

On the eve of Oklahoma's statehood, which was granted on November 16, 1907, Vernon used his position to champion the cause of Black Indians and African Americans. Oklahoma's new constitution included a "Jim Crow clause" that legalized segregation.[79] In October 1907, a delegation of Black Indians and African Americans from Oklahoma arrived in Washington, DC, to lobby against this provision. The delegation included A. G. W. Sango

Figure 2. Bishop William Tecumseh Vernon, date unknown (Library of Congress).

and J. Coody Johnson, both prominent Black Creek individuals, and W. H. Twine, an African American lawyer. The *Muskogee Cimiter*, a Black newspaper that Twine had once edited, contended that Vernon, who was still serving as Roosevelt's registrar of the treasury, gave "all possible assistance to the delegation." His actions "put the Negroes of Oklahoma and Indian Territories under lasting obligations to him." Vernon entertained the delegates in "royal style" at his "splendid" home.[80] Given his influence in Roosevelt's administration, he was probably responsible for securing the meetings between the delegation and attorney general Charles Joseph Bonaparte, Kansas senator Charles Curtis, secretary of the interior James Rudolph Garfield, and President Roosevelt himself. During their audience with the president, the delegates "briefly stated their cause," and they left feeling optimistic about his support. Nevertheless, Roosevelt still signed off on Oklahoma's constitution with its Jim Crow provisions.[81] Despite this outcome, the diverse Black residents of Oklahoma maintained deep affection for Vernon, who supported them in their "hour of need."[82]

Black people in Oklahoma soon honored Vernon for his accomplishments and his support over the Oklahoma constitution issue. The all-Black town of Taft, also founded on the allotments of Creek freedmen, named a school after the high-achieving African Methodist. The W. T. Vernon School began operations in 1908 and included Sarah Rector among its students. Rector was a Creek freedwoman minor whose allotment became an oil-producing juggernaut. The wealth that she accumulated resulted in her gaining national recognition as the "richest black girl in America."[83] While attending the W. T. Vernon School, Rector must have learned about the school's namesake. At the very least, she would have known that he was an African Methodist minister and held a significant role in the Roosevelt administration. As Rector grew into womanhood, she could draw on her knowledge of W. T. Vernon as inspiration for how to navigate a hostile world as a prominent African American.[84]

Vernon's profile in Oklahoma grew dramatically in June 1911, when Walter L. Fisher, President William Howard Taft's secretary of the interior, appointed him as assistant supervisor of schools for the Five Civilized Tribes. Vernon was meant to relocate to Muskogee to perform this work. Black people in Oklahoma must have been pleased at this development. Senator Curtis suggested Vernon for the job. Curtis, who was himself of Indigenous heritage, had sponsored the Curtis Act of 1898, the legislation that extended the Dawes Act to the Five Civilized Tribes. He had also met with the 1907 Black delegation from Oklahoma. Probably, Vernon had become acquainted with Curtis during his ten years at Western University.[85]

The reaction to Vernon's appointment was immediate and explosive. Newspapers throughout Oklahoma and beyond ran stories on the fallout. On June 8, the *Muskogee Times-Democrat* ran the headline "Negro Gets Big Gov't Job Here." The accompanying article posited that the reason for the appointment was "to line up the Oklahoma negroes for Taft before the next national convention." The newspaper also conducted an interview with Chief Moty Tiger of the Creek Nation. Through an interpreter, Tiger called it an insult that "a colored man" would be appointed supervisor over Native schools. He wondered why Fisher had not simply chosen a white man or an Indigenous man for the job. Yet, "What can the Indian do? What the government says we must accept."[86] Chief Moty Tiger's statements must have offended the diverse Black residents of Indian Territory, reminding them that generations of slaveholding had entrenched racial prejudice within the Five Civilized Tribes.

Numerous others joined the chorus protesting Vernon's appointment. These included Oklahoma officials like Senator Thomas Pryor Gore. While in Washington, DC, Gore commented on the Vernon appointment: "I regret the appointment. The Indians, the democrats and many white republicans will also regret it. Only the colored people and a few others will approve such a selection. If a negro is deemed indispensible to this place, it seems to me it should have gone to an Oklahoma negro. However, I think a white republican could and should be found for the position." Various other white state officials agreed with Gore.[87] There were violent undertones in the newspapers regarding Vernon. On June 9, the *Muskogee Times-Democrat* warned that "personally we would advise Vernon not to come to Muskogee to accept the job. This is a white man's country."[88] This barely veiled threat was typical of what Black people, particularly high-achieving Black people, faced from resentful white people in the early twentieth century.

Benjamin Franklin McCurtain, the son of Choctaw chief Green McCurtain, spoke harshly regarding Vernon's appointment. Despite his family's history with African Methodists—his father had donated a building to African Methodists in San Bois, Oklahoma, and they had named it Greenrock AME Church in his honor—Benjamin McCurtain declared that "the Choctaws and Chickasaw Indians are filled with indignation over the appointment of the negro, W.T. Vernon, as assistant supervisor of the schools of the five tribes; and will enter a vigorous protest at once." He explained that "it has always been a rule of the government that where an Indian was qualified to fill a position in the Indian service, they had the preference." This rule had not been followed in Oklahoma, and white men had often taken such jobs. Typically, McCurtain contended, the tribes had not complained. But now that the government was placing "a man of an inferior race" in such an important position, they felt compelled to speak out. McCurtain demanded that "the government should appoint Indians to fill these positions, wherever an Indian can be found who is able to qualify."[89]

The "flood of protests" had their desired effect. Vernon was instead appointed "supervisor-at-large," and according to Secretary Fisher, "it is not anticipated that his duties will take him to Oklahoma."[90] During his tenure, Vernon focused on the educational needs of Black Indians. Then, in April 1912, he visited Haskell Institute, an Indigenous school in Lawrence, Kansas. The local newspaper explained that "Prof. Vernon has been devoting his attention to the freedmen among the Indians but he is now devoting more attention to the course of study in all the schools."[91] A few months later, he was appointed president of Campbell College, an AME school in Jackson, Mississippi. He was elected an AME bishop in 1920.[92]

Despite the ugly reaction to Vernon's appointment in 1911, or perhaps because of it, Black Oklahomans rallied around him. Vernon's impressive career and his ability to rise above adversity inspired them. They valued what African Methodists like him represented: racial pride in the face of a racist society, political proficiency, and self-determination. They wanted to prove that like the African Methodists, they, too, could govern themselves. So, in 1911, when a group of migrants established another all-Black town in the Creek Nation, they named it Vernon in his honor.

Vernon's first president was Edward Woodard. Among the early residents were Professor F. E. Wesley and his sister, Louise Wesley, who established Vernon's first church and school. The town developed a strong farming community and also attracted businessmen like Mr. Holliday and Mr. Watson. In 1912, Vernon established its own post office, and Ella Woods served as the first postmaster. Eventually, the town had a high school with its own basketball team, several grocery stores, and a gas station. The town declined after World War II, but it remains in existence. Vernon's original church, New Hope Baptist Church, still stands. As of 2015, the church's pastor was Clayborn Fields, who was born and raised in Vernon. His congregation includes African American, Indigenous, Mexican, and white members.[93]

Ten years after Bishop Vernon's controversial appointment in Oklahoma, the city of Tulsa was up in flames. The notorious massacre of 1921 claimed the lives and property of numerous African Americans. It was no coincidence that Vernon AME Church, W. T. Vernon's namesake congregation, was set ablaze as well. Clearly, white Oklahomans had not forgotten the "insult" they had suffered in June 1911. Their violent actions expressed their continued hatred for Vernon and what he and other African Methodists represented. The members of Vernon AME Church worshipped in the basement for a few years until they could rebuild their edifice. In those trying times, they displayed the pride and resolve associated with African Methodism.[94]

This section has demonstrated that African Methodists like Thomas M. Haynes and Buck Colbert Franklin played crucial roles in the success of all-Black towns. AME ministers participating in the AMM formed an important part of these settlements as well. The combined efforts of AME laity and clergy ensured that diverse Black communities throughout Indian Territory knew of the AME Church and saw it as representing Black pride and self-reliance. That is why, in 1911, Black migrants named their town after William Tecumseh Vernon. They watched him withstand a racist onslaught after his appointment as supervisor of schools for the Five Civilized Tribes. His dignity in the face of this opposition convinced them that this resolute African Methodist was the appropriate namesake for their town.

Conclusion

This chapter has shown that the African Methodist Migration, which overlapped with other migration movements, facilitated the settlement of hundreds of Black ministers west of the Mississippi River. Both clergy and laity aided the growth and development of Black migrant communities throughout the West, particularly in the all-Black towns of Indian Territory. The African Methodist Migration was unique because of its duration and its association with a Black religious institution. It shows that religious motivations compelled Black migration to the West just as racial and economic concerns did.

The remaining chapters of this book are a case study of one region involved in the African Methodist Migration, Indian Territory. These chapters will show how the AME Church's work in Indian Territory began. They will also discuss the ministers who migrated to the region to establish the Indian Mission Annual Conference, the complex ecclesiastical infrastructure that they built, and their participation in citizenship battles on behalf of their parishioners.

4

"Ham Began . . . to Evangelize Japheth"

The Birth of African Methodism in Indian Territory

On the morning of October 25, 1879, a diverse group of African Methodist Episcopal (AME) clergy and laity gathered in Yellow Springs in the Choctaw Nation of Indian Territory. Their purpose was to formally organize and establish the Indian Mission Annual Conference (IMAC). They met in the home of the Chickasaw freedman Billy Keel. The meeting began at half past ten in the morning, and Bishop Thomas Myers Decatur Ward presided. Among the AME clergy present were three ministers who had been laboring in Indian Territory for several years: James Fitz Allan Sisson, a white man; Robert Grayson, a prominent Black Creek; and Dennis Barrows, an African American originally from Georgia. The laity in attendance included Indigenous people from the Five Civilized Tribes who were either African Methodists or interested observers. Although her name does not appear in the record, Annie Keel, Billy Keel's wife and a Chickasaw freedwoman, was probably in attendance. Her presence was crucial because around 1870 she helped bring the AME Church to Boggy Depot, one of the denomination's earliest sites for evangelism in Indian Territory.[1]

Annie Keel, Billy Keel, and other Black Indians were forced into Indian Territory in the 1830s as enslaved workers of the Five Civilized Tribes, which included the Cherokee, Creek, Choctaw, Chickasaw, and Seminole Nations. After the Civil War, and the various treaties that guaranteed their freedom, Black Indians fought to attain full citizenship in the tribes and acquire the land to which they considered themselves entitled. They made this demand during the same era in which the federal government promised freed Black people "forty acres and a mule" to aid their transition to freedom. Such white religious organizations as the Methodist Episcopal Church, South (MECS), commonly evangelized among these Black Indians. Annie Keel, however, invited the AME Church to her community in Boggy Depot around 1870. By that time, the denomination had established itself as a historically Black organization of longevity and geographic reach. Within AME ministerial ranks were both formally educated clergy and those with special military, missionary, and political credentials. The denomination also boasted its own national newspaper, the *Christian Recorder*, and the first historically Black institution of higher education in the United States, Wilberforce University in Ohio.[2]

This chapter argues that Annie Keel invited the AME Church to evangelize in Indian Territory because, unlike other denominations in the area, it was an autonomous, Black institution with impressive transnational accomplishments. Not all formerly enslaved people favored such institutions. AME bishop Wesley J. Gaines, who evangelized in the South for several decades after the Civil War, noted that some Black people had a "prejudice born of generations" that caused them to reject an independent Black denomination in favor of one governed by white people.[3] Annie Keel and her community, on the other hand, eagerly embraced the AME Church, recognizing that belonging to this denomination would give them access to a national network of churches, educational institutions, and prominent people. Likewise, the AME Church welcomed these Black Indians just as it had always embraced marginalized people of color from a variety of ethnicities. By highlighting the diverse population that joined the IMAC, this chapter broadens what is typically meant by the term "Black church," especially when applied to the AME denomination.

Slavery in the Five Civilized Tribes

Prior to their forced removal to Indian Territory, enslaved people like Annie Keel lived among the Five Civilized Tribes in the southeastern United States. These tribes were considered "civilized" because they incorporated certain elements of Euro-American culture into their own. The tribes, at least nominally, embraced Christianity and adopted Euro-American models of political organization and economic development. The Cherokee, whose culture was primarily oral, even developed a written form of their language in 1821.[4]

As a testament to their adaptation to Euro-American societal norms, the Five Civilized Tribes gradually embraced African slavery. The tribes' system of slavery developed from their long-held tradition of taking war captives and either exchanging them for goods or incorporating them into their communities.[5] Slaveholders among the Five Civilized Tribes tended to be wealthy people of mixed Native and European ancestry. Like their white counterparts in the South, they forced enslaved Africans to work as both agricultural and domestic laborers. Through their unpaid labor, enslaved Africans made slaveholders' lands more profitable and their home lives more comfortable.[6]

Among the Chickasaw, the development of the slavery system began in the 1750s when British traders brought the first enslaved Africans to Chickasaw lands. These lands included areas of Alabama, Mississippi, and Tennessee. The Chickasaw lived in villages and often intermarried with the Choctaw. They hunted and fished and engaged in agriculture. The Chickasaw were also fearsome warriors who successfully battled against Europeans as well as other Native people. The Chickasaw had a comparatively small tribe; whereas the Choctaw numbered about 15,000 prior to removal, the Chickasaw population was estimated at between 3,000 and 4,000. By the 1830s, the enslaved population among the Chickasaw numbered about 1,200. Annie and Billy Keel belonged in this population. The Chickasaw purchased enslaved people from other slaveholders and from slave traders. Since many enslaved people came from English-speaking backgrounds and later learned the Chickasaw language, they played crucial roles as interpreters.[7]

Very little is known about Annie Keel's early life among the Chickasaw. According to census records, she was born around 1820 either in Tennessee or Mississippi.[8] She became the property of Tennessee Keel, a Chickasaw woman. It remains unclear whether Tennessee owned Annie from birth or whether she purchased her. Tennessee, who probably lived on Chickasaw lands in northeast Mississippi, belonged to a slaveholding family that included Simon Keel (Muchenechee, her brother) and Booker Keel (her cousin). Annie and other enslaved people performed agricultural labor and domestic duties for the Keels.[9]

In the 1830s, the Chickasaw and the other southeastern tribes learned that their level of so-called civilization would not save them from white interference. All five faced relentless efforts by white people to encroach on their fertile homelands. With President Andrew Jackson leading the charge, the US government forcibly moved these southeastern tribes westward to Indian Territory. Here, they were supposed to begin anew without further intrusion from white people. The forced march from the Southeast to Indian Territory is conventionally called the Trail of Tears. The Chickasaw took this march in 1837; trudging along with them were enslaved people like Annie and Billy Keel.[10]

Upon their arrival in Indian Territory, many Chickasaw settled in Choctaw-designated areas.[11] In 1837, the Chickasaw founded the town of Boggy Depot in the Choctaw Nation. The town was located between two creeks, roughly fourteen miles southwest of Atoka. Boggy Depot became the site of the first Chickasaw agency and, from 1858 to 1860, was the capital of the Choctaw Nation. In the 1870s, the residents moved the town two miles to the south and renamed it New Boggy Depot.[12] The Chickasaw and Choctaw, along with the other tribes, continued African slavery in Indian Territory. Edmond Flint, who was enslaved by the Choctaw, explained that "slaves had been brought to the Indian Territory by the first Indian emigrants from the south." Flint further elucidated that most of these slaveholders were mixed-race people.[13] Tennessee, Simon, and Booker Keel all settled with their enslaved workers near Boggy Depot in an area now called Whitehall. Annie and the rest of the enslaved workers helped their masters establish their new homes.[14]

While the Keels made their homes in the Boggy Depot area, other Chickasaw settled on the Red River in the Choctaw Nation. It was in this fertile area that the "largest slave owners" established themselves.[15] Disease ran rampant among slaveholders and enslaved people at this location. Mary Lindsay, whose mother, Mary, was owned by the Chickasaw Sobe Love, recalled that "my mammy say dey have a terrible hard time again the sickness when they first come out into that country, because it was low and swampy and all full of cane brakes, and everybody have the smallpox and the malaria and fever all the time. Lots of the Chickasaw families nearly died off."[16] These hardships made early life in Indian Territory perilous.

As they had been in the Southeast, enslaved Africans in Indian Territory were immersed in Native cultures. Lucinda Davis, who was born around 1848 in Indian Territory, provides an example of this cultural immersion. Her master was a "full-blood Creek Indian" man named Tuskaya-hiniha. His large farm was located roughly twenty-five miles from Fort Gibson. During her enslavement, Lucinda served as a housekeeper and a nursemaid to her master's grandson, whom they called Istidji. Lucinda spoke the Creek language fluently and exclusively, only learning English after the Civil War. As evidence of her language proficiency, she recounted in a Works Progress Administration interview various words and phrases in the Creek language. She noted that her master's name meant "head man warrior," while his grandson's name meant "little man." Lucinda also recalled that in the Creek language, enslaved people were called Istilusti, which meant "black man."[17]

Lucinda recounted various Creek traditions such as the process by which the Creek named their male children. She contended that "when de boy git old enough de big men in de town give him a name, and sometime later on when he git to going around wid de grown men dey stick on some more name. If he a good talker dey sometime stick on 'yoholo,' and iffen he makes lots of jokes dey call him 'Hadjo.' If he is a good leader dey call him 'Imala' and if he kind of mean dey sometime call him 'fixigo.'"[18] One man she remembered was named Hopoethleyoholo, the "yoholo" on the end of his name indicating that he was a "good talker." Lucinda also recalled that the Creek permitted their enslaved workers to live on and cultivate their own land, provided that they gave a large portion of their produce to their masters. Such was the case for Lucinda's parents. She explained that "dey didn't have to stay on de master's place and work like I hear de slaves of de white people and de Cherokee and Choctaw people say dey had to do." Lucinda also remembered that the Creek cooked everything outdoors in large pots. Typical foods included roasted green corn, ash cakes, greens, pork, deer, wild turkey, fish, and turtle, and there was always a pot of sofki available in the house for anyone to eat. Visitors were encouraged to partake of this dish lest they offend Tuskaya-hiniha's sense of hospitality.[19]

Lucinda also witnessed busk festivals and dances among the Creek. She particularly remembered the Green Corn Ceremony in July 1863. Since many of the enslaved men had escaped to freedom by this time, it was "jest a little busk." She also witnessed big dances, which the Creek called "banga." She attended the "Tolosabanga," or chicken dance, and the "Istifanibanga," or skeleton dance. She also remembered the "Hadjobanga," or crazy dance in which the participants "dance crazy and make up funny songs to go wid de dance." At the drunk dance, which she did not enjoy, participants imbibed alcohol and quarreled. As these examples indicate, Black Indians like Lucinda were fluent in the Indigenous cultures of their masters.[20]

While enslaved in Indian Territory, Annie Keel began carving out a life for herself. In the 1840s, she became involved with a man named Tuthliotaby. In 1845, they had a son, Jacob Keel, and Tennessee's brother Simon took ownership of him.[21] Enslaved women like Annie were sometimes encouraged and sometimes forced into sexual relationships in order to produce more enslaved workers for their masters. It remains unclear whether this was why Annie became involved with Tuthliotaby. It was certainly why Mary Lindsay's mother became involved with her partner. Sobe Love chose to "marry off" Lindsay's mother to William, who was enslaved to the Chickasaw Chick-a-lathe. Love later purchased William so that "we was all Loves then." Love's enslaved workers on his vast farmland eventually numbered around one hundred.[22]

Annie's relationship with Tuthliotaby was short lived, and by the 1850s she was involved with Billy Keel. Billy Keel was born in Mississippi and was enslaved to Booker Keel. Billy and Annie had probably known each other for years, possibly even before removal. It remains unclear whether they ever formally married, but they had a long relationship and numerous children: Betsie was born in 1853, Charley was born in 1855, Daniel was born in 1856, and Lucy Ann was born in 1870. Annie's mistress took ownership of Betsie, Charley, and Daniel. Lucy Ann, born after the Civil War, never felt the lash of slavery.[23] The Keel children escaped one of the harshest aspects of slavery, separation from loved ones. Mary Lindsay was not as fortunate. Sobe Love gave Lindsay to his daughter, who had moved to Texas. Lindsay's parents were heartbroken, "but they couldn't say nothing." Lindsay recalled that "I jest cried and cried until I couldn't hardly see." Unlike so many enslaved people, Lindsay reunited with her family after the Civil War.[24]

On the eve of the Civil War, Annie Keel's family, along with numerous others, remained enslaved by the Five Civilized Tribes. Among the Chickasaw, 118 slaveholders kept 917 people in bondage, while among the Choctaw, 385 slaveholders enslaved 2,297 people. Most of these slaveholders were mixed-race people whose holdings on average numbered eight enslaved people. In the years immediately before the Civil War, Edmond Flint recalled that "anti-slavery agitators disturbed the peace of mind of the slave owners."[25] When the Civil War broke out, the governments of the Five Civilized Tribes, in part because of a vested interest in slavery, supported the Confederate cause. In June 1861, the Chickasaw and Choctaw governments signed a treaty with the Confederate States of America in which the rebel government promised them "territorial integrity and representation in the Confederate Congress, control over trading activities, and the existence of slavery."[26] Even so, in *Contested Territory: Whites, Native Americans, and African Americans in Oklahoma, 1865–1907*, Murray R. Wickett points out that "while officially the Five Civilized Tribes concluded treaties supporting the Confederate States of America, in fact, the tribes were bitterly divided in their support for the two sides."[27] As a reflection of that reality, some Chickasaw and Choctaw sided with the United States and even served in the Union army.[28]

The Confederate army established fighting forces among the tribes in Indian Territory. In 1862, Booker Keel began serving as a captain in Shecoe's Chickasaw Battalion, Mounted Volunteers. The Chickasaw Battalion was commanded by Colonel Martin Shecoe and primarily served in Indian Territory.[29] Booker Keel made himself useful in other ways besides fighting. Twice in 1863, he allowed the Confederate army to use a wagon and team that he owned. He received payment for this service at Boggy Depot in July and August of that year. According to Annie Keel's son Jacob, Booker Keel died in the war, though the details remain unknown. Simon Keel died shortly after the war.[30]

The enslaved population in Indian Territory took advantage of the chaos that the Civil War brought and fled for freedom. In 1861, numerous Black Indians enslaved by the Creek absconded with Opothleyahola, a Creek chief loyal to the Union. Along with other Creek and Seminole, the loyalist Black Indians fled to Kansas.[31] Mary Grayson's father and her uncles William and Hector were among those who ran away to Kansas. Uncle William, whose full name was William McIntosh, later joined the First Kansas Colored Volunteer Infantry. Interestingly, an African Methodist, Rev. John Turner, helped recruit for and served as a chaplain for this regiment.[32] Lucinda Davis recalled that in 1863, her own Uncle Abe led the enslaved men on her plantation to flee and join the Union army. Uncle Abe later fought in the war and gained the moniker "Abe Colonel."[33]

Some enslaved people witnessed the violence and upheaval of war firsthand. Lucinda Davis recalled the Battle of Honey Springs, which occurred on July 17, 1863. Lucinda was playing outdoors with Istidji when word came that a battle was approaching. Lucinda's master, Tuskaya-hiniha, gathered the enslaved workers and forced them to evacuate the house and flee the area. During their journey, Lucinda recalled seeing Confederate soldiers dragging "big guns on wheels" and Union soldiers burning down buildings. Lucinda also remembered hearing the sounds of battle, like the "guns going all day." Ultimately, Lucinda's master led his enslaved workers to Choctaw/Chickasaw lands, where they waited out the war. Throughout the journey, most of Tuskaya-hiniha's enslaved workers escaped, until Lucinda was the only one left.[34]

The Confederates and their Native allies faced defeat in 1865. The Creek and Seminole Nations both signed treaties with the US government in 1866 in which they formally ended hostilities and agreed to free their enslaved population. The Cherokee Nation, which had already abolished slavery in 1863, signed a similar treaty in 1866. The Cherokee treaty was ratified on July 27. In November, the Cherokee adopted into their tribe those freedmen who had resided in the Cherokee Nation at the time of the treaty or who returned to the nation within six months of the treaty's passage. Cherokee freedmen and their descendants could vote in local and national elections and hold government offices. In 1875, Joseph Brown was the first freedman elected to the Cherokee National Council. He was followed by several others in the 1880s and 1890s. The Creek and Seminole also adopted their freedmen in

1866. Soon afterward, the Creek Nation created a new constitution. Creek freedmen played an active role in both the legislative and judicial branches of the government. Within the Seminole Nation, freedmen enjoyed "equal political, economic, social, and cultural rights."[35] They used their suffrage rights to great effect and became a crucial constituency for leaders like John Chupco.[36]

The Chickasaw and Choctaw Nations surrendered to the Union in summer 1865. In 1866, the Chickasaw and Choctaw signed a joint treaty with the United States that formally ended the war and attempted to create a new status for their enslaved populations. Article 2 of the Chickasaw/Choctaw treaty abolished slavery among the tribes. Article 4 declared that the freedmen would be equal in all Chickasaw and Choctaw laws. This article stipulated that the freedmen living in the Chickasaw and Choctaw Nations "shall be entitled to as much land as they may cultivate for the support of themselves and families."[37] The treaty also stated that the two tribes had to adopt the freedmen as citizens by June 1868 or forfeit a $300,000 payment for lands in the "Leased District," a large portion of land in what is now southwestern Oklahoma that the US government had been leasing from the Choctaw since 1855. The 1866 treaty ceded this land back to the United States, with the further stipulation that if the tribes failed to abide by the June 1868 deadline to adopt their freedmen as citizens, the US government would use the $300,000 to aid and support the freedmen. The Chickasaw and Choctaw were displeased at this provision and refused to adopt the freedmen as full citizens of their nations. The question of freedmen citizenship remained an unresolved issue in the ensuing decades.[38]

In 1883, the Choctaw General Council finally passed "An Act to Adopt the Freedmen of the Choctaw Nation." This act granted limited citizenship to those formerly enslaved people who had been living in the Choctaw Nation when the 1866 treaty was ratified. Their descendants would receive limited citizenship as well. Freedmen and their descendants were allowed to vote and hold political office. They could not, however, serve as principal chief or district chief. They were permitted to improve land, but they were limited to forty-acre claims. They were also prohibited from collecting tribal annuities. Unlike the Choctaw, the Chickasaw never formally adopted their freedmen.[39]

The 1866 treaty stipulated that the Chickasaw and Choctaw freedmen could choose and cultivate their own land. Despite the uncertainty regarding their citizenship status within the tribes, the freedmen embraced the treaty's words and established homes and farms. Lemon Butler explained that "we just go out and improve such quantities as we think we can cultivate."[40] Edmond Flint settled in Atoka County with his family and "staked a claim, fenced 40

Figure 3. Freedmen cabins in Okmulgee, Oklahoma, circa 1899 (Oklahoma Historical Society).

acres and built a log house." He cultivated corn, which he used on his farm, and cotton, which he sold at market in Fort Smith. He also raised livestock and at one time owned seventy-five head of cattle, twenty-five ponies, and eighty-five hogs. He purchased his farm implements at the D. N. Robb store in Atoka.[41]

Similarly, Billy Keel lived on an "improvement" in Yellow Springs, presumably with Annie and their children. On his land, he built "a few log cabins."[42] Like other freedmen cabins, Billy's dwelling probably had "dirt floors and mud-and-stick chimneys" (figure 3). Billy Keel probably owned cows and pigs for sustenance and a horse or mule for transportation and labor. Although freedmen like Edmond Flint and Billy Keel occupied their land—and the treaty gave them the right to live there—they still had to battle against Indigenous and white people who encroached on them. Their questionable citizenship status left them vulnerable, yet they continued to create new lives for themselves as free people.[43]

Annie Keel and the IMAC

As Black Indians entered this new world of freedom, they sought to establish their own institutions. To further this goal, Annie Keel led efforts to bring the AME Church to Boggy Depot. African Methodists had begun working in nearby Skullyville around 1869, and Annie was, evidently, impressed with their efforts.[44] She could have chosen to join any number of other denominations, but she chose the AME Church. She ascribed to what AME historian Reginald F. Hildebrand has termed the "Gospel of Freedom," "a kind of black nationalism based on the premise that a corrective racial philosophy was absolutely necessary in order to undo the damage done by slavery, and combat ongoing racial oppression."[45] To achieve mental emancipation and racial equality, adherents to the Gospel of Freedom sought out venues for enterprise and independence. The AME Church, because of its history of Black self-government, served as an ideal such venue. Formerly enslaved people throughout the United States eagerly established AME churches like Emanuel in Charleston, South Carolina. Annie Keel did the same in Indian Territory.[46]

Annie and the Black Indians of Boggy Depot (or Whitehall) were deeply religious people who had worshipped and prayed throughout the arduous Trail of Tears. When they settled in the Chickasaw and Choctaw Nations in the 1830s, they continued their religious practices. With the assistance of their slaveholders, they built brush arbors, which were outdoor churches created from tree branches and limbs. The enslaved population of Whitehall had probably worshipped in brush arbors in the South, where the practice was common, and easily transplanted the custom to Indian Territory.[47] Brush arbor services were typically informal affairs. Among the enslaved people of Whitehall, "they had worship service very similar to the way we do now. They didn't have preachers, now, but they would sing and pray and things like that and they'd get happy and shout and so forth." Master Frank was an Indigenous slaveholder who helped the enslaved people of Whitehall build a brush arbor. Humorously, after he completed the task, the Black Indians "heard him hollering and carrying on and they thought he was shouting too, but later they found out he ran into a hornet's nest."[48]

From the 1830s to the 1860s, Annie Keel and the Black Choctaw and Chickasaw in the Boggy Depot area continued their informal worship in the brush arbors. Eventually, they decided that they wanted to become members of the AME Church. Toward that end, Annie Keel contacted a Presbyterian minister named Mr. Wright. According to Keel's descendant Lonnie Johnson Sr., "Mr. Wright was very friendly with them." He agreed to correspond with the African Methodists and ask them to "send a bishop to the Territory to organize them as a church." The result of this correspondence was that the Arkansas Annual Conference formally sent an AME minister to Indian Territory in 1870.[49]

Annie Keel and the Whitehall freedmen could have joined one of several other denominations already located in Indian Territory. By the 1870s, Methodists in the MECS, Baptists, and Presbyterians had all established a presence in the region and had successfully evangelized among the Five Civilized Tribes. Black Indians, though, were poorly represented in leadership positions within the white-controlled denominations in Indian Territory. In 1873, the MECS reported having only four Black ministers. Between 1870 and 1890, the Presbyterian Church had only one minister to serve its Black membership, the Black Choctaw Charles W. Stewart.[50] Annie Keel did not seek out membership in the MECS, the Presbyterian Church, or any of the other predominantly white denominations in Indian Territory because none of these institutions allowed Black Indians the leadership and governance opportunities that they desired.[51]

Annie Keel could have joined the Colored Methodist Episcopal Church, a predominantly Black denomination founded in 1870. This denomination had established an Indian Mission Conference by 1874 and had nearly three hundred members in Indian Territory by 1890. This organization, however, was established with the assistance of the MECS and remained under its influence. Keel desired membership in a denomination with both Black representation and autonomy. The AME Zion Church, another historically Black denomination, might have been another option for Keel, but it did not make inroads in Indian Territory until after 1890. She also could have established a Baptist congregation, but Black Baptist churches in Indian Territory, while important, came without the interstate structure and institutional support that the AME denomination offered.[52]

Meanwhile, African Methodists had developed a reputation for maintaining effective self-government, funding educational institutions, and cultivating powerful leaders. Since 1816, Black bishops, ministers, and lay officers had governed the denomination in accordance with its own Book of Discipline. In 1852, the church began publishing the *Christian Recorder*, a newspaper that informed its readership about domestic and international affairs as well as pertinent denominational news. Moreover, the *Recorder* was for African Americans the newspaper of record during the Civil War.[53] In 1863, the denomination purchased Wilberforce University in Ohio, the first private African American university in the United States. By the 1870s, when Annie Keel was considering her denominational options, the AME Church had expanded throughout the United States, and its leadership included some of the nation's most prominent and well-connected African Americans. Among these leaders were Bishop Daniel Alexander Payne, the crusader for an educated ministry, and Bishop Henry McNeal Turner, the Civil War chaplain and Reconstruction politician. Annie Keel realized that as an African Methodist she would have access to a national network of such leaders who could provide assistance and support to her community.[54]

Having weighed all her options, Annie Keel chose the AME Church, which W. E. B. Du Bois would call "the greatest Negro organization in the world."[55] By making this choice, she continued a pattern of formerly enslaved Black women who migrated to the West and spurred the founding of various AME congregations. Priscilla Baltimore helped initiate this pattern in the 1830s by creating Brooklyn AME Church, later named Quinn Chapel, in Brooklyn, Illinois. Bridget "Biddy" Mason continued the pattern in 1872 with the establishment of First AME Church in Los Angeles, California. Keel, who was Mason's contemporary, did the same in Indian Territory.[56] In the early 1900s, other AME women served in crucial leadership roles in western churches. "Rocky Mountain evangelists" in the Colorado Annual Conference, for example, included Lydia Allen, Olive Elliot, Dorcas Watson, Nannie J. Reynolds, and Mary Ramsey. At this time, the AME Church prohibited women from becoming ordained ministers.[57] Yet, out of necessity, these women were tasked with conducting revivals, organizing congregations, and pastoring churches.[58]

Evidence suggests that the Mr. Wright who helped bring African Methodism to Boggy Depot was in fact Allen Wright, who served as the chief of the Choctaw Nation from 1866 to 1870. He was also a Presbyterian minister and scholar in Boggy Depot whose accomplishments included translating the Psalms from Hebrew into the Choctaw language. Scholars have typically viewed Wright, a former slaveholder, as hostile toward the freedmen and desirous of their removal from Indian Territory.[59] His role in bringing the AME Church to Indian Territory complicates that characterization.[60]

Wright was born in Mississippi in 1826 and took the forced march to Indian Territory in 1834. From the 1840s to the 1850s, he attended prestigious schools in the East. He spent three years, from 1852 to 1855, at Union Theological Seminary in New York City, where he earned his MA. He might have learned about the AME Church during his tenure at Union. New York had several significant AME congregations at the time, including Bethel AME Church, Macedonia AME Church, and Bridge Street AME Church. Also, in May 1852, the AME General Conference convened in New York City, bringing hundreds of African Methodists to the city for three weeks.[61] After completing his education, Wright returned to Indian Territory, where he was ordained as a Presbyterian minister. In 1859, he moved his family to Boggy Depot, where "he assumed charge of the Presbyterian Church and all missions within a range of fifty miles."[62] He maintained a permanent home in Boggy Depot for the rest of his life, and it was here that he became acquainted with Annie Keel's community.

Throughout the 1860s, Wright took on leadership roles for the Choctaw. During the Civil War, he was one of the Choctaw who signed the treaty pledging support for the Confederacy. He also served in Captain Wilkins's Company of Choctaw Infantry. At the war's end, he was one of the Choctaw leaders who negotiated and signed the 1866 treaty between the Choctaw/Chickasaw and the victorious United States. In this treaty, the Choctaw and Chickasaw abolished slavery and agreed to adopt the freedmen into their tribes lest they forfeit the $300,000 payment for the Leased District. The Choctaw chose Wright to lead them through this new phase in their nation's history, electing him as principal chief in 1866. Freedmen and freedwomen like Annie Keel hoped that he would deal fairly with Black Indians and support their rights as guaranteed in the treaty.[63]

In his capacity as principal chief, Wright attended a meeting in Boggy Depot in August 1870 to discuss the freedmen's future in Indian Territory. The meeting included Governor Cyrus Harris, who was the chief of the Chickasaw, Captain George T. Olmstead, who was the Indian agent, and about three hundred Black Choctaw and Chickasaw. During this meeting, Wright told the freedmen that "now it seems that everybody is against you," and he questioned, "would it not be better if I were to advise you to leave the country and go to Liberia, where there is a home provided for free people?" He had already corresponded with the American Colonization Society about the plan and hoped that the freedmen would adopt it. They made it clear, however, that they were "perfectly satisfied" in Indian Territory and uninterested in migrating elsewhere. Wright, convinced of the freedmen's desire to stay in Indian Territory, focused his attention on improving their lives. He even asked them to "authorize me to send for a teacher," but they declined because they were too impoverished to financially support one.[64]

Annie Keel likely approached Wright about bringing the AME Church to Indian Territory shortly after the August meeting in Boggy Depot. Wright heeded her request, reasoning that the African Methodists could provide both educational opportunities and spiritual growth to the freedmen. Wright's invitation explains why early AME ministers to Indian Territory reported that "our church is cordially welcomed in this Territory," and why they established their headquarters and postal addresses in the Choctaw Nation.[65]

Wright's willingness to aid the freedmen via the AME Church might have been an attempt to curry favor with the federal government. He knew that according to the 1866 treaty, the Choctaw and Chickasaw would only receive the $300,000 payment for the Leased District if they formally adopted the freedmen into the tribe. Historian Barbara Krauthamer has explained how this treaty stipulation "wove" together the issues of Black citizenship and Choctaw and Chickasaw land, "effectively linking freedom and land as fungibles."[66] Wright did not adopt the freedmen during his time as principal chief, but he might have thought that his actions regarding the AME Church would help convince the federal government that his tribe was taking steps in that direction.[67]

So, having accepted Wright's invitation, the AME Church's Arkansas Annual Conference sent Aaron T. Gillett to Indian Territory in November 1870.[68] By 1872, Gillett had established two churches with a combined worth of $300. These two churches, one of which must have been within the Whitehall community, had forty-two members and seventeen probationers.[69] Although Gillett went to Indian Territory by invitation, he was still evangelizing in restricted lands. Indian Territory was closed to non-Natives until 1889. In that year, the federal government permitted settlers from the states to take possession of land in the western part of Indian Territory, land that it had acquired in the 1866 Reconstruction treaties (map 2).[70] In 1890, the federal government formally created Oklahoma Territory in this western section and opened it to further settlement. African Americans migrated there in significant numbers, compelling the AME Church to establish the Oklahoma Annual Conference in 1896.[71]

At the General Conference of 1872, a committee of bishops validated Gillett's early efforts in Indian Territory. In their report, Bishops William Paul Quinn, Daniel Alexander Payne, Alexander W. Wayman, Jabez P. Campbell, James A. Shorter, T. M. D. Ward, and John M. Brown expressed the "propriety" of organizing a conference "among the Indians."[72] Around this time, Bishop Shorter himself visited Indian Territory and helped organize churches.[73]

Over the next several years, AME ministers trickled into Indian Territory and began establishing a firm presence for the denomination. Their efforts remained under the auspices of the Arkansas Annual Conference. In 1876, this conference sent out ministers to six sites in Indian Territory: Skullyville Circuit, Boggy Depot Mission, and Red River Mission in the Choctaw Nation, Creek Mission in the Creek Nation, and Fort Gibson Mission and New Hope in the Cherokee Nation.[74]

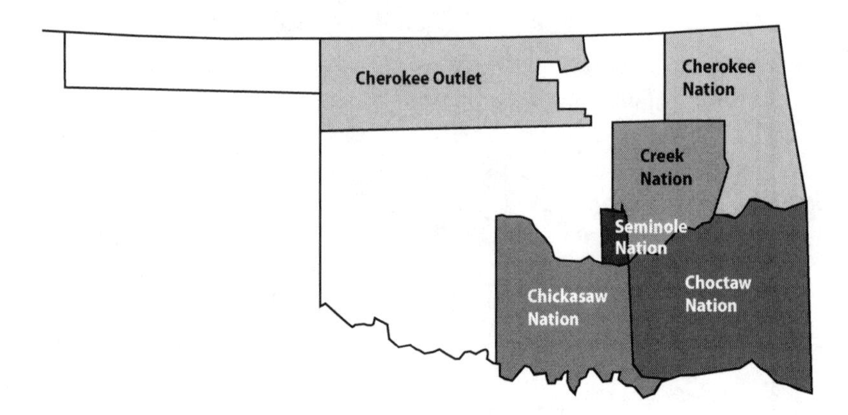

Map 2. The Five Civilized Tribes in Indian Territory, 1889

James Fitz Allan Sisson, a white AME minister, labored in Indian Territory during these early years and established his base of operations in the Choctaw Nation. In July 1877, he reported to the *Christian Recorder* that "the bounds of my District are the bounds of the Indian Territory. I have visited its tribes, and peoples raised by them [Black Indians]." Sisson remarked that he often used interpreters on his visits, a fact that made him feel that he was in a foreign country. These interpreters were likely Black Indians, who often spoke both English and Indigenous languages. Sisson contended that "we are steadily having some success." AME ministers took action when they witnessed Black Indians suffering mistreatment. Sisson decried that the Choctaw "have not adopted the colored people; and are constantly talking of driving them off of their tribes."[75] In response, a committee from the Arkansas Annual Conference "took action to bring before the authorities at Washington the outrageous treatment which the eight thousand colored people of the Indian Territory are now receiving."[76] Presumably, these AME ministers wrote a letter to secretary of the interior Carl Schurz regarding their concerns.[77]

By summer 1878, the AME Church had established at least seventeen congregations throughout Indian Territory.[78] In the Choctaw Nation, African Methodists had established Boggy Depot Mission, Skullyville Circuit, and Doaksville Mission. Sisson served at Boggy Depot Mission, probably Annie Keel's church. He called the site, "the garden spot of the west," and reported that he had thirty members.[79] In the Chickasaw Nation, there were Colbert's Station and Red River Mission.[80] In the Cherokee Nation, the church had established a congregation in Fort Gibson, at which Dennis Barrows served as pastor. In the Creek Nation, there were Creek Circuit and Webbers Falls. Creek Circuit had "the strongest membership of any," many of them farmers. In the Seminole Nation, there was the Seminole Mission, a six-year-old site that reportedly had four hundred members and seven Sunday schools.[81]

In March 1879, at the Arkansas Annual Conference meeting in Little Rock, Sisson submitted a resolution to form a separate conference for Indian Territory. He stated that "the distances by horse are very great from among the Indian raised brethren to and from the seat of the Arkansas Annual Conference." To increase efficiency in reaching these Black Indians, he argued for "the propriety, necessity, and duty of organizing an Annual Conference near Atoka, Indian Territory, on the first Thursday after the first Sabbath in September, 1879."[82] Sisson's resolution, which was unanimously passed, led to the official establishment of the Indian Mission Annual Conference a few months later.

Bishop Ward formally organized the conference on October 25, 1879. Ward, a native Pennsylvanian, was familiar with AME expansion in the West. In the 1850s, he became the "original trailblazer" for African Methodism in California. By establishing the IMAC, he continued his pattern of planting the AME Church in the West. He was a large man with a deep melodic voice. His contemporaries called him "old man eloquent" because of his superior and imaginative rhetoric.[83]

Billy Keel, as devout an African Methodist as his wife Annie, hosted the 1879 meeting at his home in Yellow Springs, Indian Territory.[84] Present at this meeting were various clergymen who had been working in Indian Territory: James Fitz Allan Sisson and Dennis Barrows, both elders; and William Henry Hynes, a deacon. Also present were seven preachers: Robert Grayson, a Black Creek; Charles Chapman, a Black Choctaw; Nelson Johnson, a Black Chickasaw; Isaac Kemp, a Black Chickasaw; Watson Brown, a Black Choctaw; and George W. McCamey and William Edwards, about whom little is recorded. Clergy from other conferences also attended the meeting at Keel's home.[85]

Bishop Ward's opening address at this meeting revealed his perceptions of Indigenous people as well as his vision for the IMAC. He began by stating, "since a boy I have heard of the Choctaw, Chickasaw and Cherokee Indians. I am glad to see you face to face and to tell you that Jesus died for the red man as well as the black man." Ward's words indicate that diverse members of the Five Civilized Tribes were present and that seeing them in person was an experience that he had long desired. Ward continued, saying,

> I remember that the red man once owned every foot of this country; but the red man is now passing away. The black man was brought here a slave, but he has increased to millions. The red man has been reduced to hundreds; the black man has no arms nor munitions of war showing that God is greater and mightier than these. In suffering there is a bond of sympathy between us, hence we bring you the black man that has equally suffered with you and been crushed; he brings to you the Gospel of Peace. We tell you of the "Man of Sorrows," who was acquainted with grief, who came to bind up the brokenhearted and to comfort them that mourn.[86]

Ward concluded by saying that the "Indian driven back from the Pacific and bereft of land may take a stand, not as a bond slave or as a warrior, but as a Christian." In this address, Ward argued that Black and Native people shared a mutual history of suffering. He contended that Indigenous people, whom he erroneously perceived as a "vanishing warrior" race, could embrace a new identity as Christians and as African Methodists. Ward believed that by adding Native people of various ethnicities to its ranks, the AME Church was fulfilling its purpose, which was to be a beacon of hope and a place of spiritual renewal for the oppressed.[87]

Those present at the meeting expressed optimism about the future of the Indian Mission Annual Conference. Elder W. R. Carson, from the West Texas Conference, declared that "you are planting good seed and I hope God may prosper you." Elder Henry Wilheit, also from the West Texas Conference, contended that "as sure as God has aided you in the past he will in the future. You have my prayers, my sympathy and all I can give you." Lastly, Rev. C. W. Porter averred that "you have no fine steepled churches or bells for us to look at or listen to, but souls are here to be saved. When sick in bed I was ordered to meet this Conference; I felt it was a heavenly call. Jehovah is with you and the brightest diamonds will be given to those who labor in this field."[88]

The AME minister John T. Jenifer sent a letter from Little Rock that was read to the assembled body. In the letter, he explained that illness prevented him from traveling to the meeting. He regretted his absence, "because I think that an act so auspicious as the formation of an Annual Conference of the A.M.E. Church, by which the sons of Ham can bring their Japhetic brothers to the cross and lift them up to the Triune God, is not only an epoch in the history of the church, which is of great significance, but it is also an event in history of each one whose privilege it is to take part in this work." By invoking the language of Ham and Japheth, Jenifer implied that the AME Church was fulfilling a biblical destiny. He expressed pride that his brethren were "now planting the banners of African Methodism upon every hilltop and in every vale in the land." He interpreted this nationwide expansion as the future of African Methodism.[89]

This 1879 conference meeting lasted for four days, during which much occurred. George McCamey and William Edwards were ordained as deacons. The conference passed resolutions for the further establishment of Sunday schools and missions and against the use of whiskey and tobacco. The conference also gave a statistical report based on the work that ministers had been doing since 1870. The conference reported 367 members, forty-three probationers, two local preachers, six exhorters, two Sunday schools, 400 students, twelve officers and teachers, and 220 books. The Indian Mission Annual Conference also had nine church buildings, worth a total of $475. Moving forward, the conference was divided into two presiding elder districts with eleven ministerial appointments.[90]

Conclusion

In 1879, the AME Church established the Indian Mission Annual Conference. By this action, the denomination formalized its outreach to diverse Indigenous people in Indian Territory. Annie Keel played an important role in this development. As a woman who had recently been freed from slavery, Keel was eager for her community to build its own institutions. She was particularly keen to do so since the Chickasaw and Choctaw were denying Black Indians a legal position in their tribes. Keel chose to join the AME Church because of its proud history of self-governance and its many institutional accomplishments. Her community had finally thrown off the shackles of slavery, and now its members would be part of a denomination founded by an enslaved man and completely controlled by people of African descent. The AME Church, as an institution for all marginalized people of color, welcomed Black Indians. In the ensuing decades, African Methodism spread throughout Indian Territory in an organized and deliberate fashion. As the next chapter shows, an ethnically diverse cadre of AME ministers worked to ensure this development.

5

"Blazing Out the Way"

The Ministers of the Indian Mission Annual Conference

Three main ethnic groups were represented within the Indian Mission Annual Conference (IMAC) clergy: Black Indian, African American, and white. Among the Black Indian ministers, there were Black Creek, Black Choctaw, Black Chickasaw, and Black Cherokee individuals. Black Creek ministers exerted the most influence and had the most longevity within the IMAC. African Americans, whose presence in Indian Territory was part of the African Methodist Migration (AMM), formed a demographic majority within the IMAC clergy. They came from Arkansas, Georgia, and a variety of other locales. They also married Black Indian women and become incorporated into their communities. There was one white minister within the IMAC, James Fitz Allan Sisson. As was demonstrated in the previous chapter, Sisson, a native of Massachusetts, played a critical role in the early growth and development of the IMAC. Because of his efforts on behalf of a historically Black denomination, he faced violence from white vigilantes.

This chapter reveals how the ministers of the IMAC came from a variety of ethnic backgrounds, demonstrating that the African Methodist Episcopal (AME) Church welcomed diversity not only in its membership, but also in its clergy. In this way, the denomination brought to fruition Richard Allen's vision of a racially and ethnically inclusive Methodist institution. Despite their differences, IMAC ministers still established ties with one another based on mutual hardships, intermarriage, and collective experiences as African Methodists. Some IMAC ministers even developed long-standing friendships. It was through their efforts that African Methodism spread throughout Indian Territory in an organized and deliberate fashion.

Black Indian Ministers

In the early years of the AME Church's development in Indian Territory, the denomination recognized the remarkable ethnic and linguistic diversity among Black Indians.[1] To succeed, the AME Church acknowledged a need to recruit ministers with the relevant cultural fluency. In that vein, the denomination elevated Black Indians, particularly among the Creek, to leadership positions. In the 1870s and 1880s, these Black Indian ministers wholly embraced African Methodism, and their contributions played a crucial role in the early success of the AME Church in Indian Territory. Their influence waned over time, in part, because of the steady influx of African American ministers. By the early 1900s, only a few Black Indian ministers were left in the IMAC.

The first AME ministers among the Creek were African Americans from the Arkansas Annual Conference. These ministers found Black Creek people to be remarkably receptive to joining the denomination. At the 1876 Arkansas Annual Conference meeting, William Jones reported that three hundred people had joined the Creek Mission, which likely included several congregations within the Creek Nation. The Arkansas Annual Conference then appointed another African American, Addison Tennyson, to the Creek Mission for the upcoming year.[2] By 1878, however, the Arkansas Annual Conference was appointing Black Creek men to pastor churches in the Creek Nation. This reflected both the conference's recognition that Black Creek individuals were needed to sustain the mission and Black Creek willingness and ability to take on such roles.[3]

Peter Stidham, a freedman, was one of the first Black Creek to serve as an AME minister. He was born around 1848 in the Creek Nation to March Coleman and Sylla Corbin. He took his last name from his master, the "wealthy Creek" slaveholder George W. Stidham. After the Civil War, he lived in Arkansas Colored town and married Bina Stidham, also a Black Creek. He embraced a leadership role in the community in the wake of the "Dunn roll." The Creek agent J. W. Dunn created this roll in 1867. It determined which Creek and Black Creek qualified for tribal citizenship and what financial benefits were associated with that status. The 1,774 people included on the "Dunn roll" were eligible to receive payments from the sale of some Creek lands to the United States. Peter Stidham collected the names of qualified Black Creek and submitted them at the "old agency." He performed this service alongside William Nero, an important community leader.[4]

When the African Methodists arrived in Creek country in the early 1870s, Stidham recognized an opportunity to serve as a spiritual leader for his community. By 1876, he was serving as a local deacon.[5] In 1878, the Arkansas Annual Conference appointed him pastor of all the churches in the Creek Nation. This appointment demonstrated that the AME Church recognized the importance of elevating Black Indians to leadership roles and that Black Creek were willing to take up that mantle. Aiding Stidham in his work was another Black Creek, George W. Grayson. Presiding elder Aaron T. Gillett visited the churches in the Creek Nation and enthused that they had the "strongest membership" of any churches in Indian Territory.[6]

Another comment that Gillett made regarding the Creek churches revealed tensions between the Black Creek and African Americans. Gillett noted that although Stidham and Grayson were "doing well," they would "do better, but they have too much fogyism." Gillett seemed to imply that the ministers were maintaining Creek traditions that he considered old-fashioned and backward. Perhaps they wore garments or accoutrements that he saw as uncouth. Perhaps they were speaking the Creek language with their congregants rather than English. These were certainly aspects of Black Creek culture that some African Americans considered off-putting. Henry Clay, an African American originally from North Carolina, gave voice to that perspective. He contended that "I never did get along good with these Creek slaves out here. . . . In fact I was afraid of these Creeks and always got off the road when I seen Creek negroes coming along. They would have red strings tied on their hats or something wild looking."[7] Another African American complained that the bilingual Black Creek "just jabber jabber and a feller can't get a word of it."[8] Gillett appeared to struggle with these same cultural differences.

For their part, the Black Creek were sometimes resistant to the presence of African Americans. Gary Zellar highlights this dynamic in *African Creeks: Estelvste and the Creek Nation*. He notes that in the 1870s and 1880s, African Americans entered the Creek Nation as farm- or railroad workers and as the spouses of Black Creek people. As this study has shown, still others came as AME ministers. Zellar contends that "enough state freed people did come into the Creek country in the early 1880s, however, to cause concern among all Creeks, no matter what their skin color." The Black Creek sometimes viewed African Americans, particularly those seeking land, as outsiders threatening Creek ways of life.[9] African Methodists recognized this attitude and willingly elevated Black Creek individuals to pastoral roles. This flexibility enabled the AME presence in the Creek Nation to grow, despite the cultural differences between the Black Creek and African Americans.

Stidham's ministry continued into the 1880s, and in 1883 he achieved the rank of local elder. He died seven years later, but by then other Black Creek ministers had already taken up the task of expanding African Methodism.[10] Robert Grayson was among them. He was born in the 1830s and lived among the Creek throughout his life. Probably, he had ties to the prominent and mixed-race Grayson family. He might have been enslaved to this family or descended from someone who was.[11] Like other Black Creek, Grayson was bilingual. He used these talents during the Civil War while serving in the First Indian Home Guard, a Union regiment.[12]

After the Civil War, Grayson became a prominent political leader. In 1867, the Creek Nation crafted a constitution that enfranchised Grayson and other Black Creek. This constitution established the National Council, the legislative branch of the government. The National Council was composed of a lower house, the House of Warriors, and an upper house, the House of Kings. Forty-seven Creek towns, including three "African" towns, elected representatives to the National Council. These three "African" towns were North Fork Colored, Arkansas Colored, and Canadian Colored. Grayson, who was raised in North Fork Colored, represented this town in the both the House of Warriors and the House of Kings.[13] In addition to serving as an elected representative from North Fork Colored, Grayson also served as one of its town kings.[14] As they had for centuries, town kings helped regulate town life. During this period, they also maintained membership rolls and ensured that residents received appropriate payments.[15]

Robert Grayson, already a significant leader in the Black Creek community, became an African Methodist in the 1870s. By 1879, he had joined the Arkansas Annual Conference as a "traveling preacher" and was appointed pastor of the churches in the Creek Nation. That October, he attended the inaugural meeting of the Indian Mission Annual Conference in Billy Keel's home.[16] Over the next several years, Grayson focused his ministerial efforts in the Muskogee area. In 1882, he reported that the Muskogee Mission had three separate churches valued at $1,000 altogether. These congregations had a combined membership of seventy-seven. Grayson also reported two Sunday schools with fifty-two students and three teachers. For the next couple of years, Grayson was assigned to the Sugar Creek Mission, also located in the Creek Nation. At this time, this mission included Sugar Creek, Pecan Creek, and Ash Creek. In 1883, Grayson reported one church building, valued at $1,000, with seventy-one members.[17] Because of his ministry, he was empowered to perform important services, like funerals, for the Black Creek community. These services added to his role as a town king.[18]

Grayson climbed the ranks of the AME ministry. During the 1882 Indian Mission Annual Conference, Presiding Elder Sisson presented Grayson for deacon's orders. Sisson took this step because he was confident in Grayson's work and his commitment to African Methodism. The Committee on Admissions and Orders examined Grayson and determined that he met the necessary academic and moral requirements. So, on the fourth day of the conference, Bishop Henry McNeal Turner ordained Grayson as a deacon, "according to the form and ceremonies of the African Methodist Episcopal Church." In addition, Turner ordained another Grayson, William, to the deaconate. William Grayson, possibly Robert Grayson's relative, was later assigned to the Okmulgee Mission in the Creek Nation.[19]

Like Peter Stidham, Robert Grayson seemed to face some cultural misunderstandings with African American ministers. At the 1884 Indian Mission Annual Conference meeting, Bishop Turner removed him from Sugar Creek and replaced him with William Grayson. Turner's reasons for moving Robert Grayson were rooted in the belief that he was a "non-progressive man." The situation angered Robert Grayson, who argued that "the Bishop should have consulted him as he could speak both languages." He implied that William Grayson was not bilingual and would, therefore, be less effective at Sugar Creek. William Grayson took over the charge and was described as "moving right forward and will make a good report this year."[20]

As a legislative representative and as an AME minister, Robert Grayson was positioned to bring educational opportunities to the Creek Nation. With the assistance of William Grayson, with whom he maintained a good relationship, he established a school at Sugar Creek. Working alongside these AME ministers were Johnson Lee and Richard Carr, both Black Creek men.[21] The Creek Nation recognized the Sugar Creek school and sent representatives to oversee its progress each quarter. In October 1885, John McIntosh, the national superintendent for the public schools in the Creek Nation, performed this task and was satisfied with what he saw.[22]

Like Grayson, John A. Broadnax used his position as an AME minister to improve education within the Black Creek community. Broadnax was born in Indian Territory in the 1860s to a Black Indian mother and an African American father. He joined the AME Church in 1882 and served as both a pastor and a presiding elder. Taking advantage of his position as an AME clergyman, Broadnax established a Sunday school and a day school in Muskogee around 1884.[23] A fellow minister effused that "[Broadnax] has one of the best Sunday and day schools on the district. If we had a few more such preachers we would be glad."[24]

In addition to bringing educational opportunities to his community, Broadnax also served as a bridge between the Black Creek and the AME

Church. In March 1885, he married Hannah Brown, the daughter of Simon Brown, who represented North Fork Colored in the House of Warriors.[25] The wedding was a society event, and even the *Indian Journal*, a popular newspaper in the Creek Nation, picked up the story. Significantly, Broadnax chose an AME minister, W. J. Smith, to perform the ceremony. In doing so, he emphasized his affiliation with the AME Church and ensured that all of his guests were aware of the denomination and its clergy. Smith conducted the ceremony at Simon Brown's home in Muskogee. Wedding guests included Black Creek individuals like Ellen Rentie and, probably, Broadnax's various AME friends and colleagues. They were perched in the sitting rooms and the gallery as they beheld the bride, who was beautifully attired in "dark and pink velvet, trimmed with rich cream colored Spanish lace" and "a flowing veil with a wreath of flowers encircling her brow and jewelry." They observed as Smith officiated the ritual according to the AME order of service. Afterward, the guests "dined sumptuously" and listened as Hannah and her friends performed "harmonious" music.[26]

After the wedding, Broadnax continued his educational work, but now with the assistance of his new family. Hannah taught at her husband's school in Muskogee. Her father served as its trustee along with L. W. Sango and H. B. Gibson.[27] In July 1885, Hannah presided over the students' final exercises for the school term. The students displayed their abilities in reading, spelling, and recitations for the "large number" of parents and friends who attended the event. Broadnax, Joe Danish, Ned Gibson, and John Kerna gave speeches, and Hannah concluded the day with music. The trustees were pleased with Hannah's success at the school and stated their desire that "she will be our teacher the next term."[28] She likely continued to assist her husband in his educational work until her premature death in March 1886.[29]

Black Creek ministers like Peter Stidham, Robert Grayson, and John A. Broadnax played crucial roles in the early years of AME expansion into Indian Territory. They pastored the Creek churches and established schools. Although African American ministers seemed to struggle with some of the cultural differences between them, they acknowledged that these Black Creek ministers were necessary for the denomination's success. The dominance of Black Creek individuals in the AME ministry reflected their status in Indian Territory. Unlike freedmen in some of the other tribes, the Black Creek played significant roles in their nation's government. Ministers like Robert Grayson and Broadnax blended their civic and spiritual roles.[30]

From the 1870s to the 1890s, a diverse mixture of Black Choctaw, Black Chickasaw, and Black Cherokee individuals joined the AME ministry as well. They lacked the same political influence as the Black Creek, but their work contributed to the early success of the AME Church in Indian Territory. These ministers included Charles Chapman and Watson Brown, both Black Choctaw, and Nelson Johnson and Isaac Kemp, both Black Chickasaw. All four men were present at the 1879 inaugural meeting of the IMAC and supported congregations in their respective communities.[31] George B. Duffin, Henry Harlin, and Fielding Evans, all Black Cherokee, joined the AME ministry as well.[32]

Watson Brown was born around 1822 and probably arrived in Indian Territory during the removal period in the 1830s.[33] He joined the AME Church because of the influence of Aaron T. Gillett. Around 1877, Gillett performed the wedding ceremony between Watson Brown and Jane, who was an African American from Arkansas. The couple felt warmly toward Gillett for his services and named their son Aaron after the AME minister. Twenty years later, when Brown applied for tribal citizenship, he explicitly stated, "I was married to [Jane] by Rev. Aaron Gellord [*sic*] a Methodist." Oftentimes, Black Indian enrollees could not recall the name of the ministers who married them, but Gillett's name was emblazoned in Brown's memory. Evidently, Gillett also influenced Brown to become an African Methodist minister, which he did in 1878. He could both read and write, educational accomplishments that the AME Church desired in its clergy. He also had the cultural fluency to work in diverse Black Indian communities. As a result, he spent his early ministry working in the Seminole Nation rather than among the Choctaw or Chickasaw.[34]

Henry Harlin, like Watson Brown, demonstrated the cultural fluidity of the Black Indian ministers. Harlin was Black Cherokee, but he preached for years among the Black Chickasaw. He began his ministry in the 1880s and recalled that his presiding elder sent him to the Chickasaw Nation to preach. He was licensed as a deacon and, eventually, pastored Wesley Chapel in Colbert.[35]

By the early 1900s, only a few Black Indian ministers were left in the IMAC. This development occurred for two main reasons. First, some of the original Black Indian ministers had died by that time. This included Peter Stidham, who died around 1890, and Henry Harlin, who died in 1901. Second, some ministers moved out of Indian Territory to serve in different districts. This was the case for John A. Broadnax, who moved to Kansas, where he remained an AME pastor and served as a grand master in the Masons. The small number of Black Indian ministers who replaced those who died or moved away tended to be Black Creek like Warrior Grayson.[36]

At the same time that Black Indian representation in the clergy declined, African American representation increased. This dynamic was not entirely new. Even in the 1880s, there were more African American than Black Indian ministers in the IMAC. The difference was a matter of scale. Whereas in 1883 there were roughly twenty IMAC ministers, most of whom were African American, in 1907 there were roughly seventy IMAC ministers. Most of them, again, were African American. This development reflected the shifting demographic realities throughout Indian Territory. According to David A. Chang, "between 1890 and 1907, the African American population of Indian Territory increased more than fourfold, surging from less than 19,000 to more than 80,000."[37] There is minimal direct evidence to explain how Black Indians in the AME Church felt about the increasingly African American clergy. They might have approached it with a combined sense of dread (as it reflected the shifting demographic dynamics of Indian Territory) and optimism (given what it said about the growth of African Methodism).

African American Ministers

Between 1870 and the early 1900s, dozens of African American ministers participated in the African Methodist Migration to Indian Territory. These ministers constituted the largest segment of AME clergy in the IMAC. As was discussed in the previous chapter, Aaron T. Gillett of Arkansas was one of the first. Ministers like Dennis Barrows, Jacob B. Young, and James Fletcher Morris followed him and, during their work, married Black Indian women. As Fay A. Yarbrough demonstrates in *Race and the Cherokee Nation: Sovereignty in the Nineteenth Century*, a significant number of non-Native individuals sought marriage partners within the Five Civilized Tribes. AME ministers like Barrows, Young, and Morris were a part of that larger nineteenth-century pattern. Their marriages integrated the AME Church within Black Indian communities and gave AME clergymen a stake in tribal citizenship battles. Ministers like A. J. Miller and G. A. L. Dykes also participated in the African Methodist Migration to Indian Territory, and their efforts significantly aided the growth of the denomination in that region.[38]

Dennis Barrows was one of the first AME ministers to join the AMM to Indian Territory. He was born in Georgia around 1852 and entered the AME ministry in the 1870s. He transferred to the Arkansas Annual Conference, and in 1876 Bishop T. M. D. Ward appointed him to the Fort Gibson Mission in the Cherokee Nation.[39] While at Fort Gibson, Barrows drew in "large and attentive congregations" and enrolled sixty students in Sabbath school. Barrows regularly wrote to Native newspapers like the *Cherokee Advocate* to publicize his church services and to inform the readership about the AME Church.[40] He built such a positive reputation in the Cherokee Nation that he was invited to preach at the Tahlequah Seminary, then the premiere educational institution in Indian Territory. His efforts helped prove the efficacy of establishing a separate conference for the churches in Indian Territory. It was appropriate, then, that he was present at the founding of the Indian Mission Annual Conference in 1879.

In the 1880s, Barrows began to pastor in the Choctaw Nation. It was here that he initiated the pattern of African American AME ministers marrying Black Indian women. Barrows pastored the McAlester Mission, where he added a new room to the parsonage, paid off debts, and added new members to the church. In the course of his work, he met and married Jane, a Black Chickasaw woman. Between 1880 and 1892, the couple had seven children: Chester, Lacey, Joseph, Edward, William, Daisy, and Annie. Barrows's marriage and children incorporated him within the Black Choctaw and Chickasaw communities. This role bolstered his influence as a minister and provided him with new civic opportunities. In the 1890s, he became a leader in the Committee of the Choctaw Colored Citizens' Association. In August 1894, he helped this organization compose a statement of grievances that they sent to the Dawes Commission. In 1898, he testified before the commission on behalf of his children and successfully had them enrolled as Choctaw freedmen. Both the 1894 statement and Barrows's 1898 testimony will be discussed in detail in chapter 7.[41]

Like Barrows, Jacob B. Young was part of the AMM to Indian Territory and became incorporated into the Black Indian community through marriage. Young was born around 1850, presumably in the South, and had migrated to Fort Gibson by the 1870s. He married Polly Vann, a Black Cherokee woman from Webbers Falls. Between 1874 and 1890, the couple had four children: Jacob, Peggy, Rosa, and Frank. During their marriage, Young served in the US Army as a so-called Buffalo Soldier. The Buffalo Soldiers belonged to all-Black regiments in the Ninth and Tenth Cavalry and the Twenty-Fourth and Twenty-Fifth Infantry. They protected the western frontier and engaged in armed combat against Indigenous groups like the Kiowa and Comanche. Young was stationed in Texas at Fort Stockton and Fort Duncan, where Polly visited him. Young retired from the army around 1880, settled in Fort Gibson, and became an AME minister. Probably, Young drew distinct differences between the Native people he fought as a soldier and the Black Cherokee whom he worked among as a minister. Young developed a strong reputation in the IMAC, as evidenced by his appointment as a ministerial delegate to the 1888 General Conference in Indianapolis.[42]

Like Barrows and Young, James Fletcher Morris was a part of the AMM to Indian Territory and became incorporated into the Black Indian community through marriage. Morris was born in Barber County, Alabama, around 1870. He migrated to Hartshorne in the Choctaw Nation, and he became a minister in the IMAC in 1894. Over the next twenty years, Morris pastored in the Choctaw and Creek Nations and served as the presiding elder of the Atoka district. Additionally, he worked as Bishop Gaines's private secretary and served on the Publication Board for the *Southern Christian Recorder*. Just as Barrows had done, Morris married a Black Chickasaw woman. She was Francis A. Stevens, and they wed in 1898. The couple had at least four children: James Wesley, Bulah, Edgar S., and Evans R. Morris. Also like Barrows, Morris parlayed his roles as an AME minister and a member of the Black Indian community into a civic leadership position. In May 1905, he was elected as the president of the Choctaw and Chickasaw Freedmen's Association, a job that he held for four years. Morris was particularly concerned with ensuring that the children of Black Indian freedmen, like his own, would receive citizenship rights. Morris later went to Washington, DC, to petition the government on behalf of the association, an event that will be discussed in detail in chapter 7.[43]

Because of their marriages, Barrows, Young, and Morris became fully incorporated into Black Indian communities. Barrows and Morris formally represented these communities through Choctaw and Chickasaw freedmen organizations. They later defended their organizations' interests before the Dawes Commission. They also advocated for their children, ensuring that they received citizenship in the tribes. These ministers' stories exemplify what happened during the African Methodist Migration. For decades, clergymen migrated to and around Indian Territory developing AME congregations and becoming integral members of the communities they served.

Many other ministers participated in the AMM to Indian Territory and played significant roles in building up the Indian Mission Annual Conference. G. A. L. Dykes was one such minister. He was born in Sherrill, Arkansas, to Jeremiah and Betsy Michell Dykes. He attended local public schools and then Shorter College, an AME institution in Little Rock. He later graduated from Jackson Theological Seminary. Sisson, undoubtedly impressed with

Dykes's academic accomplishments, requested that Dykes bring his talents to Indian Territory. Dykes arrived in 1882 and spent over a decade pastoring various churches in the Choctaw and Creek Nations. During this tenure, he became familiar with the educational needs of Black Indians. To assist them, he served as the president/superintendent of the AME Church's Sisson Mission School in Muskogee. To keep the school financially afloat, he engaged in aggressive fundraising efforts.[44]

Like Dykes, A. J. Miller was a well-educated minister who participated in the AMM to Indian Territory. Miller was born in 1858 in South Carolina to enslaved parents. After graduating from high school, he became a teacher. Then, Miller's AME mentor, Rev. M. M. Mance, helped him gain admittance to Payne Institute in Cokesbury, South Carolina.[45] After only a few months at Payne, Miller transferred to what one article lists as South Carolina University (probably either the University of South Carolina or South Carolina State University). Miller eventually attended medical school and earned an MD.[46] Miller moved from South Carolina to Indian Territory in 1880, where he worked in the Choctaw Nation. He pastored churches in Doakville and Atoka and established three additional churches himself. He later served as the presiding elder of the Atoka district.[47] While in the IMAC, A. J. Miller, like Dennis Barrows, established significant relationships beyond the Black Indian community. He worked closely with Robert A. Leslie, a Creek Baptist preacher who was married to an AME woman.[48] Leslie even wrote to the *Christian Recorder* to recount "the good work done by the Rev. A.J. Miller."[49] Miller also interacted with John Q. Tuft, the US Indian agent for Indian Territory. In 1883, Miller recalled meeting Tuft in Muskogee to discuss "some business," though he remained vague about what that business entailed.[50]

From the 1870s to the early 1900s, numerous African American ministers participated in the AMM to Indian Territory. Some of the earliest ministers included Barrows, Morris, Young, Dykes, and Miller. In 1907, the year before the IMAC became the Central Oklahoma Conference, there were around seventy such ministers.[51] They included Milton W. Austin of Texas, who pastored Bethel AME Church in Rentiesville, and James E. Toombs of Virginia, who pastored Ward Chapel AME Church in Muskogee. Additionally, C. W. Watkins pastored at Stringtown, M. D. Brookins pastored at South McAlester, R. J. Patton pastored at Atoka, William H. Buchanan pastored at Okmulgee, B. M. Mayhue pastored at Tahlequah, B. J. Nelson pastored at Fort Gibson, and A. G. Washington pastored at Vinita. Through the efforts of these clergymen, the AME Church became firmly planted throughout the Five Civilized Tribes, particularly among Black Indian communities.[52]

A White African Methodist in Indian Territory

James Fitz Allan Sisson, a white minister from Massachusetts, participated in the AMM to Indian Territory alongside his African American colleagues. He joined the AME Church in the 1860s because he believed that it was the only religious organization in the United States that truly embraced all races equally. He pastored in Maryland, Virginia, and Georgia and frequently endured violence from racist white people who resented his work within a historically Black denomination. He transferred from Georgia to Arkansas to escape the murderous mobs. In 1872, while in the Arkansas Annual Conference, he was assigned to pastor in Indian Territory, where he also faced physical threats. He played an integral role in the establishment of the IMAC and remained one of its most dedicated ministers. As a white clergyman in the AME Church, he was the living embodiment of the denomination's egalitarian ethos. His willingness to subordinate himself to Black ecclesiastical authority made him unique among the white ministers in Indian Territory.[53]

Sisson was born on November 9, 1833, in Fall River, Massachusetts. He was the second of eight children born to Thomas R. Sisson and Lydia Estes.[54] Although he was described as "a young man of fine talents and a fair education," the location of his schooling remains unknown.[55] Sisson became a trained pharmacist and likely continued in that profession until the 1860s, when he moved to the South to aid those newly freed from slavery.[56]

During his time in the postbellum South, Sisson encountered numerous white denominations. Among these were the Methodist Episcopal Church (MEC) and the Methodist Episcopal Church, South (MECS).[57] Yet, Sisson chose the AME Church.[58] According to his friend and AME ministerial colleague Theophilus Gould Steward, Sisson did so "because of its universality, or cosmopolitanism in practice." Steward also remarked that "despite that part of its name which seemed to indicate a race church, it was, according to Brother Sisson's observation, the only church he could find in the land where no race was barred and where all shared alike in its privileges. It was the African Church; but it was open to all, of whatever race or clime."[59] Sisson considered genuine racial egalitarianism to be a prerequisite for any denomination that he joined, and by his analysis only the AME Church fit this description.

Sisson's career in the AME Church started in the Baltimore Annual Conference, to which he was formally admitted in 1866. At this time, the AME Church was rapidly growing throughout the South, something that white people had prohibited prior to the Civil War. Sisson's efforts contributed to this Southern expansion. He was one of the first AME ministers to evangelize among the Black community in Cecilton, Maryland. Prior to his arrival, the residents of Cecilton had never seen "white men who believed in their educational advancement." Sisson, who protested against "color prejudice and proscription in any and every form," drastically altered their point of view.[60]

When the white residents of Cecilton discovered Sisson's efforts, they were enraged. They made their feelings clear on one Sunday in July 1866. That morning, Sisson had preached at the local church and had formally organized a missionary society. Somehow, a mob of about twenty white people discovered that a "white man was at the 'nigger' church calling the 'niggers' brother and sister." They posted themselves at the doors and windows of the church as Sisson conducted an afternoon meeting with the Sabbath school. They wanted to "hear for themselves what was said, and to prove that though Richmond had fallen, and Lee had surrendered. . . . Cecilton was one of the places not subdued."[61] They were armed with clubs, knives, and pistols.[62]

Despite the presence of the hostile crowd, Sisson continued his meeting undaunted. He spoke of the history of the AME Church and contended that its purpose was to "demonstrate to the world that the colored man was susceptible of the same development, morally, intellectually and otherwise, that any other race variety was." At this, the mob leader shouted, "That's a lie." Sisson ignored the interruption and noted the accomplishments of the AME Church. He mentioned the denomination's Book Concern in Philadelphia; its newspaper, the *Christian Recorder*; its institution of higher education, Wilberforce University in Ohio; and its eight "full-fledged" bishops. These declarations rendered the mob apoplectic with rage. They threatened violence if he continued and gave him fifteen minutes to leave. Fearing for his safety and the safety of others, he agreed to depart. As he left, the mob threw apples at him, and one man beat him with a stick. The rest of the congregation fled in terror. Sisson was rushed away to Chesapeake City and then Baltimore, where he made a complaint at the Freedmen's Bureau. The mob escaped legal retribution for the attack, but the white people were compelled to stop their harassment of the African Methodists. Some Black people responded to the event by preparing means of "self-protection." Others, at least for a time, steered clear of the AME Church.[63]

The violence that Sisson faced was typical during Reconstruction, particularly from the Ku Klux Klan and other vigilante groups. Southern white people, furious at the destruction of the former slave regime, lashed out against Black people and their white allies. Because of his efforts on behalf of the AME Church, Sisson was vulnerable to attacks. As one sympathetic

African Methodist explained, "It will be remembered that Rev. James F. Sisson is a white man, and the fact that he was doing Christian work among the colored people was considered a crime by these white 'gentlemen,' punishable with the use of pistol and club on her [*sic*] person."[64]

Despite the risks to his safety, Sisson continued his work in the AME Church. While still under the auspices of the Baltimore Annual Conference, he helped Bishop Alexander W. Wayman spread the AME Church into Virginia. Sisson was particularly active in the Portsmouth area, and he petitioned the denomination to send financial aid to a church in nearby Jolliffe. By 1867, enough work had been accomplished in Virginia that Wayman officially established the Virginia Annual Conference. Sisson was fiercely proud of his contributions to this work, and in 1887 he corrected an inaccuracy in the *Christian Recorder* regarding his part in Virginia's AME development.[65]

In addition to his church work, Sisson was also active in social justice initiatives aimed at advancing Black civil rights. In January 1866, he attended a Capital City Equal Rights League meeting at an AME church in Harrisburg, Pennsylvania. The president of the organization introduced Sisson, who spoke on the topic of "Progress and Equal Rights." Sisson's address was well received by the members of the league, who awarded him five dollars to support his mission work in the South.[66] While in Pennsylvania, Sisson also spent four days organizing missionary societies in the Williamsport area and planned to collect clothing, books, and other domestic goods for needy Southern freedmen. His efforts compelled one observer to say that "I have seen a great many men who profess to be our friends, of Mr. Sisson's color, but never came up with one equal to himself: he is both a gentleman and a Christian in every way."[67]

Around 1870, Sisson transferred to the Georgia Annual Conference. On May 11, 1870, he opened an account at a Georgia branch of the Freedman's Saving and Trust Company, more commonly known as the Freedmen's Bank. The US government created this institution in 1865. Its purpose was to make banking services available to newly emancipated Black people and to provide them with an opportunity to save money and build wealth. Unfortunately, due to mismanagement and difficult economic times, the bank failed in 1874. Nevertheless, by supporting this endeavor, Sisson demonstrated his understanding of the economic issues facing the freedmen and his commitment to alleviating them.[68]

In May 1872, Sisson began his pastorate of the Ringgold Circuit in Catoosa County, Georgia. This circuit included St. John's AME Church, an appointment where he established a day school. On July 18, 1872, he wrote an impassioned letter to President Ulysses S. Grant. In the missive, Sisson complained that white people in Ringgold were threatening him with violence. These white locals resented his educational work among freedmen and felt particularly galled that he belonged to a Black denomination and deferred to Black bishops and presiding elders. Sisson explained to the president that "indecent epithets have been applied to me. . . . Bricks and stones have been frequently thrown at me, while I have been passing through the Streets of [Ringgold]. Threats have been made to ride me on a rail, to drive me out of town, and to kill me." Other African Methodists in Ringgold faced similar physical threats. Sisson's day school teacher was pushed off the railroad veranda, hit in the head, and attacked with bricks and stones. Sisson pleaded with the president to dispatch the military to Ringgold to protect him and the Black population.[69]

Grant either ignored Sisson's entreaties or gave an insufficient response. In order to escape the violence in Ringgold, Sisson transferred to the Arkansas Annual Conference in November 1872. At the 1872 Arkansas Annual Conference meeting in Camden, Bishop John M. Brown appointed Sisson presiding elder of the Little Rock district. This district encompassed Indian Territory, so Sisson began visiting and evangelizing among the "ten thousand" Black people who were "dispersed among the Indian tribes." He continued this work throughout the 1870s and was instrumental in establishing the Indian Mission Annual Conference in 1879.[70]

During his tenure in Indian Territory, Sisson faced the same harassment that he had suffered in both Maryland and Georgia. In 1878, while he was pastoring at Boggy Depot, an unknown assailant shot up his home. Evidently, this attack occurred because Sisson was teaching school among Black Indian children. At the 1879 New England Annual Conference meeting, Sisson displayed two of the bullets that had been lodged in the walls of his cabin as proof of the assault.[71]

Sisson remained in the IMAC throughout the 1880s, earning the nickname "Apostle Sisson" because of his "labors, hardships, sacrifices."[72] He served as an IMAC delegate to the General Conference in both 1880 and 1884. At the 1884 conference, held in Baltimore at Bethel Church, his presence caught the attention of James M. Maxwell, who was covering the event for the *Independent* newspaper. He described Sisson with a mixture of admiration and disbelief saying, "the Rev. James A. Sisson, a presiding elder from the Indian Territory, was the only white preacher connected with the Conference. Mr. Sisson, like a pet lamb living with a drove of milch cows, has associated with these brethren over twenty years—all his ecclesiastical life—from choice."[73]

Although Maxwell was baffled at Sisson's denominational choice, African Methodists had long since embraced him and his work in the IMAC. Around 1886, Sisson transferred to the Mississippi Conference, where he served at Grove Circuit. He died two years later at the age of fifty-five. He never married, so only his mother and four siblings survived him.[74]

Sisson built his legacy as an AME minister in the IMAC. His presence, as a white man in a predominantly Black denomination, sent a powerful message to the residents of Indian Territory. This message was that people of color could and should govern their own institutions and that well-meaning white people should respect their authority. He also demonstrated that the AME Church was truly a racially egalitarian organization.[75]

Diverse Ministers United in Ministry

As the previous sections have demonstrated, the ministers of the IMAC were remarkably diverse. There were Black Indians from various ethnic communities, African Americans from all over the South, and even a white minister from the Northeast. There were occasions of intercultural misunderstandings and tensions, but, as this section will show, these ministers also developed close ties to one another. They built ties because they shared mutual hardships, because they intermarried within Black Indian communities, and because the traditional AME calendar required that they consistently interacted with one another. Because of these factors, some IMAC ministers created long-standing relationships.

Laboring in Indian Territory was a challenging task for the diverse ministers in the IMAC. The lack of money was one of the most consistent problems. Many churches in the IMAC could not afford to adequately pay their pastors because the members themselves were poor farmers who had "no wages" and "very little money in circulation."[76] Sisson explained that "it is not possible for the pastors to clothe themselves decently from the salaries they get, nor can they purchase ponies, saddles, bridles and blankets needful for their transportation over their missions." He recalled that "only a few days ago, I was at a pastor's house, while his children were crying for bread."[77] This financial situation also affected presiding elders, who were tasked with traveling hundreds of miles to visit all the churches in their districts.[78] Since he could not rely completely on the churches to pay for his travel expenses, Sisson solicited money from his friends on the East Coast. Even with that support, he lamented that "in so many instances I suffered for food, shelter, etc., and Nellie shared with me. She is my faithful Choctaw pony."[79] Poor harvests exacerbated the situation. In one year, both the corn and cotton crops failed, causing yet more financial hardship for the IMAC church members and, by extension, their pastors and presiding elders.[80] Black Indian ministers, who had the benefit of their well-established communities for support, complained less about these difficulties than did their African American and white counterparts.

IMAC ministers formed strong bonds because of their mutual difficulties, and they supported one another through those difficulties. In 1877, Barrows warmly recalled an occasion when Sisson came to his aid. Barrows had been recently appointed pastor of Fort Gibson and was traveling there from Little Rock, Arkansas. On the way, he stopped at Fort Smith, apparently unable to secure enough money to complete his journey. He was fretting about how to proceed when "my beloved Elder J.F.A. Sisson" appeared. Barrows informed him of his predicament. Sisson responded by securing two horses and then traveling with Barrows to Fort Gibson, an eighty-mile journey. When they finally arrived at their destination, a local family housed them. Barrows fondly recounted that "we laid down, and we slept just as good as if we were in the best of our state friends houses."[81] During the course of his ministry, Barrows maintained his relationship with Sisson, and he formed other intercultural ties within the IMAC clergy.

When Barrows married his wife, Jane, she incorporated him into the Black Choctaw and Chickasaw communities. This fact enabled him to establish a long-standing friendship with another IMAC minister, the Black Choctaw Watson Brown. Because of their relationship, Brown was both willing and able to help Barrows's children with their tribal citizenship applications for the Dawes Commission. In December 1902, Brown appeared before a notary public and signed an "affidavit of acquaintance" for Barrows's son Chester. In this document, he acknowledged that Chester had died in February 1901. In November 1903, Brown and his wife appeared before another notary public to sign affidavits for Barrows's daughters Daisy and Annie. The document for Daisy stated that "we Watson Brown and Jane Brown, on oath state that we knowed [*sic*] Jane Barrows who was a citizen, by adoption, of the Chickasaw Nation; that she was the lawful wife of Dennis Barrows, who is a citizen [of the] U.S., that a female child was born to her on the 11th day of April 1891; that said child has been named Daisy Barrows, and is now living."[82] The affidavit for Annie was virtually the same. Brown's willingness and ability to aid the Barrows children reveals the close bonds between their families, bonds that were sealed by the men's connection as IMAC ministers.[83]

IMAC ministers also established relationships because they regularly interacted at AME meetings like the district conference. District conferences were held once per year and were attended by all the pastors in a particular region of the IMAC. The presiding elder of that district governed the meeting. Pastors took turns presenting reports on their churches, and then they all came together to initiate plans for the district's success.[84]

On March 25, 1886, the Fort Gibson district commenced its district conference. Presiding elder John A. Broadnax governed the meeting. In attendance were pastors including Robert Grayson, Jacob B. Young, and G. A. L. Dykes. On the first day, all the ministers delivered reports on their churches. That evening, the conference held the first of several worship services for the conference members and the residents of Fort Gibson. The next day, the conference discussed the possibility of establishing a school in Muskogee, in the Creek Nation. Toward that end, the conference appointed a committee to discuss the matter with Joseph M. Perryman, the chief of the Creek Nation. The committee's goal was to see "what his honorable board or council will do for us in that direction."[85] Given his position in the Creek legislature and his experience with the Sugar Creek school, Grayson probably led this committee. At this time, there was already an AME school in existence in Muskogee, the Sisson Mission School. The meeting with Perryman might have been an effort to find financial support for this school or another altogether. So, at this district conference, Black Indians and African Americans heard each other's reports, attended worship services together, and worked together to create a school. This experience of intercultural interaction was duplicated every year and in every district of the IMAC.[86]

Travel to and from AME meetings also bonded IMAC ministers. These journeys varied in duration but could last for weeks. In 1880, A. J. Miller and James Fitz Allan Sisson both attended the General Conference meeting in Saint Louis, Missouri. Afterward, they sojourned together to Indian Territory.[87] Miller was new to the IMAC, so he hardly knew Sisson. Nevertheless, he recalled that the two men had "a very pleasant time" during the trip. They reached Atoka in the Choctaw Nation and remained there for two weeks. Presumably, Sisson spent that time introducing Miller to local African Methodists and relevant Choctaw leaders. Finally, the pair proceeded to Miller's new pastorate in Doaksville. During that trip, they stopped in Caddo, where Miller observed Sisson conducting a quarterly conference. The next day they attended Sunday morning worship service together.[88] This weeks-long journey in 1880 cemented a bond between the men that lasted nearly a decade. Both men later transferred to the Mississippi Conference, where they maintained their friendship.[89] It was no surprise, then, that when Sisson died in 1888, Miller wrote an obituary for the *Christian Recorder*. In it, he bade his friend to "sleep on, servant of God."[90]

The ministers of the IMAC were ethnically diverse, but their differences did not inhibit them from forming connections. Many shared the common experience of financial and material want, and they supported one another through those difficulties. African Americans who married Black Indian women were able to form close relationships with Black Indian ministers, such as in the case of Barrows and Brown. Also, IMAC ministers attended various AME meetings together, sometimes traveling with one another on the way there and back. Not all IMAC ministers were the best of friends, but their experiences in Indian Territory gave them a unique bond.

Conclusion

A diverse cadre of ministers spread African Methodism throughout Indian Territory, further demonstrating that racial and ethnic inclusivity were significant facets of the AME Church. Ministers like Grayson, Barrows, Sisson, and a host of others worked alongside one another in the IMAC. They recognized their cultural differences, but they remained committed to their common goal. J. F. Dixon, another IMAC minister, explained it well, saying that "we encounter many difficulties, adversities, prejudices and oppositions from all sides and directions . . . but we as heralds of the gospel of Christ are united in intention to plant the banner of African Methodism in every portion of this territory."[91] Together with their equally diverse parishioners, AME ministers went on to establish churches and schools among the Five Civilized Tribes. The next chapter takes an in-depth look at these developments and other institutional structures that African Methodists put into place in Indian Territory.

6

Conferences, Churches, Schools, and Publications

Creating an AME Church Infrastructure in Indian Territory

Throughout the nineteenth and twentieth centuries, the diverse residents of Indian Territory displayed a remarkable receptivity to the African Methodist Episcopal (AME) Church. Creek, Black Creek, Black Choctaw, Black Chickasaw, Black Cherokee, and Black Seminole individuals all became African Methodists. Native leaders like Green McCurtain and Pleasant Porter were unwilling to join the AME Church themselves, but they donated property to the denomination and supported its land claims. Buoyed by this assistance, African Methodists spent decades creating a firm foundation for the AME Church in Indian Territory.[1]

This chapter argues that the AME Church created a lasting infrastructure in Indian Territory by establishing the Indian Mission Annual Conference (IMAC), building churches and schools, and using AME and non-AME publications to promote the denomination's work. This development was only possible because of the openness that Indigenous people of various ethnicities showed toward African Methodism. This is, ultimately, but one example of how the denomination functioned in the numerous areas of the African Methodist Migration (AMM).[2]

The Indian Mission Annual Conference

With the support of laypeople like Annie and Billy Keel and the labor of diverse ministers like Robert Grayson, Dennis Barrows, and James Fitz Allan Sisson, the AME Church established the Indian Mission Annual Conference in 1879. Whenever African Methodists created a new conference, they constructed a complex infrastructure to support it. As part of that infrastructure, the General Conference assigned a bishop whose job it was to oversee the conference and appoint presiding elders and pastors. The new conference was tasked with fulfilling various financial obligations, holding annual meetings that served as both business and worship sessions, and establishing its own chapter of a women's missionary organization. The creation of the IMAC continued this established pattern, as the following section will discuss.

At the 1880 General Conference, the newly created IMAC was assigned to the Eighth Episcopal District, which also included conferences in Arkansas and Mississippi. Bishop Henry McNeal Turner, who was one of the most prominent African Americans in the country, was appointed episcopal leader of this district. For the churches in Indian Territory, this development represented an improvement over their previous circumstances. While under the auspices of the Arkansas Annual Conference for nearly a decade, these churches had enjoyed only limited episcopal support. But now, as an official conference, they were entitled to greater attention and oversight. Gaining Turner as their bishop added to their excitement. Turner had already achieved national stature by becoming the first Black chaplain in the US Army in 1863, serving in the Georgia legislature in 1868, being appointed the postmaster of Macon, Georgia, in 1869, and reaching the AME episcopacy in 1880. African Methodists in Indian Territory took great pride in having Turner as their first bishop, and they were eager to enjoy the fruits of his energy and expertise.[3]

There was another significant reason why African Methodists in the IMAC were pleased at Turner's episcopal appointment. Since their arrival in Indian Territory, African Methodists had faced skepticism about their denomination's legitimacy. While Black Indians like Annie Keel welcomed the denomination, others doubted the validity of this independent Black organization. In 1877, Barrows reported that a Black Cherokee man once impeded him from using a church building because he had "never heard of the African Methodist Episcopal Church and its origin and that it is controlled by colored Bishops. Such a Church is not recognized in the United States."[4] Presiding elder Aaron T. Gillett faced similar incredulity. Writing from Fort Gibson in 1878, he stated that "a great many of our people here in the Indian country do not believe there is a colored Bishop, and will not until they see one."[5] Unlike Annie Keel, some Black Indians were so accustomed to viewing people of African descent in servile positions that the idea of a self-governing Black institution seemed impossible. To counteract this impression, Barrows and others continually encouraged bishops to visit Indian Territory. Bishop T. M. D. Ward obliged during the 1879 founding of the IMAC, but the African

Methodists in Indian Territory hoped that Bishop Turner's term in the conference would permanently end Black Indians' cynicism. Their hopes were well founded; ministers ceased complaining about this issue in the 1880s.[6]

Bishop Turner played a crucial role in the early years of the IMAC's existence, serving as this conference's presiding bishop from 1880 to 1884. He recruited talented ministers for the IMAC such as A. J. Miller. He met Miller at the 1880 General Conference and immediately appointed him to Doaksville in the Choctaw Nation. As the previous chapter highlighted, Miller became an important asset to the IMAC. During his four-year tenure, Turner also served as a staunch advocate for education. Using his political connections and skill, he secured funds for freedmen schools from the commissioner of Indian affairs. This aspect of his episcopal service will be examined in detail later in the chapter.[7]

Perhaps Turner's most lasting contribution to the IMAC was simply his presence. Turner, who lived in Atlanta, visited Indian Territory at least once a year to preside over the annual conference. This meeting lasted for about one week, but Turner likely spent additional days in Indian Territory before or after the meeting to converse with IMAC members and to examine the conference's progress. During these yearly meetings, Turner offered words of encouragement to the assembled clergy and lay members of the IMAC. Given the myriad struggles that they were facing, as outlined in the previous chapter, these African Methodists embraced Turner's words. At the 1881 meeting in Fort Gibson, for example, Turner declared, "You, my dear brethren, are the pioneers of a great and noble Church. If you are wearied of your heavy burden look through the future and hear the [*sic*] now babes and unborn posterity calling you blessed, and when you are old and unable to do anything save praise God, you will see a grand assemblage of men devising and making laws for a conference of which you are fathers." In response, A. J. Miller contended that "Bishop Tuner [*sic*] is the man that the Indian Territory has been looking [for] and desiring for a long time."[8] Turner's appearance every year reassured African Methodists in Indian Territory about their important place within the connectional AME Church and silenced critics who doubted the validity of the denomination.[9]

Turner's humble demeanor surprised and delighted the residents of Indian Territory. They assumed that a man of his stature would be cold and unapproachable. A member of A. J. Miller's church in Atoka was happy to be proven wrong. He contended that "Bishop Turner is the man for me. He sent for me to come and see him. I thought he would treat me as I had before been treated, but I was much mistaken. He asked me in, shook my hand

and talked with me as though I was a man not of a lower creation than he. I tell you he is the man for us colored people out here." Other members of the IMAC expressed similar sentiments, making comments such as, "I like Bishop Turner, he is so social and friendly, I was sorry when he left. He does not treat us as if we were not human."[10] Perhaps, these Black Indians were referring to how white Christians had treated them poorly in the past.

The African Methodists in Indian Territory enjoyed Turner's episcopal stewardship. They were bewildered, however, at the financial obligations imposed on them as members of the IMAC. They were already accustomed to their local requirements, which included paying their pastors' salaries and providing them with housing accommodations. Although many of these African Methodists were impoverished, they tried to meet these requirements, even going so far as to board their pastors in their own homes.[11] With the establishment of the IMAC, they had new connectional obligations. They had to elect delegates to represent them at the General Conference and then pay for those delegates' travel expenses. Some viewed such requirements as superfluous and unfair given their own financial hardships. On the eve of the 1880 General Conference in Saint Louis, Sisson, who was elected as an IMAC delegate, complained that "when I appeal for traveling expenses to and from St. Louis, they think they are not able. Their argument is conclusive. 'We are not able to send you, and if you can't go, you can't; that's all and you'll have to tell the Bishop so and he'll have to excuse you.'" Sisson further explained that he needed fifty dollars for the round-trip journey and more for "clothes and incidental expenses."[12] Sisson did, ultimately, attend the meeting, but he remained exasperated with his lack of financial support. His frustration was understandable, but so too was the Black Indians' position. Never before had they financially supported an institution with such a complex fiscal system, and they needed time to adjust.

Over time, the members of the IMAC did adjust to their financial responsibilities as members of the connectional AME Church. Their gradual support of the Dollar Money system provides evidence of that fact. The General Conference instituted the Dollar Money system in 1868 to finance the denomination's national and international infrastructure. Under this system, ministers were required to collect one dollar from each church member annually. The Financial Department of the AME Church, which was organized in 1872, collected all the Dollar Money and used it to support the general expenses of the church, like the salaries of bishops and general officers. Dollar Money also supported the Publication Department, AME colleges, missions, the widows of ministers, the Church Extension Society, and other institutional enterprises. The AME Church continued the Dollar Money system until 1956, when it adopted a new budgetary system.[13] While under the auspices of the Arkansas Annual Conference, the churches in Indian Territory had been expected to contribute to the Dollar Money system, but that expectation increased exponentially with the creation of the IMAC.[14]

The IMAC steadily increased the amount of Dollar Money that it submitted to the Financial Department. In 1880, the newly created IMAC raised only $21.19, a very modest amount compared to what other more established conferences raised. This amount suggests that some church members paid their full dollar, while others paid whatever they could, whether it be ten cents or even less. In 1884, the IMAC's Dollar Money amount increased to $260.70, and in 1907, the conference raised well over $1,000. This steady increase shows that the members of the IMAC gradually accepted their new financial obligation.[15] The annual conference minutes of the IMAC, which were supposed to be printed every year, included the names of all church members who paid their Dollar Money. This practice was standard throughout the AME Church and encouraged widespread participation. Because of this practice, the identities of many early members of the IMAC have been preserved. Jane Ward, a formerly enslaved woman of both African and Choctaw descent, appeared on the 1883 Dollar Money list for Bethel AME Church in Atoka. Jane's mother, Meliza Flint, also paid her Dollar Money that year, as did nineteen others from Bethel.[16]

The creation of the IMAC placed another responsibility on the residents of Indian Territory, that of hosting their own annual conference meetings. Previously, they had attended Arkansas Annual Conference gatherings in cities like Little Rock. After 1879, they were obliged to hold these yearly gatherings themselves. The AME churches in Muskogee and Fort Gibson, because of their location and prosperity, often hosted the annual conference for the IMAC. During these gatherings, clergy and laity from throughout Indian Territory met for roughly a week. Ministers presented reports on the progress of their churches, and the presiding bishop handed out pastoral appointments for the new conference year. Annual conferences were also social occasions in which African Methodists could "meet, greet, and eat."[17] These meetings helped foster a sense of community among a diverse body of Black Indians and African Americans.[18]

During annual conferences, IMAC members were immersed in AME liturgy, a unifying experience for these diverse people. On the opening day of the 1883 Indian Mission Annual Conference in Brazil, Choctaw Nation, Bishop Turner read the Decalogue, or the Ten Commandments. The conference responded to each commandment in typical AME fashion, with, "Lord have mercy upon us, and help us to keep this law." Turner repeated this ritual on the fourth day of the meeting during Sunday morning services. By reciting the Decalogue, African Methodists affirmed their belief in one God and vowed not to kill, steal, lie, or covet. Committing themselves to the Law of Moses helped African Methodists order their lives and maintain good relationships with one another. Another ritual that was common during annual conferences was the singing of the Doxology. African Methodists typically sang this song at the beginning and the end of all worship services. Like the recitation of the Decalogue, the singing of the Doxology occurred throughout the 1883 annual conference meeting.[19] The AME Doxology originated in the Church of England, and its purpose was to praise and glorify God. The lyrics were:

> Praise God from whom all blessings flow
> Praise Him all creatures here below
> Praise Him above, ye heavenly host
> Praise Father, Son, and Holy Ghost.[20]

By singing this song, African Methodists expressed their conception of a generous God and affirmed their belief in the Trinity.

During annual conferences, IMAC members were also exposed to traditional AME hymnody. Richard Allen published a hymnal in 1801 while he was pastoring "Mother" Bethel in Philadelphia. In 1818, he produced the denomination's first official hymnal, *The African Methodist Pocket Hymn Book*. Revised and updated AME hymnals have been printed regularly ever since. These hymnals contain a preponderance of songs from Charles Wesley, one of the founders of Methodism. Wesleyan hymns are both poetic and instructive, their lyrics expressing Methodist principles and offering Christian encouragement.[21]

Bishop Turner was a strong proponent of Wesleyan hymnody.[22] He opened both the 1882 annual conference meeting in McAlester and the 1883 annual conference meeting in Brazil with "And Are We Yet Alive," a song that described the salvific process as understood by Methodists. It began by acknowledging God's grace: "And are we yet alive, / and see each other's face? / Glory and thanks to Jesus give / for his almighty grace!" It went on to proclaim, "Preserved by power divine / to full salvation here, / again in Jesus' praise we join, / and in his sight appear." The third stanza would have resonated with the clergymen struggling in Indian Territory: "What troubles have we seen, / what mighty conflicts past, / fightings without, and fears within, / since we assembled last!" The final three stanzas expressed God's love and the process of human perfection:

Yet out of all the Lord
hath brought us by his love;
and still he doth his help afford,
and hides our life above.

Then let us make our boast
of his redeeming power,
which saves us to the uttermost,
till we can sin no more.

Let us take up the cross
till we the crown obtain,
and gladly reckon all things loss
so we may Jesus gain.

By singing this hymn, the clergy and the lay people of Indian Territory reaffirmed their belief in Methodist theology. Other hymns sung at the 1882 and 1883 meetings included "Comfort Ye Ministers of Grace," "Soldiers of Christ, Arise," "A Charge to Keep I Have," and "Jesus, Lover of My Soul," all four hymns written by Charles Wesley. They also sang "Alas! And Did My Savior Bleed," "Together Let Us Sweetly Live," and "Jerusalem, My Happy Home." These hymns connected IMAC members to African Methodism and the broader family of Methodist religious bodies.[23]

The Indian Mission Annual Conference attracted outside visitors. Bishop Ward recalled that on the opening day of the 1891 meeting, an "Indian chief" gave a "very impressive address." Ward did not mention the man's tribal origins, but presumably he belonged to one of the Five Civilized Tribes. The man attended the meeting because he recognized a commonality of oppression between Black and Native people. To the assembled body of African Methodists, "he spoke of the prejudice that existed in the heart of the white man towards the Indian and Negro. He said that it was nothing new in the history of the world for one race to try to crush out another, but that truth crushed to the earth, will rise again for the eternal world is hers. He said we were not to become disheartened by difficulties thrown across our path."[24] Witnessing the denominational strength of the AME Church and its ethnic diversity made this man hopeful that these people of color would overcome the pernicious racism that subjugated them.

The Women's Home and Foreign Missionary Society (WHFMS) formed another part of the IMAC's infrastructure. At the urging of an evangelist, Lucy Thurman, Bishop Turner and secretary of missions William B. Derrick established this connectional organization at the 1893 Michigan Annual Conference meeting in South Bend, Indiana. The General Conference formally recognized the WHFMS in 1896, and its members primarily included AME women in the South and the West. The organization was meant to be a counterpoint to the northern-based Women's Parent Mite Missionary Society (WPMMS), which was founded in 1874 and was led by the wives of AME bishops. The WHFMS supported Turner's missionary efforts in Sierra Leone, Liberia, and South Africa. It also provided preaching opportunities for women who were interested in joining the ministry.[25] Both the WHFMS and the WPMMS operated at the same time as the Women's Convention of the National Baptist Convention, an organization that Evelyn Brooks Higginbotham highlights in *Righteous Discontent: The Women's Movement in the Black Baptist Church*. While all these female auxiliaries operated within their respective denominations, they were largely autonomous. They generally selected their own officers and raised and deployed their own funds.[26]

The IMAC branch of the WHFMS was formally established by Bishop Wesley J. Gaines at the 1897 annual conference meeting in Muskogee. It was composed of local chapters from individual churches throughout Indian Territory, each with its own officers.[27] By 1907, almost thirty churches in the IMAC had branches of the WHFMS, and that year they raised about $120.[28] Emma Tucker, the wife of presiding elder Charles R. Tucker, served as the first president of the IMAC branch of the WHFMS. She brought both an Atlantic World consciousness and an impressive level of professionalism to the organization. She demonstrated her commitment to the former at the group's first annual meeting, which took place in August 1898 in South McAlester. On August 4, she supported the suspension of all business so that the assembled body could celebrate "the emancipation of the slaves of the West Indies," which had occurred on August 1, 1834.[29] This was the same historical moment that Thomas Sunrise memorialized in 1859.[30] Tucker and the AME missionaries traveled fifteen miles to Hartshorne to enjoy orations that marked the occasion. During Tucker's presidential tenure, her contemporaries remarked on how efficiently and effectively she executed her work. At the second annual meeting of the WHFMS, the conference reporter effused that the "meeting was managed in such a graceful and intelligent manner that I tried to believe that I was dreaming. I thought could it be possible that I was here in the Indian Mission Conference or was I in Atlanta, Nashville,

Columbia, Jacksonville, Philadelphia or some city in some of our older conferences? But indeed it is here in this territory."[31]

The IMAC branch of the WHFMS continued to develop during the 1900s, and Tucker remained active in the organization. A multiethnic cadre of women joined her in this work, many of whom were also married to IMAC clergy. One of these women was Frances Walker, a Black Cherokee woman who married the African American AME minister Daniel S. Walker. Bishop Gaines handpicked Frances Walker to assist Tucker when he first created the IMAC branch of the WHFMS in 1897.[32] Walker was particularly successful at developing the organization in Webbers Falls in the Cherokee Nation. In 1898, a church member in Webbers Falls declared that the missionary society there had "shown greater improvement than any other department of the church." He attributed this growth "to the untiring efforts of the pastor and Sister Francis Walker, who have worked conjointly to advance the interest of this particular society."[33]

Working alongside Tucker and Walker were numerous other women of various ethnicities. They included Celia Boyd, a Black Choctaw who became the president of the Atoka district's WHFMS in 1898; Annie Osborne, a Black Creek; Francis A. Morris, a Black Chickasaw and the wife of the minister James Fletcher Morris; Addie R. Toombs, the wife of the minister James E. Toombs; and M. L. Brookins, the wife of the minister Matthew D. Brookins.[34] Through the WHFMS, these diverse women worked together to raise funds for the support of local and international causes. At the 1907 Indian Mission Annual Conference meeting, for example, the WHFMS branch in South McAlester reported that it had raised $86.48. The officers of this branch explained that "we have helped the poor some; we have fed the hungry, clothed them; and gave them money and the last but not least, we have gone to their homes and prayed for them and by the omnipotence of God, our lives have been spared." Toward these ends, they gave financial aid to church officials and ill church members. They also provided funds to bury the dead.[35]

The establishment of the IMAC brought greater infrastructure to Indian Territory. By and large, the members of this conference embraced the AME Church's complicated denominational apparatus. They relished having their own bishop and named Turner Chapel in McAlester after their first episcopal leader.[36] They also embraced the WHFMS, happily supporting a branch of this connectional organization in Indian Territory. Over time, they also recognized their new financial responsibilities as an integral aspect of African Methodism and took pride in belonging to a Black institution with such a complex internal organization.

Churches

Churches formed the cornerstone of the AME infrastructure in Indian Territory. African Methodists started establishing churches around 1869, beginning in locations with strong Black Indian communities like Skullyville and Boggy Depot in the Choctaw Nation. During the 1870s, 1880s, and 1890s, African Methodists expanded throughout Indian Territory, attracting a diverse population. Some of the most significant churches included Bethel and Greenrock in the Choctaw Nation, Ward Chapel and Bethel-on-the-Point in the Creek Nation, and Fort Gibson in the Cherokee Nation. By the early 1900s, a demographic shift had occurred in Indian Territory and, by extension, in the IMAC. African American migrants to the region had exponentially increased by this time. They were seeking land and opportunity, and many of them joined AME churches. The membership of the IMAC reflected this change, and Black Indians gradually found themselves in the clear ethnic minority. As the previous chapter highlighted, Black Indian ministers experienced the same dynamic. Yet, this notable change did not dissuade Black Indians from remaining African Methodists.

The first church that African Methodists established in Indian Territory was in Skullyville in the Choctaw Nation. Founded in 1832, the town of Skullyville once served as the Choctaw capital, and it attracted prominent residents like the McCurtain family.[37] After the Civil War, formerly enslaved Choctaw and Chickasaw remained in Skullyville County seeking to build new lives as free people. In 1869, Granville Ryles, an African Methodist from the Arkansas Annual Conference, began evangelizing within this Black Indian community. The AME Church's Skullyville Mission grew to include congregations in Skullyville, Fort Coffee, Hudson Hollin, Magnolia, and Peoples. Early members were Black Choctaw and Black Chickasaw like Benjamin Thompson, Treacy Colbert, Silla Clark, Smith Brown and his son Charles, and Richard Brashears and his son Edward. Annie Blackwater (formerly enslaved by Green McCurtain) and her husband, Thomas Blackwater, belonged to the mission as well. Thomas was a veteran of the Civil War, having run away from his master in 1864 to enlist in the 113th Kansas Regiment of the US Colored Infantry. By 1883, the Skullyville Mission had grown to include thirty members.[38]

Another early church that African Methodists established in Indian Territory was in Boggy Depot, the home of Annie Keel and her community of Black Choctaw and Black Chickasaw. The Arkansas Annual Conference began sending ministers to Boggy Depot in the early 1870s. By 1879 the church

Figure 4. Dr. Lonnie Johnson Sr. and family. *Sitting, left to right:* Dr. Lonnie Johnson Sr. and Gracie M. Johnson. *Standing, left to right:* Lonnie Johnson Jr., Donna Renee Johnson Rhodes, and Drew Patrick Rhodes, 2020 (Courtesy of the Johnson family).

had thirty members and an edifice valued at $500. After the Missouri, Kansas and Texas Railway bypassed Boggy Depot, its residents established a town two miles south that they named New Boggy Depot. African Methodists joined in this migration and established a church at the new site in the 1880s. Nicodemus "Demus" Colbert, who was born in the Choctaw Nation in 1864 and was the son of Treacy Colbert, was among the members of the New Boggy Depot church. His grandson Lonnie Johnson Sr. (figure 4) explained that Demus and his friends did not attend services every week, but they would "come by the church on the way home and they would leave an offering . . . many times they'd leave much as a hundred dollars, I understand." The New Boggy Depot church continued to thrive into the 1890s.[39]

Although the churches in Boggy Depot and Skullyville were established first, Bethel AME Church in Atoka became known as the "mother church" of the IMAC. The congregation was organized around 1880 and was largely composed of Black Choctaw, some of whom had migrated from the original Boggy Depot. Initially, they worshipped in a brush arbor on a hill near "a good spring of water." By 1885, the congregation numbered fifteen and replaced the brush arbor with a log cabin. In 1890, Bishop William H. Heard visited Atoka and held "a series of meetings." He also raised enough money to buy lumber for a new church building. The church was twenty by thirty feet and included a bell tower, windows, and doors. In 1895, the church was rebuilt again with dimensions of forty by sixty feet. The structure also had a "12 foot studded wall with bell tower," windows, doors, and comfortable seats. Throughout the years, the members of this church were "very active in helping to build other churches, lodges, and schools for the colored people of Atoka."[40]

The earliest members of Bethel in Atoka were Ruthie Anderson, Jane Ward, Siney Thompson, Cook Thompson, and Henry Collins. Ruthie Anderson was born in the Choctaw Nation around 1850 to Charley and Millie Thompson and was enslaved by Emma Colbert. After emancipation, Ruthie lived in Atoka and joined the brush arbor church.[41] She remained a loyal African Methodist throughout her life, even attending the 1889 district conference in Atoka. On the last day of the conference, Ruthie and Clarisa Flax, whose family also had close ties to the Atoka church, provided food for the entire conference.[42] One participant said that this meal "did credit to our inner man."[43] Perhaps this meal included a traditional hominy and meat dish that Black Choctaw called Tom Fuller, a variation on the Choctaw term *ton-fulla*.[44] Jane Ward, another founding member of Bethel, remained loyal to her church throughout her long life. She regularly paid her Dollar Money from the 1880s and onward.[45]

Although some of the earliest AME churches established in Indian Territory were in the Choctaw Nation, African Methodists also found fertile ground among the Creek. During the 1870s, they planted seeds that grew into churches like Ward Chapel in Muskogee. This church was first constructed in 1883, but it burned down in 1885. With support from churches in Kansas City and Saint Louis, as well as members of the Methodist Episcopal Church, South (MECS), G. A. L. Dykes rebuilt the edifice. The first worship service occurred on the second Sunday in May 1886. The new church had dimensions of twenty-four by thirty-six feet and was, eventually, named after Bishop Ward.[46] Over time, this church grew in status and prosperity. As a result, it hosted the Indian Mission Annual Conference meetings in 1898, 1903, and 1907. By 1907, Ward Chapel was the most prominent church in the IMAC. It raised the most Dollar Money, had the most members, and had the most valuable property.[47]

Ward Chapel had close ties to the Black Creek community. In January 1887, Alex G. W. (A. G. W.) Sango led a "surprise storm party" for the church's pastor, E. M. Willingham. Sango and several others, including his sister Nellie Sango, visited Willingham at the parsonage and gave him gifts.[48] The Sangos recognized the significance of Ward Chapel and wanted to ensure their good relationship with its pastor. The Sangos were crucial allies for Willingham, as well. Their father was Scipio Sango, a noted Black Creek leader who represented Canadian Colored town in the House of Warriors. A. G. W. became a leader in his own right. He was an attorney, a school administrator, and a founder of the Creek Citizens Realty Bank and Trust Co. He also served in the House of Warriors, like his father. Sango was friends with Booker T. Washington and hosted a dinner for him when Washington visited Muskogee in November 1905. In turn, Washington included a detailed biography of Sango in his book *The Negro in Business*.[49]

Ward Chapel hosted speakers from throughout the African Diaspora, displaying the same Atlantic World consciousness that Emma Tucker showed in the WHFMS. In June 1896, Mary Russell Webb, a Jamaican evangelist, gave a "series of lectures and talks" at the church.[50] In 1903, E. E. Budonauro of Havana, Cuba, preached there as well. An observer recounted the event: "At 3 p.m., Rev. E.E. Budonauro, A.M., B.D., M.D., of Havana, Cuba, preached to one of the largest crowds that ever was witnessed in Ward's chapel, and while he preached, it seemed that two hundred people at once shouted and cried out 'Amen.'" Bishop Moses B. Salter later appointed Budonauro the pastor at South McAlester.[51]

In 1904, the Ward Chapel congregation built a new church at the corner of Ninth and Denison Streets, where the church still stands today. By 1904, Muskogee had grown to include "two well represented colored banks, ten or fifteen colored grocery stores, one colored jewelry store, one colored Photograph Gallery, four colored hotels, ten colored lawyers and eleven colored doctors." The new Ward Chapel contributed to the thriving Black community in Muskogee by hosting a variety of cultural events. On September 30, 1904, the church hosted a meeting of the Fortnightly Culture Club. The meeting, which was open to the public, included an invocation, musical solos, essay presentations, and a debate. During the debate, Professor Charles Arthur Biggers and William S. Pesters, Esq., argued over the merits of Oklahoma statehood.[52] On July 28, 1905, Ward Chapel hosted the "Piano, Song and Dramatic Recital" of Miss Alberta Guy of Topeka, Kansas. Guy was then a student at the music conservatory at Washburn College in Topeka. Local Muskogee musicians accompanied her during the performance.[53] Then, on February 22, 1907, Ward Chapel hosted the "Musical and Literary Recital" of the Dunbar Literary Society at Dunbar High School.[54]

In part because of their success at Ward Chapel, African Methodists established their flagship school in Muskogee. This school was originally named Sisson Industrial Institute. While African Methodists also considered Atoka and Fort Gibson as possible sites, they ultimately chose the place where they had been the most effective at building community relationships and owning valuable property. The school expanded in 1916 and was renamed Flipper-Key-Davis University. The minister G. T. Sims hosted a reception for Bishop James M. Conner at Ward Chapel to celebrate this expansion.[55]

In the early 1880s, African Methodists established another church in the Creek Nation, Bethel-on-the-Point. This church was placed within the Eufaula Mission and initially shared its pastor with congregations in Eufaula, Muskogee, and Elk Creek. In 1883, these four churches had a combined membership of seventy-two.[56] The precise site of Bethel-on-the-Point remains unknown, but its inclusion within the Eufaula Mission suggests that it was located somewhere between Eufaula and Muskogee.[57] John A. Broadnax, a Black Creek who was the presiding elder over that church, remarked in the *Christian Recorder* that "most of the members are full blooded Indians."[58] By the term "full blooded Indians," Broadnax was not referring to Black Creek people, whom he typically called "colored."[59] Instead, he was referring to Creek people of exclusively Indigenous heritage. Broadnax highlighted the ethnic makeup of Bethel-on-the-Point to demonstrate that the AME Church was successfully evangelizing among a diverse population of Native people. Little is known about these parishioners beyond Broadnax's description, but their existence indicates that some Creek were willing to openly affiliate with a historically Black denomination. Perhaps, like Thomas Sunrise and John Hall, they saw the AME Church as a desired venue because of its resistance to white hegemony and its embrace of different kinds of worship. Perhaps these Creek people had kinship ties to Robert Grayson (the noted Black Creek legislator who pastored Bethel in the mid-1880s) and desired to join his church. Regardless of their exact motivations, their acceptance of

African Methodism speaks to their intercultural openness. By 1891, Pugh A. Edwards, an African American married to a Black Choctaw, was pastoring the church.[60]

African Methodists also established churches in the Cherokee Nation, the most prominent of which was in Fort Gibson. Fort Gibson was one of the oldest "non-Indian settlements" in Indian Territory. The history of the town began in 1824 when Colonel Matthew Arbuckle built the military base of Fort Gibson. American military families and diverse Native people settled around the fort and established the town. The fort remained in use during and after the Civil War, until it was largely abandoned in 1890. The town continued to develop and was incorporated in 1898.[61]

James Fitz Allan Sisson began preaching and "sowing seed" in Fort Gibson in 1872. Then, Bishop Ward appointed Dennis Barrows pastor in 1876.[62] The Fort Gibson church made slow but steady progress, and in 1879, Barrows reported having seventeen members.[63] During the 1880s, C. K. Petty organized the church's missionary society, maintained a successful Sabbath school, and obtained seventy library books. The Presbyterian Board of the Bible Society of Saint Louis, Missouri, donated some of these books and gave the church six months' worth of Sunday school materials as well.[64] Despite this progress, the church was also in debt, and its edifice remained "unfurnished and unseated."[65] By the 1890s, the church had installed a new floor and purchased a parsonage.[66]

The AME church in Fort Gibson was tuned in to the problems facing Cherokee freedmen. E. C. King, who pastored the church during the 1890s, witnessed how untoward characters robbed this vulnerable population of government funds. The roughly 4,500 Cherokee freedmen throughout the Cherokee Nation were due to be paid $903,000 from the Department of the Interior. They were also due funds from land sales.[67] One untoward character at this time was a Mr. Stevens, a merchant from Muskogee, who tricked freedmen into signing their power of attorney over to him, failing to explain that this permitted him to "draw their checks." This arrangement angered the freedmen, for he was able to "pay himself and give back to them what he wanted them to have." They related their plight to E. C. King and appealed to the authorities. Still, Stevens was unwilling to relent. He waited until the freedmen received their checks and then had the US marshals arrest them and force them to sign over their checks to him. If they refused, "the marshalls would beat the men over the head with winchesters and pistols; and they would continue to beat, curse and kick women until they sign their checks." The freedmen, angry at the treatment of the women, "rose up" in defiance against the marshals. Several newspapers related this story, but only the *Christian Recorder* fully explained why the freedmen were "threatening to attack" the marshals. In a letter to the *Christian Recorder*, the sympathetic King asserted that "I never saw people treated as badly as the U.S. Marshals treated [Cherokee freedmen] in Fort Gibson."[68]

As African Methodists continued their work of church building in the 1890s, they accepted direct assistance from Native leaders like Green McCurtain, who served as treasurer and eventually principal chief of the Choctaw Nation. McCurtain lived in San Bois, Oklahoma, and possessed significant land and property holdings in the Choctaw Nation. In 1894, McCurtain donated a building, located just north of San Bois, to African Methodists, among them the Black Choctaw Harriet Stewart.[69] They converted the building into Greenrock AME Church, a name that paid homage to McCurtain. Pugh A. Edwards, Harriet Stewart's husband and the former pastor of Bethel-on-the-Point, became Greenrock's first pastor and called it "the finest AME Church in the Indian Mission Conference." He announced that the church would be dedicated in July 1894 and that "all ministers and friends are cordially invited."[70]

McCurtain, a former slaveholder, probably donated the building for Greenrock AME Church to gain the favor of the Black Choctaw, whose support he needed to fulfill his political ambitions. Representing the Tuskahoma Party, he ran for principal chief throughout 1894 and 1895 in anticipation of the election in 1896. McCurtain's overture toward Black Choctaw African Methodists was very much in line with the Tuskahoma Party's efforts to gain the support of freedmen. The Tuskahoma Party promised, "the protection of intermarried and freedmen citizens' rights," and it also called for "each freedman to receive forty acres of land as his proportion of the public domain."[71] The 1883 Act to Adopt the Freedmen of the Choctaw Nation had already guaranteed land rights and citizenship for Choctaw freedmen and their descendants.[72] The Tuskahoma Party's pitch to the freedmen in the 1890s represented a commitment to maintain this status quo as the Choctaw Nation navigated the uncertain terrain of the Dawes Commission era. As a member of the Tuskahoma Party, McCurtain assured the freedmen that they would receive their just due under his administration. He did indeed win the election of 1896 and in subsequent elections continued reaching out to the Black Choctaw community as an important part of his constituency.[73]

The early 1900s was a period of change for the IMAC. Several early congregations declined due to the migration of their members. Skullyville was bypassed by the Kansas City Southern Railway in 1895, leading to the town's demise. African Methodists and other residents moved elsewhere, resulting in Skullyville's designation as one of the "ghost towns" of Oklahoma. These African Methodists likely joined the new AME church in nearby Spiro, where the Kansas City Southern Railway placed its depot.[74] Residents of New Boggy Depot also migrated to different locations, most notably Atoka. The town's AME church ceased to be viable, while Bethel in Atoka thrived with the population infusion.[75] Bethel-on-the-Point disappeared, too, its members probably joining different congregations. Despite these changes, other churches like Ward Chapel remained stable. Also, new churches were established, such as those in the all-Black towns of Boley, Clearview, Redbird, Tatums, and Rentiesville.[76]

Just as the IMAC reflected the larger migration patterns occurring in Indian Territory, the institution also mirrored the shifting demographics of the region. David A. Chang has explained that by 1907, the African American population of Indian Territory had exploded to over eighty thousand.[77] IMAC churches reflected this dramatic shift as an increasing number of Black migrants joined AME churches in Indian Territory. African Americans had been attending these congregations for years, but by the early 1900s they formed a clear demographic majority within the IMAC. For members like Jane Ward, who had been a part of the IMAC for decades and had already seen a decline in Black Indian clergy (highlighted in the previous chapter), this development must have been worrying. It underscored the reality that the residents of Indian Territory felt under siege by African American and white migrants seeking land and opportunity.[78]

The African Americans who moved to Indian Territory and joined AME churches during this period came from various regions of the South. Henry Augustus Guess, for example, was born in McLennan, Texas, in the 1860s, and by the 1890s he was living in the Choctaw Nation and attending Bethel in Atoka.[79] In 1901, he married Minnie Jackson, an African American from Tennessee who lived in Guthrie, Oklahoma. After Henry graduated from law school, the couple moved to South McAlester, where they attended the local AME church.[80] Joining the Guesses in the South McAlester congregation were Mamie and James W. Thompson, an African American couple from Arkansas. Mamie, who worked as both a music teacher and a hairdresser, later served as the president of the WHFMS for the Central Oklahoma Conference.[81] At the same time that the Guesses and Thompsons attended the church at South McAlester, Virginia and Robert Larry of Alabama belonged to the AME congregation in Hartshorne, and Ozella and Henry Slaughter of Georgia attended Salter's Chapel.[82]

Despite the IMAC's demographic shift in favor of African Americans, Black Indians maintained their presence in various AME churches in the early 1900s. Jane Ward, a Black Choctaw and a founding member of Bethel in Atoka, was still part of that congregation in 1907. One of her fellow parishioners was the Black Choctaw James Osborne, whose mother, Ruthie Anderson, was also a founding member of the church. James attended with his wife, Annie, a Black Creek. Meanwhile, the Black Creek family of Sonie and Peggie Grayson and daughter Julia attended the AME church at Pecan Creek. At the same time, the Salt Creek Mission counted Black Creek members as well, including spouses Rentie and Mollie Sango.[83]

In the early 1900s, the Black Indians in IMAC churches worshipped alongside the new African American migrants. At Bethel in Atoka, Jane Ward and the Osbornes shared their congregation with the Claytons, who were originally from Texas.[84] In Pecan Creek, the Graysons attended church with Arkansas natives like Alice Legrand. At Redland Station, Ibby McClure and her husband, William, both Black Cherokee, worshipped with Thunie Green of Arkansas and her three children. In some instances, blended Black Indian and African American families attended services together. Such was the case at Redland Station, where Susie Campbell, a Black Cherokee, and her African American husband, B. C. Campbell, belonged to the congregation along with their daughter Octavia.[85] The influx of African Americans from all over the South and the continued presence of Black Indians meant that AME churches were culturally diverse. Some Black Indians primarily spoke Indigenous languages. Lucy Trice, for example, belonged to the AME church in Fort Smith. She was fluent in the Choctaw language and only spoke minimal English.[86]

Despite their differences, African Americans and Black Indians found a commonality through African Methodism. These diverse IMAC members attended weekly church services, quarterly and annual meetings, and church-related social events together. They recited the same liturgy, sang the same hymns, and submitted the same Dollar Money. These unifying experiences did not negate the understandable concern that Black Indians felt about the shifting demographics in Indian Territory. They did, however, provide opportunities in which Black Indians could find common ground with their new African American neighbors.

So, from 1869 to the 1900s, African Methodists established churches throughout Indian Territory. In so doing, they created a vital aspect of their denomination's infrastructure. Over time, the IMAC reflected the demographic shift in Indian Territory, and African Americans became a clear ethnic majority. While Black Indians may have felt alarm at this change, they remained committed to African Methodism. Perhaps some of this loyalty was due to the AME church's long-standing efforts to give them access to education. This aspect of the denomination's work is the subject of the next section.[87]

Schools

Schools formed another significant part of the AME infrastructure in Indian Territory. When African Methodists first arrived in the region, they discovered communities of Black Indians with limited access to education. This situation was particularly pronounced in the Choctaw and Chickasaw Nations. In 1877, the commissioner of Indian affairs reported that the freedmen in these two nations "are deprived of all participation in the school-funds of the Indians, and consequently have no advantages of an education except what is furnished to them by the Government of the United States." As a result, these two nations had only five freedmen schools, which were inaccessible to most of the population. African Methodists, along with members of other denominations, stepped into this void and sought to educate freedmen in all the Five Civilized Tribes. Many of these ministers' early efforts occurred in the Choctaw Nation, where educational opportunities were particularly sparse. By the 1870s, the AME Church had already established various schools throughout the country, most notably Wilberforce University in Ohio. From their first years in Indian Territory, African Methodists continued in this pattern by founding day schools and colleges, performing a much-needed service to the freedmen.[88]

Throughout their tenure in Indian Territory, AME ministers established day schools that provided a rudimentary education to Black Indian children. In 1877, Nelson Coleman, a member of the AME church in Skullyville, reported that the African Methodists had created one such school in the Choctaw Nation. In May of that year, Aaron T. Gillett preached at the school before a large crowd of students and their families. He "told the scholars to be true in every thing, and all things would soon be theirs." The service ended with the hymn "Blow Ye the Trumpet Blow," and then Henry Harris, the pastor of Skullyville Circuit, spoke a few words.[89]

Sisson commenced his educational efforts in Atoka, where he lamented that "no day school had been opened, for the benefit of the colored youth, in the town, when I took charge of this mission." He opened his school in 1878 and enrolled thirty-five students. He initially charged his pupils a small sum but later waived this fee. Barrows visited the school in June 1878 and attended the students' examination exercises. Barrows also gave "an interesting and profitable address" to the assembled students, teachers, and families.[90] Encouraged by these early efforts, the 1880 General Conference appropriated $500 for "educational work" in Indian Territory.[91] Sisson continued to travel throughout the Choctaw and Chickasaw Nations and identified additional sites that needed schools. These sites included Blue Branch, New Boggy Depot, McAlester, Stringtown, Sam Boyd's, Double Springs, Spring Bluff, Caddo, Brazil, and Colbert Station.[92]

The AME minister C. H. Hopkins tried to create a school in Blue Branch in the Choctaw Nation. In 1881, Hopkins explained that the freedmen in Blue Branch were begging for assistance in educating their children. They had already built a schoolhouse and simply needed a teacher. Hopkins appealed to the *Christian Recorder*, explaining that "if we can get a lady to come from the States and teach us and our children, we will board her and give $15 per month; and she can carry on school all the year if she likes to, and after the first or second vacation we will by that time have enough children for the School Board to take hold of it."[93] Clearly, Hopkins recognized the urgency of the freedmen's plight and considered the AME Church equipped to meet their needs.

The African Methodists founded a school in New Boggy Depot in the Choctaw Nation. On June 24, 1881, this school held an "examination and exhibition of day school children" at Emmanuel Chapel. J. F. Dyson attended the event and claimed that it "excelled any similar demonstration in decorum and talent ever held by the Indians or freedman heretofore." Dyson also noted that a large number of "our red brethren" attended the occasion. Presumably, they were Choctaw and Chickasaw. According to Dyson, these attendees were impressed by what they witnessed, and "they left commending the conduct of the meeting with panegyric that would do a royal feast credit."[94]

African Methodists were not alone in creating schools for the freedmen. As historian Daniel F. Littlefield explains in *The Chickasaw Freedmen*, AMEs regularly competed with white Baptists over educational development in Indian Territory. The US government initially favored the Baptists and financially supported their schools. A. J. Miller complained that the superintendent of US schools in the Choctaw and Chickasaw Nations would not even allow African Methodists to teach in these Baptist institutions. When Dyson attempted to do so, the superintendent declared that "I have orders to employ no one to teach unless they are Baptist." Meanwhile, a local AME minister began teaching a pay school for the freedmen community in McAlester. This community attempted to get funds from the government, but the superintendent contended that "he could get the government aid for them but he could not employ the same teacher because he was a Methodist, but he would send them a Baptist teacher." The freedmen at McAlester refused to give up their AME teacher, and as a result, their school temporarily closed.[95]

During his term as the IMAC's episcopal leader, Bishop Turner appealed to the US government for support for the AME schools. In November 1880, he wrote to secretary of the interior Carl Schurz, who oversaw the Bureau of Indian Affairs. Turner knew that the government was financially supporting Baptist schools with interest from the $300,000 originally allotted to the Choctaw and Chickasaw Tribes.[96] Turner charged that the Baptists were using this money both to run their schools and to "disseminate their peculiar religious creeds and dogmas." He contended that the government should remain impartial to the various denominations and show "no special favors" to the Baptists. He asked for $1,500 to run six or seven schools. To persuade Schurtz, Turner emphasized the stable infrastructure that his denomination had already developed in Indian Territory. He asserted that "as the African M.E. Church has an Annual Conference in the Territory with a number of educated ministers in her rank, some of whom are teaching schools at the present time, and as we are laboring almost entirely in the interests of the colored people that it would be reasonable and just that our ministers who are teaching, and other schools under our auspices, should be . . . in part, the recipients of the government appropriation." Turner's arguments had the desired effect, and Schurtz helped him attain a government contract for $2,000 per year for educating the freedmen.[97]

After this initial victory, Turner continued to advocate for the AME schools. In July 1881, he wrote to Hiram Price, the commissioner of Indian affairs, imploring him to renew his (Turner's) government contract. Turner explained that he had effectively deployed the funds to organize schools in the Choctaw and Chickasaw Nations. He contended that "it would be a great calamity to suspend the said schools, and to prevent their continuance after they have been put in successful operation."[98] He later provided Price with a list of five locations where he wanted to maintain schools, including Atoka, Blue Station (probably Blue Branch), and Double Springs. Unfortunately for Turner, Price was also corresponding with the prominent Baptist minister Henry Lyman Morehouse. Morehouse wrote to Price that September, complaining about the dueling interests of the Baptists and the African Methodists. He claimed that the AME school in Atoka would be in direct competition with the Baptist school, and he wanted to prevent such an occurrence. Price listened to Morehouse and refused to renew Turner's contract.[99]

Turner protested in a letter to Price in December 1881. He explained that he had recently visited Indian Territory and had seen that "I am the only one out there doing any thing for the colored people." He acknowledged the presence of the Baptists but remained unimpressed with their efforts. To ensure the financial support of his schools, Turner informed Price that he would appeal directly to Congress. He reminded the commissioner that "I am well known throughout the country." He planned to compose a petition and send it to "every member" in both the House and the Senate. Particularly, he would seek out the congressmen from Georgia, as some of them "can not be reelected without my consent." Evidently impressed, Price agreed to help Turner with his petition. Turner formed a committee with several members of the Arkansas Annual Conference. These men included T. P. Johnson, G. T. Rutherford, Cyrus Berry, Jessee Asberry, and S. J. Hollinsworth. In March 1882, this committee met in Hot Springs, Arkansas, composed the petition, and sent it to Congress.[100]

The 1882 petition contended that the AME Church had a well-developed infrastructure that could, with government assistance, support freedmen schools. The opening statement explained that the African Methodists had been preaching and teaching in Indian Territory for several years and had established the IMAC. AME ministers not only aided the freedmen but also "extended our services to thousands of Indians, and half-breeds also, who have been greatly benefited by our moral and literary toils." Additionally, the IMAC included in its membership "a large number of Christian ministers and school teachers" who were equipped to educate the freedmen.[101]

The petition also explained that the African Methodists were fulfilling a desperate need. Black Indian parents traveled between fifty and seventy-five miles to attend AME schools. They would "camp under trees for weeks and months to have their children taught at our schools, sleeping beneath the open heavens, subjected to rain, snow and all kinds of weather, and thus exhibiting a desire for learning that might make the cheeks of civilization blush." To finance their educational endeavors, the African Methodists asked for $10,000 or "as much as will give those unfortunate people a system of schools."[102] Several significant politicians endorsed the petition, including Arkansas governor Thomas James Churchill and Arkansas senator Augustus Hill Garland.[103]

The petition effectively argued the African Methodists' case, and Turner received a contract for $2,000 in spring 1882.[104] The IMAC reported on this outcome at the 1883 Annual Conference, declaring that Bishop Turner made "a strong and elaborate appeal to the Commissioner of Indian Affairs for some money to aid in starting and running some schools for the children of the Freedmen of the [Choctaw and Chickasaw] Nations."[105] The members of the IMAC rejoiced at this success. Their own bishop, citing their well-established infrastructure and using his substantial political clout, had effectively lobbied on their behalf.

In September 1882, Turner applied to Price for a renewal of this new contract.[106] Evidently, his request was granted because that November, a member of the Board of Indian Commissioners visited the AME "contract schools" and gave a bleak report on their progress. This board member, E. Whittlesey, began his visit at the school near McAlester. He reported that "I found the house, a rough board structure, but no school. I was told that the conference had ordered the teacher to another station." Whittlesey moved on to the school in Atoka, finding that the "building is made of rough boards with no desks." During his visit, he met with A. J. Miller, who informed him that he had eighty students, but that their attendance was irregular. Whittlesey found "11 scholars present, all primary, just beginning to read. The teacher had just been ordered to a new station, and the school was not fully organized."[107] Concerning the school in Caddo, Whittlesey contended that "I found the building, but not teacher or scholars. The building is a wretched room, with no desks, with rough board seats without backs, and abundance of dirt. The colored population of Caddo is large, and a good school should be organized there."[108] Despite this negative report, the African Methodists forged ahead. By 1883, George H. Brown had built up the Caddo school into "one of the largest in the Choctaw Nation run by the AME Church."[109]

Over the next several years, African Methodists established additional schools, primarily in the Creek Nation. In 1891, G. A. L. Dykes, who was then serving as the general agent for missionary and school work in Indian Territory, reported on four of these: the Muskogee school, the Blue Creek school, the Vinita school, and the Eufaula school.[110] All four schools convened for nine or ten months. The Muskogee school had two teachers and thirty-eight students, and its property was valued at $650. The Blue Creek school had two teachers and forty students, and its property was valued at $3,075. The Vinita school had one teacher and thirty students, and its property was valued at $500. The Eufaula school had one teacher and twenty-five students, and its property value was unknown. The African Methodists also opened schools in Blue Jacket and Wagoner. The former had one teacher and twenty-five students, met for nine months, and had property worth $75. The latter had one teacher and twenty students, met for nine months, and had property worth $100.[111]

Throughout the 1890s, African Methodists also established several high schools in Indian Territory. In 1893, they created View High School in the Cherokee Nation.[112] A few years later, they decided to build a high school in Atoka and named it after William B. Derrick, DD.[113] They also created Gaines High School in Ardmore, Chickasaw Nation, naming it for Bishop Wesley J. Gaines.[114]

Unequivocally, the Sisson Mission School (later renamed as the Sisson Industrial and Agricultural School, and ultimately dubbed the Sisson Industrial Institute) was the most successful educational endeavor that the African Methodists established in Indian Territory. The school was named after Sisson in honor of his pivotal role in creating and expanding the IMAC and his devotion to the cause of education. A few years before his death, he declared that "we greatly need to place our educational institutions upon a firm basis. We need to educate our own youth in our own way in order to retain them in our Church, and some of them as teachers and pastors in our schools and congregations. To allow other peoples to educate our young people is to relinquish our hold upon them in our Church."[115]

African Methodists had founded institutions of higher education elsewhere in the United States before they established Sisson Industrial Institute. In 1863, they purchased Wilberforce University in Ohio, the first private African American university in the United States, and made it their own. African Methodists also created Payne Institute in Cokesbury, South Carolina, doing so in 1870. In 1880, this school relocated to Columbia and was renamed Allen University. In 1881, they founded both Morris Brown College in Atlanta, Georgia, and Paul Quinn College in Waco, Texas.[116] Sisson Industrial Institute, situated on five acres of land in the Creek Nation, was simply another example of African Methodists establishing institutions of higher education.

African Methodists first opened the Sisson Mission School in 1884 in Muskogee. The General Conference, on the recommendation of the Board of Missions, formally recognized the school shortly after Sisson's death in 1888.[117] By then, it had one teacher, who conducted classes for nine months, and twenty-nine students. The president of the school was then Julia Casey. In 1889, the school's board of trustees held a meeting in Muskogee attended by Bishop Benjamin W. Arnett and board secretary Robert J. Manuel. At the meeting, Arnett decided to organize an additional campus in Blue Creek to serve as the agricultural branch of the Sisson Mission School. Over the next several years, the expanded school steadily increased its faculty and students.[118] G. A. L. Dykes became the president/superintendent of the Sisson Mission School and was instrumental in maintaining and soliciting funds for it from 1888 to 1897.[119]

In 1896, the Sisson Mission School was renamed the Sisson Industrial and Agricultural School. Eventually, it was simply known as the Sisson Industrial Institute. The school maintained its two campuses, the industrial campus in Muskogee and the agricultural campus in Blue Creek. African Methodists recognized that the school was crucial for "the children of the new-born freedmen" because "they do not get any benefits of the Indian Funds; they suffer greatly for proper facilities of education." Also, African Methodists were pleased that the school could "perpetuate the name of one of our illustrious missionaries."[120] African Methodists made an arrangement with the Creek Nation in order to establish the school on Creek lands. Perhaps prominent Black Creek individuals like Robert Grayson and Simon Brown, both of whom had close ties to the AME Church, assisted in the negotiations.[121]

Several observers noted the significant work of Sisson Industrial Institute. In 1897, the *Christian Work: Illustrated Family Newspaper* contended that "it is entirely safe to say [that no] work among the colored people in this country and elsewhere is more practical in its aims and more worthy of generous support by the Christian public than the Sisson Industrial School, located at Muscogee [*sic*], Indian Territory." This article praised Dykes, who "has labored successfully among the ex-slaves of the Cherokee, Creek, Seminole, Chocktaw [*sic*] and Chickasaw tribes for fifteen years, after building churches at Muscogee, Eufaula, Tahlequah, Vinita and Blue Creek."[122] The article also recognized Dykes's fundraising efforts on behalf of the school and encouraged readers to offer their assistance. Another religious publication, the *Churchman*, recognized the importance of the Sisson school. In 1899, the weekly magazine related that the Black Indians "have been almost utterly neglected, and what they would be to-day were it not for the efforts of such institutions as the Sisson Industrial School at Muskogee, it is hard to conceive."[123]

Although the Sisson school received acknowledgment for its positive work, the AME Church still had to defend its rights to the school's land. In 1899, Henry Blanton Parks, the secretary of the AME Home and Foreign Missionary Department and a future bishop, wrote to the secretary of the interior. He complained that "two other parties" were encroaching on the school's land and that the AME Church wanted "exclusive rights" to the "quarter section" on which the school was located. He claimed that this was the "original agreement" that the denomination had made with the Creek Nation and that it should be honored. Parks further contended that the denomination had already invested $2,000 in the property.[124] The matter remained unresolved for several years. In the intervening time, the 1898 Curtis Act, which forced the Five Civilized Tribes to break up their lands into individual allotments, was beginning to take effect. The Curtis Act reserved land for schools, churches, and parsonages. The land reserved for schools was "not to exceed five acres."[125]

In 1902, Rev. Tyson, then president of the Sisson Industrial Institute, contacted the Dawes Commission to reassert the school's land rights. The Dawes Commission, which was created by President Grover Cleveland in 1893, was in the process of creating membership rolls for the Five Civilized Tribes and reorganizing their lands. Tyson wrote to the Dawes Commission to ensure that AME land rights would be respected. He contended that the Creek Nation had given the AME Church permission to open the Sisson Industrial Institute. He insisted that the denomination should be allowed to control the five acres of land that had been "set aside for the school in accordance with the Curtis Bill and which it is now the intention of the Commission to allot." The Dawes Commission contacted Pleasant Porter, then the chief of the Creek Nation, to verify Tyson's statements. Porter must have affirmed Tyson's assessment because the Sisson school remained open on its five acres of land.[126]

The Sisson Industrial Institute continued to operate in this way for over a decade. Then, at the 1916 Northeast Oklahoma Annual Conference meeting in Okmulgee, G. A. L. Dykes convinced Bishop James M. Conner to expand the institution. He informed Bishop Conner that the US government was selling the Tullahassee Colored Boarding School and advised him that the AME Church should purchase it. The Creek Nation originally established this school for Creek children in 1850 but converted it to a freedmen school in 1881.[127] The school was located in Tullahassee, an all-Black town five miles from Muskogee. The federal government later took over the school and, in 1914, opted to sell it. Dykes's appeal swayed Bishop Conner, and he agreed to purchase the school and fund its improvements.[128]

The AME Church established Flipper-Key-Davis University at the site of the Tullahassee Colored Boarding School. At the time, the university was "the only private institution" for Black people in Oklahoma.[129] The school was named for three of its most devoted patrons: Bishop Joseph Simeon Flipper, who presided over Oklahoma from 1908 to 1912; John B. Key, about whom little is known; and George Winton Davis. Davis was born in Muskogee in 1878 and was educated at both Langston University in Oklahoma and Hampton Institute in Virginia. He became "Oklahoma's most useful

Negro citizen" by establishing a successful ranching business on his family homestead. The Davis Ranch bred Aberdeen Angus cattle, Hampshire hogs, horses, and mules. Davis was a devoted African Methodist and donated considerable funds toward AME schools, like the institution that bore his name. He served as the treasurer for Flipper-Key-Davis for many years.[130]

Flipper-Key-Davis stood on forty acres, over thirty of which were used for "agriculture and horticultural purposes."[131] The Sisson Industrial Institute and its five-acre property became a part of this new school. On the main campus of Flipper-Key-Davis were six buildings, including two women's dormitories and one men's dormitory. The school also housed a library and a museum. Students at Flipper-Key-Davis could enter the College of Liberal Arts and Sciences, from which they could earn a bachelor's degree. Students could also enter the Department of Fine Arts, the Department of Education, the Theological Department, the Normal Department, the Academic Department, or the Industrial Department. They could also participate in extracurricular activities like athletic teams and glee clubs.[132]

Attending Flipper-Key-Davis were Black Indians and African Americans from various parts of Oklahoma. Rosella Grayson was enrolled for the 1918/1919 academic year as a second-year student in the English Preparatory class. She was the granddaughter of Robert Grayson, the prominent Black Creek and AME minister. Joining Rosella in her second-year class were Pearlie and Fred "Eddie" Murrell, both the children of Creek freedmen.[133] Meanwhile, fifteen-year-old Ruth Larry was in the second-grade class within the Department of Fine Arts. Her parents, Virginia and Robert Larry, were from Alabama and had been attending the AME Church in Hartshorne since at least 1907.[134] Black Indians held important leadership roles at the school. Pink Thompson, a Black Choctaw and a member of the AME church in Fort Towson, served on the board of trustees for Flipper-Key-Davis during the 1920s.[135]

Flipper-Key-Davis attracted high-quality faculty members. Eva Jessye taught at the school from 1920 to 1925 and served as president of the Literary Society. Jessye, a talented vocalist and choir director, went on to gain national acclaim. In 1935, George Gershwin chose her to be the "choral director for the original production" of *Porgy and Bess*. In 1963, at the invitation of Dr. Martin Luther King Jr., the "Eva Jessye Choir" performed at the March on Washington. Joining Jessye on the faculty at Flipper-Key-Davis was Richard Berry Harrison, who later achieved fame for playing "De Lawd" in the stage version of *The Green Pastures*. During his time at Flipper-Key-Davis, he also performed recitals at Ward Chapel in Muskogee.[136] P. W. DeLyles, an AME minister who pastored churches throughout Oklahoma and Arkansas, served as dean of the Theological Department at the school from 1939 to 1941. He was also a trustee of Flipper-Key-Davis from 1922 to 1941.[137]

Flipper-Key-Davis held annual exercises to celebrate the end of the school year. During this "commencement week," students gave demonstrations of their knowledge, talents, and skills. At the 1920 commencement week exercises, which lasted from May 27 to June 3, Beatrice Rentie performed an instrumental solo. Rentie was a fourteen-year-old Black Creek from Tulsa. Her older sister, Mozell Rentie, performed a reading of "The Knight and the Lady."[138] Professors and local leaders also gave agricultural lectures on subjects like "Hog Cholera Control" and "Conservation of Vegetables." Both Eva Jessye and Richard Berry Harrison participated in the week's activities, the former leading the program of the Girl's Physical Culture Club and the latter leading the program of the Conner Literary Society. Harrison also directed "Yesterday and Today," which was a pageant "depicting in song and story the life of the Negro since first landing in America." The performance was held in the Dreamland Theatre in Muskogee. AME clergy such as Bishop Evans Tyree and ministers C. R. Tucker and J. S. Smith attended the 1920 commencement week. Bishop Tyree presided over the commencement exercises on the morning of June 3, during which the senior class received their diplomas.[139]

Flipper-Key-Davis University continued to educate students from across the region into the 1930s. Future AME ministers like Abner Davis, who attended around 1920, received vital training at the institution. In 1932, the board of trustees refashioned the school as Flipper-Davis Junior College.[140] By establishing day schools and institutions of higher education like Flipper-Key-Davis, African Methodists created another vital aspect of their infrastructure in Indian Territory. Their efforts also provided an invaluable service both to their parishioners and to those unaffiliated with their denomination.[141]

Publications

Publications formed the final aspect of the AME Church infrastructure in Indian Territory. African Methodists publicized their work through newspapers, annual conference minutes, and historical pamphlets. They wrote letters detailing their progress to the *Christian Recorder*, the *Cherokee Advocate*, and the *Indian Journal*. They also produced and sold copies of the IMAC's annual minutes. Then, in 1882, Rev. John Thomas Jenifer wrote *The First Decade of African Methodism in Arkansas and in the Indian Territory*.

This twenty-four-page work detailed the origins of the IMAC and the people who helped establish it. Through such publications, African Methodists ensured that readers not only in Indian Territory but throughout the country recognized their work.[142]

African Methodists all over the nation sent in letters to the editor of the *Christian Recorder*, who then published them in the newspaper. Ministers laboring in distant regions often wrote about their experiences, informing readers about their trials and triumphs. Sisson, Barrows, Miller, Broadnax, and other clergymen in the IMAC participated in that tradition. From 1868 to 1884, Benjamin Tucker Tanner served as the editor of the *Christian Recorder*. His tenure in this position coincided with the formative years of the IMAC, and so he was the one who published these ministers' missives.[143]

Sisson regularly submitted letters to the *Christian Recorder*. His letters informed readers about the hardships that he faced as one of the first AME ministers in Indian Territory. In 1877, he remarked that "almost insurmountable difficulties have hindered my writing to the RECORDER for a long time, to wit money, and long rides; usually entertained in homes of but one small room; often without a table to write upon; often so much smoke no one can write; often made sick beyond the power of writing, by tobacco fumes, etc."[144] Later that year, he wrote about the physical obstacles that he was facing, explaining that "since my last letter was sent to you, I have been dangerously and seriously ill, and a great sufferer. A council was held over me; a brother directed to obtain a coffin; and the time fixed for my funeral, and the place for my burial place for my body determined upon. I yet live! I am engaged in my work again, though an invalid." Sisson ensured that the residents of Indian Territory would read his letters and those of the other IMAC ministers because, as he noted, "I distribute my RECORDER, free where I cannot sell it and I think it will be useful."[145] Indeed, by 1882, the IMAC reported twenty-two subscriptions to the *Christian Recorder*.[146]

While they wrote to the *Christian Recorder*, African Methodists also corresponded with Native newspapers like the *Cherokee Advocate*. The Cherokee Nation established the *Cherokee Advocate* in 1844 and published it in Tahlequah. Its articles were printed in both English and the Cherokee language.[147] In 1877, Barrows publicized the AME Church in the *Cherokee Advocate*. Beginning that January, the bilingual newspaper began running the following advertisement:

> Preaching by the Rev. Dennis Barrows, (col.) at Fort Gibson on Sundays at 11 o'clock, a.m., and 7 o'clock, p.m.

> Sunday School at 9 o'clock, a.m. Bible Class at 1 o'clock.
> Tuesday, night Class Meeting. Thursday night preaching.
> At Tahlequah 2nd Sunday in each month.

The *Cherokee Advocate* ran this advertisement for several months. Providing a detailed schedule of his activities in the *Cherokee Advocate* allowed Barrows to build a following in both Fort Gibson and Tahlequah.[148]

Barrows maintained a good relationship with the editors of the *Cherokee Advocate* and regularly provided them with information on the AME Church. In 1878, the newspaper reported that "Rev. Dennis Barrows (colored), of Fort Gibson informs us that the colored people of that place have a thriving Sunday school under his supervision." The newspaper praised Barrows, saying, "he deserves great credit for the interest he is taking in the cause of Christianity among his people; and other colored [divines] should imitate his noble example."[149] At that time, the editor of the *Cherokee Advocate* was George W. Johnson. Johnson was a fierce defender of Cherokee autonomy and land rights. He was also against allowing Cherokee freedmen to serve in the Cherokee legislature. Nevertheless, he was willing to promote African Methodism in his newspaper.[150]

The *Cherokee Advocate* also reported on Broadnax's activities, noting in 1886 that he preached at the Colored Baptist Church on Saturday, February 1, and Sunday, February 2. At this time, the newspaper's editor was Elias Cornelius Boudinot Jr., the son of the assassinated Cherokee leader and newspaperman Elias Boudinot.[151] The newspaper contended that "there was a good deal of curiosity manifested by our citizens to hear, the Reverend Gentleman [Broadnax], and he had a promiscuous house-full as long as he staid [*sic*]." Based on the opinions of the knowledgeable critics they consulted, the editors asserted, "Mr. Broadnax is a sincere and formidable exhorter, and is full worthy of the responsible position he fills."[152]

The *Indian Journal* was another Native newspaper that reported on AME news. The Creek Nation began publishing this newspaper from Muskogee in 1876.[153] Some of its earliest issues included information about the AME Church. In June 1879, the *Indian Journal* reported that "Rev. James Sisson, of Atoka, presiding elder for this district held quarterly meeting last Saturday and Sunday on Sugar creek. The Sabbath school is flourishing, having 46 scholars in regular attendance." The article also noted that Hector Robins, a Black Creek born around 1854, was serving as the school superintendent.[154] Significantly, this newspaper also reported on the founding of the IMAC. An article appeared in November 1879 stating that "Right Rev. T.M.D. Ward,

Bishop of the dioces [*sic*] of Texas, has organized an annual conference in the Indian Territory." To inform their readership about the Black denomination growing in their midst, the editors of the *Indian Journal* later explained that "there are 300,000 members on the rolls of the African Methodist Episcopal Church, that Church having been organized in 1816. It has one college, a publishing department, six bishops and many schools." Later, the newspaper added that "the African Methodist Episcopal Church claims that it has 387,566 members and probationers, against 215,000 reported in 1879."[155] Probably, African Methodists working in the Creek Nation provided this statistical information to the *Indian Journal*.

The *Indian Journal* also reported on various AME events.[156] In 1881, it mentioned Bishop Turner's visit to Muskogee and two-day trip to Fort Gibson. The newspaper included biographical information about Turner, explaining that he "was at one time Senator from Georgia, and was also the first colored man who received the appointment of postmaster—that at Macon, Ga, which fact caused considerable stir some years ago, during Grant's administration." The newspaper also reported on such happenings as G. A. L. Dykes's plans for building churches in Muskogee and Eufaula. In March 1885, it even chronicled the society wedding of Broadnax and Hannah Brown.[157]

The *Indian Journal* reported on AME meetings and on new ministerial appointments. In October 1884, during the Indian Mission Annual Conference, the newspaper reported that "our colored brethren captured the town Sunday, holding services in all the churches." That Sunday, Bishop Ward, W. J. Smith, and Broadnax preached throughout the day at the Methodist Episcopal church. Meanwhile, A. J. Imboden and Sisson preached at the Presbyterian church, and Nuck Churchill, Henry Collins, and G. A. L. Dykes preached at the AME church. The newspaper singled out the sermons by Imboden and Bishop Ward for particular praise. The next week, the newspaper listed the ministerial appointments for the new conference year.[158]

AME ministers like Sisson sent in letters to the *Indian Journal*, which the newspaper willingly published. In one such letter from 1883, Sisson praised Dykes's progress in building churches in Muskogee and Eufaula:

> I came here last Friday to hold Quarterly meeting in the pastorate of Eld. G. A. L. Dykes. I find his work in a prosperous condition; he reached here the second week in January, 1883. Since that time he has succeeded in erecting a chapel here and one at Muskogee; the one at Muskogee is under roof, and the floor laid, and $50 assured for the carpenters when they call for the money. The chapel here is under cover, and the doors and windows are ready to be

> put in, with $25 dollars [*sic*] in the treasury toward completing it. Elder Dykes has made a good impression on red, white and colored people.[159]

With this report on Dykes, Sisson informed Native readers that the denomination had the financial and organizational means to build and expand among the territory's diverse populations.

In addition to submitting materials to existing newspapers, AME ministers in Indian Territory published their own local newspapers. In 1890, while pastoring a church on South Second Street in Muskogee, T. H. Tyson established and edited *Our Brother in Black*. It was the Indian Territory's "first newspaper for a black audience," and Tyson derived the newspaper's name from a book by Bishop Atticus Greene Haygood. Tyson's newspaper only survived for a year, and there are no extant copies. The paper undoubtedly included significant material on the IMAC and its members. In 1893, another AME minister, C. R. Tucker, served as one of the founders of the *Muskogee Sun*. A. G. W. Sango, the prominent Creek freedman who would later work alongside William Tecumseh Vernon, served as the newspaper's editor.[160]

African Methodists went beyond newspapers to promote their work in Indian Territory. They also publicized their efforts through annual conference minutes. As was the custom throughout the AME Church, African Methodists in the IMAC kept detailed records of their annual meetings. During every meeting, a conference secretary wrote down what occurred each day. At the 1882 Indian Mission Annual Conference in McAlester, Sisson was elected the conference secretary, a position he had held the previous year as well. Each day of the conference, which lasted from October 26 to October 31, Sisson called the roll. He also read the minutes from the previous day and had them approved by the conference. At the 1883 annual conference, which was held from October 24 to October 29 in Brazil, A. J. Miller was elected as the conference secretary. Sisson was elected as the recording secretary, a role that was excluded in 1882 due to budget constraints. Sisson and Miller compiled the minutes from 1882 and 1883 into the *Minutes of the Fourth and Fifth Sessions of the Indian Mission Annual Conference*. The IMAC had these minutes printed and sold them for ten cents.[161] In this way, African Methodists ensured that the history of the IMAC would be preserved.

The prominent minister John Thomas Jenifer was the first to write a history of the AME Church in Indian Territory.[162] In 1882, he composed *The First Decade of African Methodism in Arkansas and in the Indian Territory*. This twenty-four-page work detailed the origins of the IMAC and the people who helped establish it. He advertised the book in the *Christian Recorder* and sold it for fifteen cents per copy. By the time he wrote *The First Decade*, Jenifer had spent several years pastoring in Arkansas, where he built relationships with African Methodists like Sisson and Bishop Ward. Undoubtedly, these two men, who played prominent roles in founding the IMAC, provided him with material for his pamphlet. In 1915, Jenifer reprinted most of the information from *The First Decade* in his *Centennial Retrospect History of the African Methodist Episcopal Church*. Then, in 1916, Richard R. Wright Jr. summarized Jenifer's writings in his *Centennial Encyclopedia of the African Methodist Episcopal Church*.[163]

Jenifer was not the first African Methodist to write about the denomination's history. Richard Allen wrote about the origins of the AME Church in his autobiographical work, *The Life, Experience, and Gospel Labours of the Rt. Rev. Richard Allen*, which was published posthumously in 1833. Thomas W. Henry discussed the denomination's history in Maryland and rural Pennsylvania in the *Autobiography of Rev. Thomas W. Henry, of the AME Church*, which was published in 1872. After Jenifer's *First Decade* appeared in 1882, numerous other African Methodists produced historical works about the denomination. In 1888, Bishop Daniel Alexander Payne, who had been elected the denomination's historiographer in 1848, composed *Recollections of Seventy Years*, which included crucial details about his life and the development of the AME Church. Then, in 1891, Payne compiled his comprehensive *History of the African Methodist Episcopal Church*.[164] Charles S. Smith published a second volume of this work in 1922.[165] Clearly, African Methodists had a sense of their denomination's historical significance and wanted to ensure that posterity recognized it. Jenifer certainly felt this way, and he demonstrated it by writing *The First Decade* and by serving as the AME Church historiographer from 1912 to 1920.[166]

Jenifer had firsthand knowledge of the early years of both the Arkansas Annual Conference and the Indian Mission Annual Conference. The AME Church established the Arkansas Annual Conference in 1868. Jenifer was transferred there in 1870 and pastored Bethel Church in Little Rock for several years. He also served as the secretary for the Arkansas Annual Conference for eight years.[167] Jenifer always supported efforts in Indian Territory. At the annual conference meeting in 1876, which he hosted at Bethel, he wrote a special note to Bishop Ward, saying, "Inclosed [*sic*] you will please find $10, being a little above half of the proceeds of our exhibition last night, which I hope you will place in the hands of those whom you may appoint in the Oklahoma field, or mission, to labor among the Indians." He offered this money because, the previous day, a committee including Sisson had proposed that Indian Territory form its own presiding elder district called the Oklahoma District. The conference adopted the suggestion, and Jenifer wanted to help.[168]

Jenifer continued to support work in Indian Territory over the next several years. At the 1878 annual conference, he led a three-person committee that sought to defend the rights of Black Indians. This committee "took action to bring before the authorities at Washington the outrageous treatment which the eight thousand colored people of the Indian Territory are now receiving."[169] Then, at the 1879 Arkansas Annual Conference meeting, Jenifer supported Sisson's resolution to create the IMAC.[170]

In 1880, Jenifer was transferred to Charles Street AME Church, a venerable congregation in Boston. During his tenure there, the AME Church held a "Tricennial Celebration" to honor the thirtieth anniversary of the election of Bishop Payne to the episcopacy. Jenifer wrote and presented *The First Decade* for this event, which was held in Sullivan Street Church in New York on May 11–13, 1882. Other African Methodists composed histories for the occasion as well. Bishop Ward wrote "History of the Introduction of African Methodism on the Pacific Coast," and T. G. Steward composed "History of African Methodism in the Island of Hayti."[171] After his presentation, Jenifer sent a copy of *The First Decade* to Tanner, who noted the gesture in the *Christian Recorder*: "To the Rev. Dr. J. T. Jenifer we are indebted for a pamphlet copy of the very able paper he read at the Bishop Payne tercentennial Episcopal celebration. Thoughtfully and intelligently prepared it is one of those productions that will resist the tooth of time. To anyone wishing to know of 'African Methodism in Arkansas and the Indian Territory,' let them read 'Jenifer's First Decade.'"[172] Perhaps encouraged by Tanner's praise, Jenifer had *The First Decade* published in Boston later that year. From August 1882 to January 1883, Tanner ran advertisements in the *Christian Recorder* to promote the book, which Jenifer was selling for "15 cents per copy or 9 copies for $1."[173]

In *The First Decade*, Jenifer began his discussion of the IMAC by laying out the geographic parameters of Indian Territory. He explained that "Indian Territory embraces an area of seventy-one thousand square miles of fertile and diversified land called the Indian Reservation, lying between Kansas on the North, Arkansas on the East, and Texas on the South and West, inhabited by the Cherokee, Chickasaw, Choctaw, Seminole, and Osage Nations." Jenifer, then, admitted the limits of his knowledge. He contended that "who the pioneers of African Methodism were, the date or year or the points of their first operations in this field it is not easy to ascertain." Yet, he identified early ministers in Indian Territory like Gillett, Sisson, and Barrows. He also gave a detailed account of the founding meeting of the IMAC in 1879 and statistics indicating the development of the conference.[174]

Jenifer viewed the work of the African Methodists in Arkansas and Indian Territory as counteracting the lingering effects of slavery. He described the region as a "land of crushed manhood, stifled aspirations and stunted intellect" that was the "home of malaria and lurking place of fever, where a people were found homeless and penniless." Into this field, African Methodists spread "the virtue of self-help," along with religious and academic instruction. As a result, "the people who were taught the advantage of self-help with Divine aid, have reaped the benefits of self-development."[175] He considered this a vital step for Black Americans still struggling to find their place after slavery.

African Methodists in Indian Territory used a variety of means to publicize their work. They sent in information to various newspapers, including those that they founded themselves. They also produced annual conference minutes. Through writing *The First Decade*, Jenifer ensured that the early work of the IMAC ministers would be preserved. He, like many of his contemporaries, recognized the historical significance of the AME Church. He acknowledged that if he failed to chronicle the denomination's work, it would be lost to posterity. This sense of history guided many African Methodists.

Conclusion

The AME Church developed a lasting infrastructure in Indian Territory. The denomination established the IMAC and numerous churches and schools. African Methodists also promoted their work through AME and non-AME publications. This infrastructure firmly entrenched the AME Church within Indian Territory. Ministers participating in the African Methodist Migration engaged in similar efforts in locations like California, Montana, and New Mexico. That is how the AME Church grew to include 1,354 churches and 97,337 members in the West by 1916 (see table 2).

While building an infrastructure in Indian Territory, African Methodists worked closely with Black Indian communities. The bonds created between them became crucial during the Dawes Commission era as Black Cherokee, Black Creek, Black Choctaw, Black Chickasaw, and Black Seminole people fought for tribal citizenship. Those battles and the roles that African Methodists played in them is the subject of the next and final chapter.

7

"All the Rights . . . of Citizens"

African Methodists and the Dawes Commission

The Dawes Commission operated from 1893 to 1914. During its existence, commissioners heard testimony and examined documentary evidence to determine who qualified as a member of the Five Civilized Tribes and was, therefore, entitled to tribal citizenship and land allotments. Successful applicants were placed on either "By blood" citizenship rolls or "Freedmen" citizenship rolls, the latter being reserved for formerly enslaved individuals and their descendants. Throughout this process, African Methodists represented the interests of Black Indians. Cornelius King, a Black Cherokee and Bishop Henry McNeal Turner's son-in-law, worked directly for the Dawes Commission as a representative for Native people. Dennis Barrows and James Fletcher Morris worked through freedmen's organizations to guarantee that the Dawes Commission heard and responded to Black Indians' grievances. Various other African Methodist Episcopal (AME) ministers testified before the Dawes Commission on behalf of their parishioners, friends, and relatives. Additionally, many Black Indians, regardless of their religious affiliation, relied on AME birth, marriage, and death records to support their citizenship cases.

This chapter argues that the AME Church played crucial roles for Black Indians during the Dawes Commission era. The denomination's assistance helped ensure that Black Indians attained tribal citizenship and its corresponding benefits. This was the logical extension of the denomination's longstanding work in Indian Territory. African Methodists understood that their denomination was about more than Sunday church services and social events. It was about supporting marginalized people of color in their quest to make better lives. AMEs knew that for Black Indians, attaining tribal citizenship was essential for achieving that end. Scholars have underappreciated the denomination's impact during this critical period for the Five Civilized Tribes. This chapter rescues the story of the AME Church and the Dawes Commission from historical obscurity.[1]

The Dawes Commission

The Dawes Commission, which began in 1893 and continued into the early twentieth century, was named for Senator Henry Dawes of Massachusetts, a reformer whose well-intentioned efforts proved catastrophic for Indigenous communities. Dawes considered himself an advocate for Native people, and he encouraged them to become assimilated into American society. Part of that "civilization" effort involved changing how tribes viewed land ownership. Generally, tribes throughout the United States held lands communally. Dawes and other reformers wanted tribes to adopt an American-style individualistic approach. They planned to "pressure the federal government into adopting a policy that would destroy tribal governments based on communal ownership of land and give each Indian his or her own piece of real estate."[2] Toward that end, Congress passed the General Allotment Act of 1887, colloquially known as the Dawes Act. By this act, the federal government forced tribes to break up their lands into individual plots for individual owners. Conveniently, this act also made available to white settlers all the surplus land that was left over after all allotments were assigned. As a result of allotment policy, Native landholdings were reduced from 138 million acres in 1887 to only 48 million acres in 1934.[3]

The Dawes Act did not initially apply to the Five Civilized Tribes. To compel these tribes to move to Indian Territory in the 1830s, the federal government had signed various treaties, guaranteeing them their lands there. The federal government hesitated to ignore these legally binding treaties. However, this hesitancy was short lived because white settlers desperately wanted access to the twenty million acres of land in Indian Territory. They believed that this land, in Native hands, was "blocking commerce between the East and West" and that this impediment "had to be removed so the nation could prosper."[4]

So, the federal government pursued allotment for the Five Civilized Tribes. Toward that end, on March 3, 1893, Congress passed a crucial appropriation bill. This bill permitted the president to create a three-person commission to negotiate allotment agreements with the Five Civilized Tribes and report back to the secretary of the interior. In accordance with this legislation, President

Grover Cleveland named Dawes the chairman of this Commission to the Five Civilized Tribes, now generally referred to as the Dawes Commission. Other members of the commission were Meredith Helm Kidd and Archibald S. McKennon. On December 8, 1893, the commissioners held an "organizational meeting" in Washington, DC. While in that city, Dawes wrote to tribal leaders to inform them of the commission's intentions. The Dawes Commission finally arrived in Indian Territory in January 1894 and took ten rooms at the Hotel Adams in Muskogee. In March, they moved their headquarters to South McAlester in the Choctaw Nation because it was more "centrally located." The commissioners traveled throughout Indian Territory, visiting its villages and towns, trying to garner support for allotment. Unsurprisingly, the tribes greeted the proposal of allotment with skepticism and anger. Many resented that the federal government was reneging on legally binding treaties and had no desire to change their traditional patterns of land ownership.[5]

The commission's initial efforts to convince the tribes to accept allotment were largely unsuccessful. In 1895, Congress added two members to the commission and replaced Kidd with Brigadier General Frank C. Armstrong. In 1896 and 1897, the commissioners, empowered by congressional actions, began creating citizenship rolls for each tribe while still trying to negotiate allotment.[6]

The tribes sent representatives to Washington to lobby for their interests. Nevertheless, Congress passed the Curtis Act in 1898. This act forced the Five Civilized Tribes to dissolve their tribal governments and accept allotment. To determine who was eligible to receive allotments, Congress empowered the commission to continue creating citizenship rolls. Members of the Five Civilized Tribes had to testify before the commission in order to be enrolled and, therefore, become eligible for an allotment. Essentially, Congress left it up to the commission to decide who was and who was not a Native person. The process of tribal enrollment lasted from 1899 until the rolls officially closed in 1907. Even after that, litigation for some cases dragged on for several more years, and additional enrollees were added.[7]

Black Indians were eager to become official citizens of the Five Civilized Tribes and receive land allotments. They followed the Dawes Commission's instructions and went to prescribed sites to apply for enrollment, hoping to be placed on the "Freedmen" rolls. For example, freedmen from throughout Indian Territory descended on Fort Gibson from 1899 until 1901. They established camps and waited for their turn to present their cases before the commission (figure 5). Some enterprising freedmen even set up stores to accommodate their fellow sojourners.[8]

Figure 5. Freedmen camped at Fort Gibson preparing to apply for enrollment with the Dawes Commission (Oklahoma Historical Society).

First and foremost, Black Indian applicants had to prove that recognized members of the Five Civilized Tribes had enslaved them or their ancestors. In determining the outcome of enrollment cases, the Dawes Commission considered each applicant's personal testimony, the testimony of witnesses, previous tribal membership rolls, and birth, marriage, and death records. Commissioners sometimes based their decisions on arbitrary measures. They could deny enrollment to applicants who had not returned to Indian Territory after the Civil War by a prescribed date. For Black Cherokee applicants, this date was February 11, 1867, six months after the 1866 treaty was ratified. Some in the Five Civilized Tribes were suspicious of the process of freedmen enrollment. The Creek Nation complained that "state negroes" were trying to pass themselves off as Black Indians to gain the privileges of citizenship. It is unclear how prevalent this practice was, but such accusations prompted commissioners to carefully examine all applications.[9]

The Dawes Commission rejected numerous applications, but ultimately over twenty thousand freedmen were enrolled throughout the Five Civilized Tribes, including African Methodists like Annie Keel and Jane Ward. The enrolled Black Indians included 6,807 Creek freedmen, 5,522 Choctaw freedmen, 472 minor Choctaw freedmen, 4,924 Cherokee freedmen, 4,670 Chickasaw freedmen, and 830 Seminole freedmen. These enrollees became eligible for land allotments, which they eagerly accepted.[10] The next section will demonstrate the role that the African Methodist Cornelius King played in the early years of this Dawes Commission process.

Cornelius King and the Dawes Commission

Cornelius King's relationship to Bishop Turner, and his Cherokee ancestry, helped him secure a job as "special Indian Agent" for the Dawes Commission from 1894 to 1897. During this three-year tenure, his role was multifaceted. He served as a messenger, a porter, and a waiter, but he also functioned as a "liaison man" between the commissioners and the tribes. King was the only member of the Five Civilized Tribes on the Dawes Commission, and he used his platform to support the commissioners' allotment policy. He did so because, having already spent time working in Washington, DC, he was convinced that "allotment was bound to come."[11] He considered it his duty to ensure that the tribes received as fair a deal as possible from the US government. Though King's efforts during the Dawes Commission era offer a fascinating look at how Black Indians navigated this complex period, scholars have made scant note of him. This section corrects this historiographic oversight.[12]

Cornelius King was born on March 17, 1861, to Phyllis Williams, an enslaved Cherokee, and George King, an enslaved African American. Cornelius believed that Phyllis was "seven-eighths Indian and one-eighth white," while George was of mixed race, with his white father/master, Ben King, being a preacher and state senator in Mississippi. In 1863, George purchased his family's freedom and sent them to live in Jackson, Tennessee, where Cornelius and his sister attended school.[13] When Phyllis died in 1876, the family moved to Fort Smith, Arkansas, and then to Indian Territory, where Cornelius became well acquainted with a diverse cross section of Cherokee people.[14]

Cornelius King met (Lincolnia) Victoria Turner in Indian Territory in the 1880s. At the time, her father, Bishop Turner, was presiding over the Indian Mission Annual Conference (IMAC), and she was accompanying him during his duties. Victoria was born to Bishop Turner and his wife, Eliza Ann, on August 25, 1864. She was educated at both Wilberforce University in Ohio and Berea College in Kentucky. She and Cornelius were betrothed in Indian Territory in 1882 and married in Atlanta on December 14, 1887. Bishop Richard R. Disney performed the ceremony.[15] The couple lived in Little Rock, Arkansas, until 1889, when Victoria's mother died and they moved to Atlanta to provide companionship for Bishop Turner. During their marriage,

Cornelius and Victoria had three sons, all of whom died in childhood: Henry McNeal, George, and Cornelius Victor. On May 28, 1892, Victoria herself died and was buried at West View Cemetery in Atlanta. Even after he remarried, Cornelius remained close to Bishop Turner. He also remained a devoted African Methodist, becoming a lifelong member of Big Bethel AME Church in Atlanta and serving as chairman of its board of trustees.[16]

While living in Atlanta in the early 1890s, King worked in the law office of Hoke Smith, the man who would later appoint him to the Dawes Commission. Bishop Turner had connections with Smith and he likely helped his son-in-law secure this position. In 1893, President Grover Cleveland appointed Smith as secretary of the interior, and Smith offered King a job on his staff. The recently widowed King accepted the offer, later explaining that "when Mr. Smith went to Washington I went with him as his private messenger."[17] In the course of his work, King "talked with many of the Senators and Congressmen who were interested in the Indian affairs." These interactions convinced him that although allotment policy was "unjust," it was inevitable because of white men's "lust for land."[18]

On January 16, 1894, in his capacity as secretary of the interior, Smith appointed King as a "special Indian Agent" to the Dawes Commission at a salary of $1,500 per year. He was to be stationed in Muskogee and receive $3 per day whenever he had to work away from the headquarters. His annual pay actually amounted to about $2,000 per year, indicating that he spent almost half the year in the field. King's duties were multifaceted. He accompanied the commissioners into the field and served as a messenger, a porter, and a waiter. Also, because of his professed Cherokee heritage, he served as a "liaison man" between the commissioners and the tribes. Before he left for Muskogee, he married Nina Culver, a graduate of the prestigious Spelman College in Atlanta, and she accompanied him to Indian Territory.[19]

African Americans greeted King's appointment with pride and excitement. Among the enthusiasts was Edward R. Carter, then the pastor of the historic Friendship Baptist Church in Atlanta. Carter profiled King for his 1894 book *The Black Side: A Partial History of the Business, Religious and Educational Side of the Negro in Atlanta, GA*. In the book, which included an introduction by Bishop Turner, Carter contended that King's appointment to the Dawes Commission was "an important and honorable place, only to be held by men of undoubted ability and well-tried fidelity." Carter also remarked that King's accomplishment was "extensively noted and commented upon by the press throughout the country, and many letters and telegrams of congratulation were received from distinguished colored men all over the country."

Some white people were more cynical about King's new job, concluding that Bishop Turner's political relationship with Hoke Smith played a role in his former son-in-law's appointment. Their suspicions had merit, especially given the fact that Smith also gave lucrative positions to Turner's sons and to Mary Brown, the daughter of Bishop John M. Brown. Smith's courting of the Black vote haunted him during his ultimately successful gubernatorial race in Georgia in 1905 and 1906.[20]

King served on the Dawes Commission from 1894 until 1897, later recalling that "I attempted to charge my duties faithfully, and believe I did so to the satisfaction of Mr. Smith. I certainly heard no complaint."[21] During his tenure, the commissioners were visiting each of the Five Civilized Tribes, attempting to convince them to accept allotment. They were also beginning to compose citizenship rolls. The commissioners arrived in Indian Territory in January 1894 and spent the next two years holding meetings with tribal governments and visiting tribal members. Since Dawes was often infirm, Meredith Helm Kidd and Archibald S. McKennon did most of the traveling. McKennon later testified that "I have been there almost all of my time for two years; I have visited almost every section of that country; I have gone through the country and talked to all classes of people, the citizen and non-citizen, the white, the black, and the red; all of them."[22] Cornelius was there right along with McKennon and the other commissioners.

In his capacity as a "liaison man," King likely attended meetings between the Dawes commissioners, tribal leaders, and various Native communities. He was able to provide insight to the commissioners about the tribes' concerns and grievances. He was also able to speak to the tribes about what he considered the inevitability of allotment. His view was in line with that of Green McCurtain, who "argued that the tribes should make the best possible agreement they could while they still had the chance."[23] Few other tribal leaders agreed with them, and instead they resisted the commissioners' attempts at negotiation. King's view, though, was in tune with Black Indians, most of whom welcomed the opportunities for land ownership that allotment would bring.[24] During meetings that the commission held with the Choctaw Colored Citizens' Association (CCCA), King might have conversed about the prospect with Dennis Barrows, a fellow African Methodist who led the organization.[25]

King's position on the Dawes Commission did not immunize him from discrimination in Indian Territory. At the Hotel Adams in Muskogee, he was forced to eat in a racially segregated section. In March 1894, Dave McCurtain, a train porter for the Missouri, Kansas and Texas Railway, spoke rudely to

King when the latter attempted to board the train and also refused to let King adjust the window curtain at his seat.[26] King and McCurtain came face to face again in the "colored dining room" at the Hotel Adams, and a physical altercation occurred. According to reports, King threw cayenne pepper in McCurtain's face and then whipped him with a cowhide. King was arrested and charged with assault and battery. The Dawes Commission apparently viewed King as too valuable to lose, and he was permitted to resume his duties.[27]

After completing his official time on the Dawes Commission, King continued to promote its work. In 1901, he published a lengthy statement in support of the commission in the Philadelphia newspaper the *Times*. He identified himself as a "Cherokee Member of the Dawes Commission" and pled with Cherokee readers to accept allotment or risk losing everything. He asserted his Cherokee heritage and his relationship to Bishop Turner, crediting his movement between the Native, African American, and white worlds with showing him all sides of the "Indian question." He claimed that in his youth in Indian Territory, he "knew the old treaty of Andrew Jackson as well as a Catholic knows his paternoster." To him—and by extension to the Cherokee—the 1835 Treaty of New Echota was Bill of Rights, Magna Carta, and Constitution, for it guaranteed them government support and title to their lands in Indian Territory. Now, as King put it, "the government offered allotment and asked the Indian leave to abrogate his ancient pledge, and instead of letting the Indian roam over the whole reservation assigned, tried to fix him to his quarter section." He contended that he too was opposed to the allotment proposal, but he advised his brethren to "submit gracefully." King contended that he joined "the first Dawes commission" in order to facilitate this process and ensure that the Five Civilized Tribes received a fair deal. Despite his acquiescence, King still asserted that Native people were "the true lord of North America" and that their struggle was similar to what the Cubans, Hawaiians, and Filipinos were enduring from the increasingly imperialist United States.[28]

In one of the great ironies of his life, King failed to gain Cherokee citizenship for himself and his children. He applied to the Dawes Commission for enrollment in 1907. According to his understanding, his mother was a "full blooded Cherokee." King, then, felt entitled to apply for admission on the Eastern Cherokee membership rolls rather than the Cherokee freedmen rolls. In 1908, the commission responded to King, questioning why his mother's name did not appear on the Cherokee Rolls of 1851. The commission requested more information about his ancestry and asked him to appear on July 8, 1908, to give additional testimony. In 1911, his application was formally rejected. The commission gave the following reasons for its decision: "Neither applicant or ancestors ever enrolled. Does not establish fact of descent from a person who was a party to the Treaty of 1835—36–46."[29] So, while King worked as a "Cherokee member of the Dawes Commission," that very commission denied his Cherokee heritage.[30] Nevertheless, he continued to assert his ancestry in public ways. He worked with a tennis ball company called Indian King and, "with his Indian looks and his Indian headdress, posed for the picture that became the company's trademark." He also established a forty-five-acre resort that became a popular destination for Atlanta's Black elite. In a nod to his cultural heritage, he named it King's Wigwam. It should be noted that neither feather headdresses nor wigwams were traditional aspects of Cherokee culture. King seemed to be playing on stereotypes of Native people for marketing purposes. While these actions are certainly problematic, they demonstrate King's continued desire to be recognized as an Indigenous person.[31]

Cornelius King played an important role in the history of the Dawes Commission, a role that he was only able to play because of his connection to the leading African Methodist in the nation, Bishop Turner. His was the only Native voice on the commission itself. In his position as a "liaison man," he spread the message that allotment policy was an unjust inevitability and that tribes would be best served by negotiating. Shortly after he completed his tenure on the Dawes Commission, the Curtis Act passed. Afterward, he continued to advocate for the commission's work, recognizing the benefits that Black Indians would reap from allotment. The fact that the Dawes Commission later rejected his own application for Cherokee citizenship did not stop him from professing his Indigenous heritage. The next section will examine the roles that other African Methodists played in the Dawes Commission.[32]

Dennis Barrows, James Fletcher Morris, and the Dawes Commission

Like Cornelius King, Dennis Barrows and James Fletcher Morris were African Methodists who had significant interactions with the Dawes Commission. Unlike him, they did so as leaders in freedmen organizations. They attained these leadership positions because they had high standing as AME ministers and because, during religious work, they became deeply incorporated into Black Indian communities through marriage. Barrows, who was one of the first AME ministers to arrive in Indian Territory, married Jane, a Black Choctaw, and the couple had seven children. Morris married Francis A. Stevens, a Black Chickasaw, and they had at least four children. Through their efforts, both Barrows and Morris ensured that the Dawes Commission heard and responded to the grievances of Black Indians like their family members.[33]

Barrows's ministerial efforts as well as his familial connections enabled him to become one of the leaders of the Choctaw Colored Citizens' Association. This organization included Choctaw freedmen and their descendants as well as any Choctaw who had intermarried with persons of African descent. Working alongside Barrows was another African Methodist, Wesley McKinney. McKinney was a Black Choctaw and deputy sheriff who was married to Lucinda, a Black Cherokee. The couple lived near Alderson in Indian Territory, where they attended the local AME church. The purpose of the CCCA was to address the freedmen's grievances. Toward that end, the group hired two attorneys to serve as their counsel, Robert V. Belt of Washington, DC, and Joseph P. Mullen of Fort Smith.[34]

The formation of the Dawes Commission in 1893 provided an opportunity for the CCCA to make its concerns known. The CCCA wrote to secretary of the interior Hoke Smith, and he advised its members to speak to the Dawes Commission directly. On February 1, 1894, the CCCA held a convention in Goodland, Kiamichi County, to discuss how to proceed. Ultimately, a committee including Barrows, McKinney, and E. D. Colbert composed a "Memorial of the Choctaw Colored Citizens' Association." In August 1894, they met with Dawes commissioners, and probably Cornelius King as well, in Goodland and presented them with the document.[35]

In the "Memorial of the Choctaw Colored Citizens' Association," Barrows helped argue that freedmen's rights had been ignored since the treaty of 1866 and that they were owed recompense. Slavery had not been their choice. Yet, as was the case for Black people in the South, slavery and all its misfortunes had been heaped on them. It was only because of "the great war of the rebellion" that they had gained their freedom. The CCCA members reminded the commissioners that during the Civil War "the Choctaw Indians generally threw their aid and influence against the United States."[36] They asserted that the freedmen should have received full citizenship rights in the 1866 treaty, which ended the war between the United States and the Choctaw Nation. Because they did not receive such rights, "they had no adequate legal security in any kind of property; no place they could call their own; were not encouraged by any sufficient legal protection, they could not build themselves homes, or surround themselves with even the barest means of existence."[37] As a result, they were in a worse position than African Americans, who had gained their citizenship rights in the Fourteenth Amendment. Ultimately, the CCCA members contended that

> Choctaw freedmen . . . should have and enjoy, and should be secured by the United States in the full possession and enjoyment of, all the rights, privileges, and immunities, including the right of suffrage, of citizens of the Choctaw Nation, and also including the right to share per capita in the annuities, moneys, and public domain claims by or belonging to said nation. They claim that these rights should have been fully secured to them by the United States when the treaty of 1866 was negotiated and concluded; and that the loss, damage, and injury suffered by them by reason of the failure to secure them in the full and equal rights of Choctaw citizens, including the estate of the Choctaw Nation, should be repaired and provided for as far as possible."[38]

Through this "Memorial," Barrows and the CCCA made clear the grievances of the Choctaw freedmen. They hoped that their statement would compel the Dawes Commission to act on their behalf.

The Chickasaw Freedmen's Association (CFA) likewise presented a petition to the Dawes Commission in 1894. In it, the Chickasaw freedmen made similar arguments to the Choctaw freedmen and requested similar redress. Isaac Kemp belonged to the committee that composed the CFA's statement. He was a Chickasaw freedman and an AME minister. In fact, he had been present at the inaugural meeting of the Indian Mission Annual Conference in 1879.[39] He received assistance in his work from John A. Broadnax, who reported in 1894 that he was an "agent for the Chickasaw, to assist them in getting the rights of the colored people and have them adopted in that nation as full-blooded Indians."[40]

Both the CCCA and the CFA remained active in the ensuing years. The organizations eventually merged to create the Choctaw and Chickasaw Freedmen's Grievance Association (CCFGA).[41] The advocacy of Barrows and the Choctaw and Chickasaw freedmen proved successful. The 1898 Curtis Act affirmed that Black Choctaw were "entitled to citizenship under the treaties and laws of the Choctaw Nation, and all their descendents [*sic*] born to them since the date of the treaty [of 1866]." Black Chickasaw were "entitled to any rights or benefits under the treaty made in eighteen hundred and sixty-six between the United States and the Choctaw and Chickasaw tribes." In addition to citizenship, Black Choctaw, Black Chickasaw, and their descendants born after 1866 were entitled to "forty acres of land, including their present residences and improvements." To receive these benefits, they had to be placed on the Dawes Commission's "Freedmen" rolls.[42]

In 1905, James Fletcher Morris became the president of the CCFGA. Morris, an African American, had become a part of the Black Indian community because of his marriage to the Black Chickasaw Francis A. Stevens.[43] Other leaders in the CCFGA at this time were Edward Colbert, who was the chairman pro tem, and William Justice, who was secretary. David K. Pierson, who had close ties to the AME Church, Wesley McKinney, A. J. Johnson, William Glover, and William Seitz also belonged to the organization.[44]

The CCFGA met in South McAlester in May 1905 to discuss the problem of freedmen's children being excluded from tribal citizenship rolls. This issue resonated with Morris because he had Black Indian children.[45] The freedmen discovered that a select committee of five US senators would be holding meetings in Indian Territory in November 1906. The chairman of the committee was Senator Clarence D. Clark of Wyoming. The other members were Chester I. Long of Kansas, Frank B. Brandegee of Connecticut, Henry M. Teller of Colorado, and William A. Clark of Montana. The CCFGA met in South McAlester again on October 20, 1906, and appointed a seven-person committee to compose a statement for the visiting senators.[46]

On November 20, 1906, the Senate committee convened at nine o'clock in the morning at the Busby Hotel in McAlester. The committee members received the CCFGA's statement, and Morris highlighted portions of it in his testimony before them. He complained that the Dawes Commission had only given the freedmen eight days rather than the requisite nine months to enroll their children for tribal citizenship. As a result, about four hundred freedmen minor applications remained in limbo. Morris requested an application extension and asked that freedmen who had already settled and made improvements on coal lands be permitted a "preference right to purchase [them] if the surface is sold."[47]

The CCFGA's written statement, which Morris helped compose, applauded the achievements of the Choctaw and Chickasaw freedmen. The statement contended that "since emancipation . . . the freedmen of the Choctaw and Chickasaw nations have been secure in the use of land for cultivation, in the erection of permanent homes, and have never occupied a position of servile poverty." They had also become educated and believed that "no community of the United States containing an equal number of persons of African blood can make an equal showing with themselves." Furthermore, they, unlike some of their counterparts in the Five Civilized Tribes, spoke fluent English. The cumulative effect was that Black Choctaw and Chickasaw were far along on the path to "civilization" and thus deserved the respect and attention of the US government.[48]

After Morris's testimony, Wesley McKinney addressed the Senate committee. He contended that certain freedmen had not received a $100 payment that was due to them. After the 1866 treaty, the Choctaw had made an agreement with the freedmen that they could either take the forty acres of land stipulated in the treaty or forfeit the land and take a payment of $100. McKinney asserted that thirty to forty freedmen had agreed to the $100 and had been placed on a list, but had never received payment. These freedmen were later denied enrollment on the Dawes roll and, therefore, "had neither land nor money, and occupy the position of any ordinary men of colored blood in this country, although they are properly classed as freedmen." The committee was largely dismissive of McKinney's testimony and declared the subject too complicated to be addressed during the session. Senator Clark ordered him to put his complaint in writing.[49]

Because they married Black Indian women, Barrows and Morris also interacted with the Dawes Commission as they attempted to enroll their own children as tribal citizens. On October 18, 1898, Barrows appeared before the Dawes Commission at Colbert's Station. He testified, "I am a U.S. citizen. My wife Jane deceased, is daughter of Matilda Cutchlo who belonged to Robert Boyd. My children are: Chester, 18; Lacey, 15; Joseph, 13; Edward, 12; William, 10; Daisy, 8; and Annie, 6." All the children were successfully enrolled, but they were later switched from the Chickasaw to the Choctaw rolls.[50] On April 14, 1904, Barrows also appeared at the Choctaw Land Office in Atoka in order to redeem a disputed land allotment for his daughter Annie.[51] Like Barrows, Morris fought for his children's rights as tribal citizens. In August 1901, in support of his son, James Wesley, and daughter, Bulla, he sent a letter to the Dawes Commission containing his marriage license and certificate. These records assisted in their official enrollment as Chickasaw freedmen.[52]

Barrows and Morris, like Cornelius King, were African Methodists who had significant interactions with the Dawes Commission. Both men worked through freedmen's organizations to ensure that the commission addressed Black Indians' grievances. Then, they fiercely defended their children's rights to tribal citizenship. The influence of African Methodist voices in the Dawes Commission era multiplied as AME ministers directly and indirectly assisted their parishioners and relatives in their efforts to become recognized members of the Five Civilized Tribes. That subject is addressed in the next section.

The AME Church Aids in Citizenship Cases

By the time that the Dawes Commission began its work, the AME Church had been laboring in Indian Territory for decades. Previous chapters have demonstrated how African Methodist ministers established churches and schools and formed significant relationships with diverse Indigenous communities, sometimes through marriage. This section shows how they participated in tribal citizenship cases. AME ministers testified on behalf of their Black Indian parishioners, family, and friends. Also, the birth, marriage, and death records that they had provided over the years served as critical evidence in support of these cases. Successful applicants took ownership of land, setting up their families for a more stable future. Whether or not the citizenship cases succeeded, the ministers' participation in the process highlighted the denomination's integral role in Black Indian communities.

The AME minister Albert Alexander Sears testified on behalf of Black Indian African Methodists to aid their citizenship cases. He performed this service for Fannie Love, a member of Bethel AME Church in Rentiesville who attempted to register her deceased daughter, Susie Love, as a Creek freedman. On November 29, 1902, in support of the Loves' case, Sears made an official statement at the office of J. B. Morrow, a notary public in Checotah.[53] In his testimony, Sears identified himself as a roughly forty-year-old "ordained Minister of the AME Church." He declared that "on or about April 1st, 1899 I in company with Jackson Smith passed the home of Susie Love daughter of Fannie Love, who resides near Checotah. At the time we passed Susie Love was washing clothes. I went from there to Okmulgee, to attend the quarterly conference as the presiding Elder of the District." When Susie died only a week later, word reached Sears, who was still in Okmulgee. He testified that "according to my established custom of keeping a record of the Births, and Deaths of my friends and Church members and their families, I made a note of this death and upon my return to my home I entered it upon my record."[54] Sears explained that he later visited Fannie Love, who confirmed the death of her daughter. Sears also swore that just as he had noted Susie's death, he had also recorded her birth, which occurred on July 7, 1879.[55] To bolster his testimony, Sears signed an "Affidavit of Acquaintance" attesting to the fact that he knew Susie Love and that she died on April 7, 1899.[56] Sears's testimony helped Fannie Love's application succeed, and Susie was posthumously declared a Creek freedman. As a result, Fannie was able to secure Susie's land allotment for herself.[57]

In 1904, Sears also testified on behalf of Phyllis Franklin, whom he identified as a distant relative. Franklin was attempting to have her deceased daughter, Mary Canard, registered as a Creek freedman. Sears's testimony was particularly important in this case because Franklin was nearly deaf and, therefore, unable to adequately answer the commissioners' questions. As he had done in the Loves' case, Sears identified himself as a minister and explained to the commissioners that he kept a detailed record of births and deaths for church members and family. For that reason, he was able to declare that Canard died on Saturday, November 11, 1899. In addition to providing this information, Sears also identified George Turner as Mary's father and explained that she took her surname from her uncle, Sam Canard, with whom she had lived. Sears testified again in 1905, this time bringing his memorandum book as evidence. His efforts contributed to the success of the case, and Mary Canard was officially declared a Creek freedman.[58]

The marriage licenses that Sears provided to Black Indians also helped them in their citizenship cases. In 1905, Sears solemnized the union of Melissa Paul and James Love.[59] Two years later, Love submitted the marriage license that Sears had signed and dated to the Dawes Commission. He used it as evidence for his son Earl's citizenship case. The proceedings turned into an uncomfortable interrogation about whether his wife was pregnant when they got married and whether Earl was James's biological son. In the end, Sears's document helped prove that Earl was born within the bounds of wedlock, and the commissioners registered him as a Creek freedman.[60]

As was the case with Sears, Alfred Gross provided marriage documents to Black Indians that later aided their citizenship applications. Also as with Sears, some of the people that Gross assisted were his own family members. Gross, an African American, joined the Black Indian community through his marriage to Mary, a Black Choctaw. In Doaksville on December 2, 1900, he officiated the wedding of Mary's niece Emma Thompson, an enrolled Chickasaw freedman. Emma's parents, Pink and Lucy Thompson, who belonged to the AME church in Fort Towson, attended the event as well. Two years later, Mary, an accomplished midwife, delivered Emma's son Lying Hampton. When Emma applied to the Dawes Commission on her son's behalf, she submitted the marriage certificate that Gross had provided and signed. She also sent in her aunt Mary's "affidavit of attending physician or midwife." These two pieces of evidence helped secure Lying Hampton's Chickasaw freedman citizenship.[61]

There were several other instances in which Gross helped his Black Indian relatives. In 1900, Gross performed the wedding of Mary's niece Rosa Jackson

Brunner. The next year, the family applied to the Dawes Commission to register Otta May Brunner, Rosa's daughter, as a Chickasaw freedman. Three documents that Gross had signed served as crucial evidence: Rosa's marriage license, an "affidavit of mother," and an "affidavit of attending physician or midwife." All three helped secure Otta May's tribal citizenship. In 1902, Gross officiated the wedding of his and Mary's granddaughter Cornelia. The marriage document helped ensure that she was successfully registered as a Choctaw freedman. Gross also assisted Black Indians outside of his family. In 1899, he performed the wedding of Patsy Graham and Sam Hall. The marriage document helped Patsy successfully enroll as a Chickasaw freedman.[62]

M. W. Austin, an African American AME minister, also provided marriage certificates that Black Indians used in citizenship cases. On March 4, 1905, Austin officiated the wedding of Daniel and Charlotte Grayson. Daniel was a Creek freedman from North Fork Colored, and Charlotte was an African American from Texas.[63] In 1906, the couple had a son, Roosevelt. To complete his application to the Dawes Commission, they needed to present proof of their marriage. Thankfully, they still possessed their marriage certificate, and Roosevelt was successfully enrolled as a "new-born" Creek freedman.[64]

In some instances, Black Indians lost the marriage certificates that AME ministers provided to them. So, during their testimony before the Dawes Commission, they invoked the names of the specific clergymen who solemnized their weddings, hoping to lend credence to their applications. Such was the case for Morris Battiest. In 1905, Battiest applied to the commission as a "Choctaw by blood," explaining that "I am mixed a little but I always go as a full blood." He contended a "Gentleman named Sisson" performed his wedding to Rhody, a Black Choctaw, since deceased, around 1879. According to Battiest, Sisson gave the couple a marriage certificate, but they lost it. Thankfully, Battiest was not the only one who remembered the wedding and the minister who performed it. Rhody's brother Wesley McKinney, who had served with Dennis Barrows in the CCCA, testified that the wedding occurred at his mother's house in the Choctaw Nation. He also recalled that the wedding was officiated by "James F.A. Sisson, a missionary." Adeline Folsom, Rhody and Wesley's sister, supported her brother's testimony. She stated that the wedding took place at her mother's house near Spiro and that the man who performed the ceremony was "Preacher Sisson," who was "a missionary and a white man." The testimony of Battiest's in-laws about Sisson's identity as the wedding officiant helped secure Battiest's petition. Both he and his children, Ella Eubanks and Leandes Battiest, were registered as "Choctaws by blood."[65]

Like Battiest, Jeff Campbell lacked a marriage certificate, so he invoked the name of his wedding officiant. During his testimony before the Dawes Commission, he declared that his marriage to Mary Campbell, a Black Choctaw, occurred around 1884 in Oaklodge (Skullyville). He contended that they were married by "Sisson, a preacher." When the examiner asked whether he had a marriage certificate, he replied, "No, sir, at that time we didn't need any. The man who married us moved off and I never got one."[66] Campbell's application succeeded, and he was enrolled as a Choctaw freedman.

Family members of Annie Keel, the woman who helped bring the AME Church to Indian Territory, also relied on their connection to the denomination to secure their tribal citizenship. Both Simon and Robert Keel, whose exact relationship to Annie Keel is unclear, appeared before the Dawes Commission in 1898 and testified that the Chickasaw Simon Keel had owned their family. Then, critically, they used their connection to the AME Church to validate their marriages and, therefore, legitimize their children. Simon contended that "my wife Katie is a U.S. citizen. I was married to her at Lehigh by an elder of the AME Church," while Robert averred that "my wife Laura is a U.S. citizen. I was married to her by Rev. Tyson of the AME Church in the Choctaw Nation." The Dawes Commission registered the Keel brothers and their children as Chickasaw freedmen.[67]

Because of their enrollment as Chickasaw freedmen, both Simon and Robert Keel received land allotments. According to the commission's regulations, their allotments had to have an appraised value of $130.16, "the standard value of an allotment to Choctaw and Chickasaw freedmen." On May 25, 1903, Simon appeared before the Dawes Commission in Atoka to receive a twenty-acre plot worth $110. During his testimony, he declared that he had visited this designated allotment and was aware of the "character of the soil." Furthermore, he contended that he already had twelve of the twenty acres of land fenced and in cultivation. Simon's allotment, while satisfactory to him, was still not equivalent to the $130.16 he was owed. So, on June 22, 1905, Simon appeared in Ardmore and received an additional allotment of ten acres that was worth $15.[68] Robert had a similar experience. On November 20, 1903, he appeared in Tishomingo to receive a twenty-acre plot worth $100. He testified that he had visited his designated allotment and was aware of the "character of the soil." He was still owed land valued at $30.16 but had to wait years to receive the rest of his allotment. On February 25, 1908, Robert Keel appeared in Ardmore and received an additional twenty-acre plot worth $30 (figure 6).[69]

Figure 6. Chickasaw freedmen filing on allotments in Tishomingo (Oklahoma Historical Society).

Extant evidence suggests that Simon Keel fared better than some other freedmen who received allotments. Some lacked the funds to properly improve their land. Others fell prey to speculators who took advantage of them, purchasing their lands for low prices. Simon, however, had already improved twelve acres of his land before it was officially allotted to him in 1903. He was living and working on his 1903 allotment in Wilson Township in Atoka County in 1910. His children Leonard, Adeline, and Levi lived with him. In 1930, he was still living there, but with his brother, Daniel Keel. His nearly thirty years of continuous land ownership was remarkable for a person of African descent at this time. The AME Church helped him achieve this feat.[70]

AME ministers helped Black Indians attain tribal citizenship directly, through their personal testimony, and indirectly, through the records that they had provided over time. Their willingness and ability to do so demonstrated the integral role that they had been playing in Black Indian communities for decades. Because of their intervention, Black Indians and their future progeny would have access to tribal citizenship and its corresponding benefits.

Conclusion

Through the cumulative efforts of King, Barrows, Morris, and a host of other AME ministers, the AME Church helped shape the Dawes Commission era, particularly for Black Indians. King, employed by the Dawes Commission, strongly advocated the interests of Native communities. Although he resented the policy of allotment, he encouraged these communities to accept it. Barrows and Morris served as leaders in freedmen's organizations and worked to ensure that the commission heard and responded to Black Indians' concerns. They achieved these positions because of their blended status as AME ministers and members, by marriage, of Black Indian communities. Then, throughout the enrollment period, AME ministers' testimony and records assisted Black Indian applicants in achieving tribal citizenship. Not all of these cases were successful. But without the aid of the African Methodists, fewer would have gained their citizenship rights and become landholders like Simon Keel.

Helping marginalized people of color from diverse ethnicities was a central purpose of the AME Church, as envisioned by Richard Allen. Thomas Sunrise, who was pastoring AME churches in New England as the Dawes Commission began its work, understood this fact. John Hall, who was pastoring in Michigan at roughly the same time, knew it too. In their efforts for Black Indians, the African Methodists discussed in this chapter embodied that goal as well.

Notes

Introduction

1. "Pink Thompson," *United States, Native American Applications for Enrollment in Five Civilized Tribes, 1898–1914* (database; hereafter *Native American Applications for Enrollment*), Ancestry.com, dataset uploaded 2013, https://www.ancestry.com.

2. "Emma Thompson Hampton," interview 12,968, Indian-Pioneer Papers Collection (hereafter IPPC), Western History Digital Collections, University of Oklahoma, https://digital.libraries.ou.edu/whc/pioneer/.

3. "Emma Thompson Hampton," IPPC.

4. *Proceedings of the Twenty-Eighth Session of the Indian Mission Annual Conference of the African Methodist Episcopal Church, Held in Ward Chapel AME Church, Muskogee, Oklahoma, October 30th, November 4th, 1907* (Nashville: AMEC Sunday School Union, 1907), 57, 60, church statistical tables; Marlynn Fleck O'Keefe, "Fort Towson (Town)," *Encyclopedia of Oklahoma History and Culture* (online; hereafter *EOHC*), accessed November 28, 2020, https://www.okhistory.org/publications/encyclopedia online; "Pink Thompson," *Native American Applications for Enrollment*; "Pink Thompson," *United States, Enrollment Cards for the Five Civilized Tribes, 1898–1914* (database; hereafter *Enrollment Cards for the Five Civilized Tribes*), Ancestry.com, dataset uploaded 2008, https://www.ancestry.com; "Minerva McChristian," *Native American Applications for Enrollment*; "Minerva McChristian (Thompson)," *Enrollment Cards for the Five Civilized Tribes*; "Mary Gross," *Enrollment Cards for the Five Civilized Tribes*; "Mary Gross," *Native American Applications for Enrollment*; *Flipper-Key-Davis University Annual Catalog, 1919:1920*, 13, 17–18, Alice M. Robertson Collection, Oklahoma Historical Society, Oklahoma City.

5. See Angie Debo, *And Still the Waters Run: The Betrayal of the Five Civilized Tribes* (Princeton, NJ: Princeton University Press, 1940); and Theda Perdue and Michael D. Green, *The Cherokee Nation and the Trail of Tears* (New York: Viking, 2007).

6. "Emma Thompson Hampton," IPPC.

7. For excellent examinations of this process, see Claudio Saunt, *Black, White, and Indian: Race and the Unmaking of an American Family* (New York: Oxford University Press, 2005); and Celia Naylor, *African Cherokees in Indian Territory: From Chattel to Citizens* (Chapel Hill: University of North Carolina Press, 2008).

8. Richard Allen, *The Life Experiences and Gospel Labors of Rt. Rev. Richard Allen* (Nashville: AMEC Sunday School Union, 1990), 4, 13–19; Richard S. Newman, *Freedom's Prophet: Bishop Richard Allen, the AME Church, and the Black Founding Fathers* (New York: New York University Press, 2008), 27–45; Gary B. Nash, "New Light on Richard Allen: The Early Years of Freedom," *William and Mary Quarterly* 46, no. 2 (April 1989): 337–39.

9. Nash, "New Light on Richard Allen," 339. This reference to Allen's work among Native people comes from a letter of introduction that three Baltimore Methodists wrote on Allen's behalf in 1785.

10. Kenneth J. Collins, "Wesley's Life and Ministry," in *The Cambridge Companion to John Wesley*, ed. Randy L. Maddox and Jason E. Vickers (Cambridge: Cambridge University Press, 2010), 46; Geordan Hammond, *John Wesley in America: Restoring Primitive Christianity* (Oxford: Oxford University Press, 2014), 148–53.

11. William Douglass, *Annals of the First African Church in the United States of America* (Philadelphia: King and Baird, 1862), 1–17.

12. Allen, *The Life Experiences and Gospel Labors*, 23. There has been some dispute among scholars regarding the exact date of this incident. Allen's testimony, however, remains authoritative, and 1787 is the most likely date.

13. Dennis C. Dickerson, "Heritage and Hymnody: Richard Allen and the Making of African Methodism," in *African Methodism and Its Wesleyan Heritage: Reflections on AME Church History*, by Dennis C. Dickerson (Nashville: AMEC Sunday School Union, 2009), 23.

14. Allen, *The Life Experiences and Gospel Labors*, 20.

15. Dickerson, "Heritage and Hymnody," 20–24.

16. This church is typically referred to as Mother Bethel since it is the "mother" church of the denomination.

17. Allen, *The Life Experiences and Gospel Labors*, 24–33; Daniel A. Payne, *History of the African Methodist Episcopal Church* (Philadelphia: Book Concern of the AME Church, 1891), 4–9; James A. Handy, *Scraps of African Methodist Episcopal History* (Philadelphia: AME Book Concern, 1902), 32–35.

18. Dickerson, "Heritage and Hymnody," 22.

19. Dennis C. Dickerson, "Canaan in Canada: The Founding of the British Methodist Episcopal Church," in *Religion, Race and Region: Research Notes on AME Church History*, by Dennis C. Dickerson (Nashville: AMEC Sunday School Union, 1995), 49–68; Dennis C. Dickerson, "Henry M. Turner and Black Latinos: The Mission to Cuba and Mexico," in Dickerson, *Religion, Race and Region*, 121–30.

20. Jarena Lee, *The Religious Experiences and Journal of Mrs. Jarena Lee* (Nashville: AMEC Sunday School Union, 1991), 69, 73–74, 85–86.

21. I first discussed Hall in "'I Call You Cousins': Kinship, Religion, and Black-Indian Relations in Nineteenth-Century Michigan." *Ethnohistory* 61, no. 1 (Winter 2014): 79–98.

22. Charles Simpson Butcher, *The Ecumenical Budget of the African Methodist Episcopal Church: Giving the Status of the African Methodist Episcopal Church, Numerically, Financially, Educationally, and a List of the Delegates to the Ecumenical Conference, London, September 4th, 1901* (Philadelphia: AME Church, 1901), historical table; *Journal of the Twenty-Third Quadrennial Session of the General Conference of the African Methodist Episcopal Church, Held in St. John AME Church, Norfolk, Virginia, May 4–21, 1908* (Nashville: AMEC Sunday School Union, 1908), 236–38; *Journal of the Twenty-Fourth Quadrennial Session of the General Conference of the African Methodist Episcopal Church, Held in Allen Chapel, African M.E. Church, Kansas City, Missouri, May 6–23, 1912* (Nashville: AMEC Sunday School Union, 1912), 16.

23. Lawrence S. Little, *Disciples of Liberty: The African Methodist Episcopal Church in the Age of Imperialism, 1884–1916* (Knoxville: University of Tennessee Press, 2000), 85–90.

24. The newspaper was established in 1852. Throughout the 1860s, it had several editors including Jabez P. Campbell, Elisha Weaver, A. L. Stanford, and James Lynch. Benjamin Tucker Tanner then served from 1868 to 1884. Richard R. Wright Jr., *The Centennial Encyclopedia of the African Methodist Episcopal Church* (Philadelphia: Book Concern of the AME Church, 1916), 302.

25. Barry M. Pritzker, *A Native American Encyclopedia: History, Culture, and Peoples* (New York: Oxford University Press, 2000), 266–67; Keith A. Murray, *The Modocs and Their War* (Norman: University of Oklahoma Press, 1959).

26. T. M. Malcolm, "The Modoc Indians," *Christian Recorder*, October 23, 1873.

27. Quoted in Philip Sheldon Foner and Robert J. Branham, eds., *Lift Every Voice: African American Oratory, 1787–1900* (Tuscaloosa: University of Alabama Press, 1998), 577.

28. Quoted in Foner and Branham, 578.

29. "Presiding Elder Malone's Appointments," *Christian Recorder*, September 4, 1884.

30. J. W. Malone, "Dakota Gleanings," *Christian Recorder*, October 9, 1884.

31. Richard R. Wright Jr., *The Encyclopedia of the African Methodist Episcopal Church* (Philadelphia: AME Church, 1947), 360.

32. Little, *Disciples of Liberty*, 90.

33. Little, 84–90; Dickerson-Cousin, "I Call You Cousins."

34. Allen Wright supported early AME efforts in the Choctaw Nation in the late 1860s and early 1870s. He was elected principal chief of the Choctaw Nation in 1866. Green McCurtain donated property to the AME Church in 1894 while he served as Choctaw national treasurer. He was elected principal chief of the Choctaw Nation in 1896.

35. John T. Jenifer, *Centennial Retrospect History of the African Methodist Episcopal Church* (Nashville: AMEC Sunday School Union, 1915), 102; Lonnie Johnson, pers.

comm., June 16, 2015; Pearl Wadkins, "Brief Sketch of Bethel A.M.E. Church," in *Tales of Atoka County Heritage* (Atoka, Oklahoma: Atoka County Historical Society, 1983), 64; "Notice," *Christian Recorder*, July 5, 1894.

36. Charles Spencer Smith, *A History of the African Methodist Episcopal Church* (Philadelphia: Book Concern of the AME Church, 1922), 30–37, 286.

37. Kenneth Marvin Hamilton, *Black Towns and Profit: Promotion and Development in the Trans-Appalachian West, 1877–1915* (Chicago: University of Illinois Press, 1991), 120–33; Larry O'Dell, "All-Black Towns," *EOHC*, accessed February 16, 2017; Bill Sherman, "94-Year-Old Bixby Pastor on Jim Crow Era," *Tulsa World*, February 12, 2017; Tonya Bolden, *Searching for Sarah Rector: The Richest Black Girl in America* (New York: Abrams, 2014), 34.

38. Nell Irvin Painter, *Exodusters: Black Migration to Kansas after Reconstruction* (New York: W. W. Norton, 1976).

39. James T. Campbell, *Songs of Zion: The African Methodist Episcopal Church in the United States and South Africa* (Chapel Hill: University of North Carolina Press, 1998); Dickerson, "Henry M. Turner and Black Latinos." Dickerson's most recent monograph brings a fresh perspective to Richard Allen's life by placing him within an Atlantic World context. See Dennis C. Dickerson, *The African Methodist Episcopal Church: A History* (New York: Cambridge University Press, 2020), 17–55.

40. Tash Smith, *Capture These Indians for the Lord: Indians, Methodists, and Oklahomans, 1844–1939* (Tucson: University of Arizona Press, 2014).

41. Theda Perdue, *Slavery and the Evolution of Cherokee Society* (Knoxville: University of Tennessee Press, 1979); Tiya Miles, *Ties That Bind: The Story of an Afro-Cherokee Family in Slavery and Freedom* (Los Angeles: University of California Press, 2005); Tiya Miles, *The House on Diamond Hill: A Cherokee Plantation Story* (Chapel Hill: University of North Carolina Press, 2010); Naylor, *African Cherokees in Indian Territory*; Saunt, *Black, White, and Indian*; Barbara Krauthamer, *Black Slaves, Indian Masters: Slavery, Emancipation, and Citizenship in the Native American South* (Chapel Hill: University of North Carolina Press, 2013); Gary Zellar, *African Creeks: Estelvste and the Creek Nation* (Norman: University of Oklahoma Press, 2007); Tiya Miles and Sharon P. Holland, eds., *Crossing Waters, Crossing Worlds: The African Diaspora in Indian Country* (Durham, NC: Duke University Press, 2006).

42. For more on Native Americans and Christianity, see Edward E. Andrews, *Native Apostles: Black and Indian Missionaries in the British Atlantic World* (Cambridge: Harvard University Press, 2013); Joel W. Martin and Mark Nicholas, eds., *Native Americans, Christianity, and the Reshaping of the American Religious Landscape* (Chapel Hill: University of North Carolina Press, 2010); Clara Sue Kidwell, Homer Noley, and George E. Tinker, *A Native American Theology* (New York: Orbis Books, 2001).

43. Theda Perdue, *Cherokee Women: Gender and Culture Change, 1700–1835* (Lincoln: University of Nebraska Press, 1998), 3–11. See also Carolyn Ross Johnston,

Cherokee Women in Crisis: Trail of Tears, Civil War, and Allotment, 1838–1907 (Tuscaloosa: University of Alabama Press, 2003), 1–7.

44. See Jimmie Lewis Franklin, *Journey toward Hope: A History of Blacks in Oklahoma* (Norman: University of Oklahoma Press, 1982); Hamilton, *Black Towns and Profit*; Painter, *Exodusters*.

Chapter 1. Richard Allen, John Stewart, and Jarena Lee

1. Allen, *The Life Experiences and Gospel Labors*, 17.

2. Nash, "New Light on Richard Allen," 339.

3. L. L. Berry, *A Century of Missions of the African Methodist Episcopal Church, 1840–1940* (New York: Gutenberg, 1942), 41–48.

4. The First Great Awakening occurred in Britain and the British colonies from the 1720s to the 1740s. John Howard Smith, *The First Great Awakening: Redefining Religion in British America, 1725–1775* (Madison: Fairleigh Dickinson University Press, 2015); Frank Lambert, *Inventing the "Great Awakening"* (Princeton, NJ: Princeton University Press, 1999); Barry Hankins, *The Second Great Awakening and the Transcendentalists* (Westport, CT: Greenwood Press, 2004); State Historical Society of Iowa, "The Robert Lucas Journal," *Iowa Journal of History and Politics* 4 (1906): 429; Ira Berlin and Leslie M. Harris, eds., *Slavery in New York* (New York: New York Historical Society, 2005).

5. Charles H. Wesley, *Richard Allen, Apostle of Freedom* (Washington, DC: Associated, 1935); Newman, *Freedom's Prophet*, 46–47, 56–57.

6. Allen, *The Life Experiences and Gospel Labors*, 28.

7. Allen, 13–20; Russell E. Richey, Kenneth E. Rowe, and Jeanne Miller Schmidt, *American Methodism: A Compact History* (Nashville: Abingdon Press, 2012), 9–25; Hammond, *John Wesley in America*, 148; Collins, "Wesley's Life and Ministry," 46.

8. Allen, *The Life Experiences and Gospel Labors*, 17.

9. The Haudenosaunee (Iroquois) Confederacy includes the Mohawk, Onondaga, Oneida, Seneca, Cayuga, and Tuscarora Nations. The Haudenosaunee, or "People of the Longhouse," created their confederacy between 1450 and 1600 in order to halt the constant warfare between them. The members of the confederacy primarily resided in upstate New York and Canada. For more on this confederacy, see Daniel K. Richter, *The Ordeal of the Longhouse: The Peoples of the Iroquois League in the Era of European Colonization* (Chapel Hill: University of North Carolina Press, 1992).

10. Newman, *Freedom's Prophet*, 46; Charles L. Blockson, *African Americans in Pennsylvania: A History and Guide* (Baltimore: Black Classic Press, 1994), 113–14; Colin Calloway, *The Indian World of George Washington: The First President, the First Americans, and the Birth of the Nation* (New York: Oxford University Press, 2018), 1, 107, 223–24, 243; Allen, *The Life Experiences and Gospel Labors*, 8.

11. Peter Douglass Gorrie, *The Lives of Eminent Methodist Ministers* (New York: Miller, Orton, 1857), 249–70.

12. Allen, *The Life Experiences and Gospel Labors*, 17.

13. Newman, *Freedom's Prophet*, 47, 145.

14. Mixed-race communities of Native and African people were not completely foreign in New Jersey. The Ramapough, whose ancestors were Munsee and Tuscarora, have resided in the Ramapo Mountains since the eighteenth century. They later intermarried with Africans and white people, and, partly because of this intermixing, they have been unable to achieve federal recognition for their tribe. See Amy E. Den Ouden and Jean M. O'Brien eds., *Recognition, Sovereignty Struggles, and Indigenous Rights in the United States* (Chapel Hill: University of North Carolina Press, 2013), 43–65.

15. Benjamin Abbott and John Ffirth, *The Experience and Gospel Labours of the Rev. Benjamin Abbott* (n.p.: John Totten, 1805), 159.

16. Abbott and Ffirth, 160; Acts 10:34 (King James Version).

17. Abbott and Ffirth, 67, 161.

18. Abbott and Ffirth, 169.

19. Allen, *The Life Experiences and Gospel Labors*, 17.

20. Nash, "New Light on Richard Allen," 339.

21. Ethan A. Schmidt, *Native Americans in the American Revolution: How the War Divided, Devastated, and Transformed the Early American Indian World* (Denver, CO: Praeger, 2014), 8. Schmidt's book provides a comprehensive examination of the Revolution from an Indigenous perspective. Colin Calloway called for such an analysis in *The American Revolution in Indian Country: Crisis and Diversity in Native American Communities* (New York: Cambridge University Press, 1995).

22. Allen, *The Life Experiences and Gospel Labors*, 16.

23. Newman, *Freedom's Prophet*, 56–57.

24. Newman, 57.

25. "Four Dollars Rewards," *Pennsylvania Gazette*, August 13, 1788; "Four Dollars Reward," *Pennsylvania Gazette*, October 5, 1791.

26. Allen, *The Life Experiences and Gospel Labors*, 24–33; Payne, *History of the African Methodist Episcopal Church*, 4–9; Handy, *Scraps of African Methodist Episcopal History*, 32–35.

27. *Reprint of the First Edition of the Discipline of the African Methodist Episcopal Church*, 4th printing (Nashville: AMEC Sunday School Union, 2013).

28. Allen, *The Life Experiences and Gospel Labors*, 24–33; Payne, *History of the African Methodist Episcopal Church*, 4–9; Handy, *Scraps of African Methodist Episcopal History*, 32–35.

29. Allen, *The Life Experiences and Gospel Labors*, 23; Dennis C. Dickerson, "The Case for a Wesleyan Interpretation of AME Church History," in Dickerson, *African Methodism and Its Wesleyan Heritage*, 8–12; Dickerson, "Heritage and Hymnody," 18–39; Dennis C. Dickerson, "Richard Allen: A Quintessential Wesleyan," *Evangelical Journal* 18, no. 2 (Fall 2000): 53–61; Dickerson, *The African Methodist Episcopal Church*, 30–38; James H. Cone, *Black Theology and Black Power* (New York: Orbis Books, 1969); James H. Cone, *The Black Theology of Liberation* (New York: Orbis Books, 1970).

30. Theophilus Gould Steward, "The Church on the Road to Success," *Christian Recorder*, May 1, 1902.

31. Sandi Brewster-Walker, "J. Hunter's Property," *Amityville Record*, October 15, 2014.

32. John A. Strong, *The Montaukett Indians of Eastern Long Island* (Syracuse, NY: Syracuse University Press, 2001), 83–106; Frank C. Cummings et al., *The First Episcopal District's Historical Review of 200 Years of African Methodism* (Philadelphia: First Episcopal District, 1987), 240; Peter R. Eisenstadt, ed., *The Encyclopedia of New York State* (Syracuse, NY: Syracuse University Press, 2005), 78; Jerry Domatob, *African Americans of Western Long Island* (Charleston, SC: Arcadia, 2001), 61; Brewster-Walker, "J. Hunter's Property"; Sandi Brewster-Walker, "The Miller Cemetery, a Final Resting Place for Civil War Veterans," *Amityville Record*, May 27, 2015.

33. "Babylon Marks Historical Locations in Town," *Amityville Record*, February 2, 2017.

34. Linford Fisher has noted that some Shinnecock and Montaukett people also attended Bridge Street AME Church in Brooklyn, New York, into the 1890s. See Fisher, *The Indian Great Awakening: Religion and the Shaping of Native Cultures in Early America* (New York: Oxford University Press, 2012), 210–11.

35. James Bradley Finley, *History of the Wyandot Mission, at Upper Sandusky, Ohio* (Cincinnati, OH: J. F. Wright and L. Swormstedt, 1840), 108, 141–44.

36. Finley, 215.

37. Older works omitted this aspect of John Stewart's life and ministry. See, for example, Nathaniel Barrett Coulson Love, *John Stewart: Missionary to the Wyandots* (New York: Missionary Society of the Methodist Episcopal Church, 1900); William Walker, *The Missionary Pioneer; or, A Brief Memoir of the Life, Labours, and Death of John Stewart, (Man of Colour) Founder, under God of the Mission among the Wyandotts at Upper Sandusky, Ohio* (New York: J. C. Totten, 1827); and Thelma R. Marsh, *Moccasin Trails to the Cross: A History of Mission to the Wyandott Indians of the Sandusky Plains* (Sandusky, OH: John Stewart United Methodist Church, 1974). Even more recent scholarship on Stewart omits his defection to the AME Church. See, for example, Sakina M. Hughes, "The Community Became an Almost Civilized and Christian One: John Stewart's Mission to the Wyandots and Religious Colonialism as African American Racial Uplift," *NAIS: Journal of the Native American and Indigenous Studies Association* 3, no. 1 (Spring 2016): 24–45; and Mark R. Teasdale, *Methodist Evangelism, American Salvation: The Home Mission of the Methodist Episcopal Church, 1860–1920* (Eugene, OR: Pickwick, 2014), 123. A notable exception is Larry G. Murphy, J. Gordon Melton, and Gary L. Ward, eds., *Encyclopedia of African American Religions* (New York: Routledge, 2011), 726–27, which explicitly mentions Stewart's defection to the AME Church.

38. Leon Litwack, *North of Slavery: The Negro in the Free States, 1790–1860* (Chicago: University of Chicago Press, 1961), 70–74; James Oliver Horton, "Race and Region: Ohio, America's Middle Ground," in *Ohio and the World, 1753–2053: Essays Toward a New History of Ohio*, ed. Geoffrey Parker, Richard Sisson, and William Russell

Coil (Columbus: Ohio State University Press, 2005), 43, 46; *The History of Wyandot County, Ohio: Containing a History of the County* (Chicago: Leggett, Conaway, 1884), 65–73.

39. Finley, *History of the Wyandot Mission*, 74–78; Samuel Gregg, *The History of Methodism within the Bounds of the Erie Annual Conference of the Methodist Episcopal Church*, vol. 1 (New York: Carlton and Porter, 1865), 143.

40. Finley, *History of the Wyandot Mission*, 103–4.

41. *The History of Wyandot County, Ohio*, 264–73; Pritzker, *A Native American Encyclopedia*, 478–79.

42. Finley, *History of the Wyandot Mission*, 78; *The History of Wyandot County, Ohio*, 264–73; William Alexander Taylor, *Centennial History of Columbus and Franklin County, Ohio*, vol. 2 (Chicago: S. J. Clarke, 1909), 84; C. W. Butterfield, *An Historical Account of the Expedition against Sandusky under Col. William Crawford in 1782* (Cincinnati, OH: Robert Clarke, 1873), 385; Abraham J. Baughman, ed., *Past and Present of Wyandot County, Ohio: A Record of Settlement, Organization, Progress, and Achievement*, vol. 2 (Chicago: S. J. Clarke, 1913), 133–35; *Correspondence on the Subject of the Emigration of the Indians, between the 30th November, 1831, and 27th December, 1833, with Abstracts of Expenditures by Disbursing Agents, in the Removal and Subsistence of Indians, &c. &c.*, vol. 5 (Washington, DC: Duff Green, 1835), 121–25; "Traditional History of the Wyandot," *Times-Democrat* (Lima, OH), November 19, 1874; "Jonathan Pointer," *US General Land Office Records, 1796–1907* (database), Ancestry.com, dataset uploaded 2008, https://www.ancestry.com; "Jonathan Pointer," *Ohio, Rutherford B. Hayes Presidential Center Obituary Index, 1810s-2013* (database), Ancestry.com, dataset uploaded 2010, https://www.ancestry.com.

43. Wells was present during American colonel William Crawford's expedition against the Wyandotte and Delaware during the Revolutionary War. In the midst of this violent conflict, Wells hid at a camp near Tymochtee Creek. He was also present when the Delaware and Wyandotte burned Colonel Crawford at the stake. After the war, Wells remained among the Wyandotte. He was present at Sandusky during John Stewart's ministry, though it remains unclear whether he participated in it. Like Pointer, Wells remained in Sandusky after the Wyandotte were forced to migrate to Kansas. By 1850, he was living with a Black family, the Stansleys. Probably, he died in Sandusky in either the 1850s or 1860s. "Samuel Wells" (Tymochtee, Wyandot, OH), *1850 US Federal Census* (database), Ancestry.com, dataset uploaded 2009, https://www.ancestry.com; Michael A. Leeson, *History of Seneca County, Ohio* (Chicago: Warner, Beers, 1886), 212; Butterfield, *An Historical Account of the Expedition against Sandusky*, 174, 380, 385.

44. John L. Steckley, *The Eighteenth-Century Wyandot: A Clan-Based Study* (Waterloo, ON: Wilfrid Laurier University Press, 2014), 124. The Wyandotte had also been exposed to Indigenous religious figures like Handsome Lake and Tenskwatawa; see Finley, *History of the Wyandot Mission*, 102–3, 351–52.

45. Finley, *History of the Wyandot Mission*, 79–93.

46. Finley, 104.

47. David Hempton, *Methodism: Empire of the Spirit* (New Haven, CT: Yale University Press, 2005), 68–74.

48. Finley, *History of the Wyandot Mission*, 80 (quoted), 77, 84, 218–21.

49. State Historical Society of Iowa, “The Robert Lucas Journal,” 429.

50. Hughes, “The Community Became an Almost Civilized and Christian One,” 32.

51. Hughes, 32–33; Finley, *History of the Wyandot Mission*, 79, 106–8, 414.

52. Finley, *History of the Wyandot Mission*, 93–95.

53. Reginald F. Hildebrand, “Methodist Episcopal Policy on the Ordination of Black Ministers, 1784–1864,” *Methodist History* 20, no. 3 (April 1982): 126–29.

54. Finley, *History of the Wyandot Mission*, 96–98.

55. Finley, 143.

56. Finley, 144.

57. Finley, 108, 141–44.

58. Love, *John Stewart*, 13; J. Gordon Melton, *A Will to Choose: The Origins of African American Methodism* (New York: Rowman and Littlefield, 2007), 217.

59. Love, *John Stewart*, 13; Finley, *History of the Wyandot Mission*, 144.

60. Hughes, “The Community Became an Almost Civilized and Christian One,” 27.

61. Horton, “Race and Region,” 46.

62. Smith, *A History of the African Methodist Episcopal Church*, 15–16; Wright, *The Centennial Encyclopedia*, 342.

63. Finley, *History of the Wyandot Mission*, 215.

64. Payne, *History of the African Methodist Episcopal Church*, 88–92; A. R. Green, *The Life of the Rev. Dandridge Davis of the African M. E. Church* (Pittsburgh, PA: Benjamin F. Peterson, 1850), 6–29; Daniel A. Payne, *Recollections of Seventy Years* (New York: Arno Press, 1968), 72–74.

65. *An Historical Sketch Published on the Occasion of the Eightieth Anniversary of Bethel AME Church, Detroit, Mich.* (n.p.: n.p., 1921); Donald L. Huber, “White, Red, and Black: The Wyandot Mission at Upper Sandusky,” *Timeline* 13, no. 3 (May/June 1996): 2–17; Finley, *History of the Wyandot Mission*, 215; Love, *John Stewart*, 14–15.

66. Lee, *The Religious Experiences and Journal of Mrs. Jarena Lee*, 1–4.

67. Lee, 13.

68. Lee, 22 (quoted), 15–19.

69. Lee, 30–31.

70. Jarena Lee first published her autobiography in 1836, under the title *The Life and Religious Experience of Jarena Lee*. She published an expanded version of this text in 1849, under the title *Religious Experience and Journal of Mrs. Jarena Lee*. In 1991, the AME Sunday School Union reprinted the 1849 version of the book, under the title *The Religious Experiences and Journal of Mrs. Jarena Lee*.

71. Frederick Knight, “The Many Names for Jarena Lee,” *Pennsylvania Magazine of History and Biography* 141, no. 1 (January 2017): 59–68; William L. Andrews, ed., *Sisters of the Spirit: Three Black Women's Autobiographies of the Nineteenth Century*

(Bloomington: Indiana University Press, 1986), 4–7; Joycelyn Moody, *Sentimental Confessions: Spiritual Narratives of Nineteenth-Century African American Women* (Athens: University of Georgia Press, 2003), 51–76; Martha S. Jones, *All Bound Up Together: The Woman Question in African American Public Culture, 1830–1900* (Chapel Hill: University of North Carolina Press, 2009), 32–35.

72. Lee, *The Religious Experiences and Journal of Mrs. Jarena Lee*, 69.

73. Lee, 73.

74. Pritzker, *A Native American Encyclopedia*, 465–66.

75. See Arthur C. Parker, "The Code of Handsome Lake, the Seneca Prophet," *Education Department Bulletin*, no. 530 (November 1912).

76. Bruce Elliott Johansen, ed., *The Encyclopedia of Native American Legal Tradition* (Westport, CT: Greenwood Press, 1998), 110.

77. Andrews, *Sisters of the Spirit*, 6.

78. Nell Irvin Painter, *Sojourner Truth: A Life, a Symbol* (New York: W. W. Norton, 1996), 73–74; Knight, "The Many Names for Jarena Lee," 61.

79. Lee, *The Religious Experiences and Journal of Mrs. Jarena Lee*, 69.

80. Lee, 73.

81. Lee, 73.

82. Lee, 74.

83. Barbara Alice Mann, *Iroquoian Women: The Gantowisas* (New York: Peter Lang, 2000), 115–82; Richter, *The Ordeal of the Longhouse*, 110–11.

84. Lee, *The Religious Experiences and Journal of Mrs. Jarena Lee*, 74.

85. Lee, 74.

86. James Bradley Finley, *Life among the Indians; or, Personal Reminiscences and Historical Incidents Illustrative of Indian Life and Character* (Cincinnati, OH: E. P. Thompson, 1859), 492.

87. Finley, 503.

88. Finley, 500–503; Finley, *History of the Wyandot Mission*, 405; Mary Stockwell, *The Other Trail of Tears: The Removal of the Ohio Indians* (Yardley, PA: Westholme, 2014), 285–86; Lee, *The Religious Experiences and Journal of Mrs. Jarena Lee*, x, 85–86; Love, *John Stewart*, 13–14.

89. Stockwell, *The Other Trail of Tears*, 283–318.

90. Polly, along with her brother-in-law, sold her husband's sixty-acre plot of land after his death and probably returned to Negrotown. Finley, *History of the Wyandot Mission*, 144.

91. Lee, *The Religious Experiences and Journal of Mrs. Jarena Lee*, 85–86.

92. Lee, 86.

93. Lee, x, 85–86; Love, *John Stewart*, 13–14.

94. Love, *John Stewart*, 14–15.

95. Knight, "The Many Names for Jarena Lee"; Andrews, *Sisters of the Spirit*, 6; Berry, *A Century of Missions*, 41–48.

96. Lee, *The Religious Experiences and Journal of Mrs. Jarena Lee*, 73–74, 85–86.

97. Berry, *A Century of Missions*, 41–48.

98. Berry, 41–42.

99. Berry, 41–42; Payne, *History of the African Methodist Episcopal Church*, 174–78.

100. Payne, *History of the African Methodist Episcopal Church*, 477.

101. Payne, 477; *Sentinel and Democrat* (Burlington, VT), July 30, 1824; Julie Winch, "American Free Blacks and Emigration to Haiti" (paper, 11th Caribbean Congress, Puerto Rico, August 1988), 1–14; Laurie F. Maffly-Kipp, "The Serpentine Trail: Haitian Missions and the Construction of African American Religious Identity," in *The Foreign Missionary Enterprise at Home: Explorations in North American Cultural History*, ed. Daniel H. Bays and Grant Wacker (Tuscaloosa: University of Alabama Press, 2003), 32; Sara Fanning, *Caribbean Crossing: African Americans and the Haitian Emigration Movement* (New York: New York University Press, 2015), 77, 89–91, 109–11; William Steward and Theophilus Gould Steward, *Gouldtown, a Very Remarkable Settlement of Ancient Date* (Philadelphia: J. B. Lippincott, 1913), 94–95.

102. Payne, *History of the African Methodist Episcopal Church*, 57–58, 64–66, 104–6, 475–79.

103. Berry, *A Century of Missions*, viii.

104. Berry, 91–104.

105. Theophilus Gould Steward, "The Church on the Road to Success," *Christian Recorder*, May 1, 1902.

Chapter 2. Seeking Their Cousins

1. The best-known example of these dynamics occurred among the Dakota and Lakota. See, for example, Gary Clayton Anderson and Alan R. Woolworth, eds., *Through Dakota Eyes: Narrative Accounts of the Minnesota Indian War of 1862* (Saint Paul: Minnesota Historical Society, 1988); and Dee Brown, *Bury My Heart at Wounded Knee: An Indian History of the American West* (New York: Bantam Books, 1976). For information on the Indian boarding school experience, see Clifford E. Trafzer, Jean A. Keller, and Lorene Sisquoc, eds., *Boarding School Blues: Revisiting American Indian Educational Experiences* (Lincoln: University of Nebraska Press, 2006).

2. My 2014 article in *Ethnohistory* was the first serious and singular examination of John Hall; see Dickerson-Cousin, "I Call You Cousins."

3. For more on Occom and Apess, see William DeLoss Love, *Samson Occom and the Christian Indians of New England* (Boston: Pilgrim Press, 1899); Joanna Brooks, ed., *The Collected Writings of Samson Occom, Mohegan: Leadership and Literature in Eighteenth-Century Native America* (New York: Oxford University Press, 2006); Jason E. Vickers, ed., *The Cambridge Companion to American Methodism* (New York: Cambridge University Press, 2013), 248–50; Philip F. Gura, *The Life of William Apess, Pequot* (Chapel Hill: University of North Carolina Press, 2015); and Jean M. O'Brien, *Firsting and Lasting: Writing Indians Out of Existence in New England* (Minneapolis: University of Minnesota Press, 2010).

4. He is also referred to as Thomas Sunrise Dana.

5. Pritzker, *A Native American Encyclopedia*, 443–44; "Religious Notices," *Brooklyn Daily Eagle*, December 13, 1851.

6. Jan DeAmicis, "Slavery in Oneida County, New York," *Afro-Americans in New York Life and History* 27, no. 2 (July 2003): 69–76; "Oneida Fugitive Slave Act Repeal Petition," New York Heritage Digital Collections, accessed December 8, 2020, https://nyheritage.org/collections/oneida-county-anti-slavery-petitions.

7. "Religious," *Rock Island Argus and Daily Union*, August 9, 1879.

8. "Indian Preacher at Putnam," *Morning Journal and Courier* (New Haven, CT), October 4, 1888.

9. "News Brevities," *Evening Bulletin* (Maysville, KY), October 23, 1882.

10. "Wesley Grove Southern M.E. Camp Meeting," *Baltimore Sun*, August 12, 1875.

11. "Transformation Extraordinary," *Brooklyn Daily Eagle*, October 22, 1882; "An Indian Lecturer," *Worcester Daily Spy*, August 8, 1888.

12. Thomas Sunrise became so well-known that a man in Philadelphia falsely claimed to be his relative. The man, John Denvey, apparently sought to benefit from Sunrise's positive reputation. "To the Public," *Sun* (Philadelphia, PA), April 17, 1851.

13. William T. Catto, *A Semi-Centenary Discourse, Delivered in the First African Presbyterian Church, Philadelphia* (Philadelphia: Joseph M. Wilson, 1857), 105–11. For more on John Gloucester, see Anthony B. Pinn, ed., *African American Religious Cultures* (Denver: Greenwood, 2009), 38–48.

14. *Public Ledger* (Philadelphia, PA), April 3, 1852.

15. *Baltimore Sun*, May 10, 1852.

16. In 1855, First African finally secured William Catto, a man of both AME and abolitionist associations, as its pastor. Under his leadership, William Still, the prominent Underground Railroad conductor, joined the church. See Daniel R. Biddle and Murray Dubin, *Tasting Freedom: Octavius Catto and the Battle for Equality in Civil War America* (Philadelphia: Temple University Press, 2010), 1–25, 59–75, 88–102.

17. While in Baltimore, Sunrise and Johnson engaged in at least one business venture together. In 1853, they endorsed the "herb medicines" of Dr. Robert Delaney. They lent their support as "moral, dignified, truly God-like Clergymen" and were most likely paid for their endorsement, which ran in a Baltimore newspaper. In the advertisement, Sunrise described himself as an "Indian Missionary," and he described Johnson as his "Secretary." *American and Commercial Daily Advertiser* (Baltimore, MD), July 25, 1853.

18. Alexander W. Wayman, *Cyclopaedia of African Methodism* (Baltimore: Methodist Episcopal Book Depository, 1882), 88–89. In his account of their relationship, Wayman implied that Johnson did not become an African Methodist until he reached Ohio in the 1860s. In actuality, he became one in 1852 at the same AME meeting at which Bishop James A. Handy was converted.

19. Robert A. Johnson, "Letter from Cleveland, O.," *Christian Recorder*, October 5, 1867; "First on the List," *Christian Recorder*, June 15, 1872; "Commencement at Wilberforce," *Christian Recorder*, July 10, 1873; "Last Day's Proceeding of the A.M.E. Conference at Frankfort," *Christian Recorder*, September 10, 1874.

20. Earl Francis Mulderink, "'We Want a Country': African-American and Irish-American Community Life in New Bedford, Massachusetts, during the Civil War Era" (PhD diss., University of Wisconsin-Madison, 1995), 77.

21. "Religious Intelligence," *Springfield Republican*, November 25, 1854; "Lecture," *Newburyport Morning Herald*, October 2, 1854; Jesse Fillmore Kelley and Adam Mackie, *History of the Churches of New Bedford* (New Bedford, MA: E. Anthony, 1869), 6, 55–57, 68, 99–100, 118.

22. At this time, according to the 1854 New England minutes, other AME churches in New England were located in Providence, Newport, and Barrington, Rhode Island; Boston, Stockbridge, Lee, Pittsfield, Lenox, and Williamstown, Massachusetts; New Haven, Bridgeport, and New London, Connecticut; Portland, Maine; and a city listed only as Bristol (probably Rhode Island, but possibly New Hampshire). *Minutes of the New England Annual Conference of the African Methodist Episcopal Church, Held in the City of Providence, R.I., from June 17th to the 26th, 1854* (New Bedford, MA: Standard Steam Press, 1854), 7.

23. Payne, *History of the African Methodist Episcopal Church*, 287, 321, 382–83; *Reprint of the First Edition of the Discipline of the African Methodist Episcopal Church*. By 1916, preachers had to receive a recommendation from the district conference rather than the quarterly conference. Wright, *The Centennial Encyclopedia*, 283. Richard R. Wright Jr., *The Doctrines and Discipline of the AME Church* (Philadelphia: Book Concern of the AME Church, 1916), 191; Works Progress Administration in Ohio, *Annals of Cleveland, 1818–1935*, vol. 40, *1857* (Cleveland: Works Progress Administration, 1936), 37–38; J. A. Warren, "A Letter from Cleveland," *Christian Recorder*, March 12, 1864.

24. "Religious Intelligence," *Springfield Republican*, November 25, 1854; Kelley and Mackie, *History of the Churches of New Bedford*, 6, 68, 99–100, 118.

25. *Minutes of the Third Annual Conference of the New England District of the African Methodist Episcopal Church in America, Held in Bethel Church, Providence, from June 16th to 25th, 1855* (Providence, RI: Knowles, Anthony, 1855), 9 (quoted); Dickerson, "Canaan in Canada."

26. *Minutes of the Third Annual Conference of the New England District*, 10.

27. *Minutes of the Third Annual Conference of the New England District*, 7; Payne, *History of the African Methodist Episcopal Church*, 295.

28. "Portland Freedom Trail Self-Guided Walking Map," n.d., Maine Historical Society (website), accessed April 10, 2021, https://www.mainehistory.org/programs_walkingtours.shtml; H. H. Price and Gerald E. Talbot, *Maine's Visible Black History: The First Chronicle of Its People* (Thomaston, ME: Tilbury House, 2006), 148–49; W. Jeffrey Bolster, *Black Jacks: African American Seamen in the Age of Sail* (Cambridge, MA: Harvard University Press, 1997).

29. *Minutes of the Fourth Annual Conference of the New England District of the African Methodist Episcopal Church in America, Held in Plymouth Hall, Boston, from June 21 to 30, 1856* (Providence, RI: Knowles, Anthony, 1856).

30. Payne, *History of the African Methodist Episcopal Church*, 361–83; Dickerson, "Canaan in Canada."

31. Payne, *History of the African Methodist Episcopal Church*, 383.

32. Payne, 361–83; Dickerson, "Canaan in Canada"; Wright, *The Centennial Encyclopedia*, 15.

33. "Religious Notice," *Cleveland Leader*, December 24, 1856; J. A. Warren, "A Letter from Cleveland," *Christian Recorder*, March 12, 1864; Robert A. Johnson, "Letter from Cleveland, O.," *Christian Recorder*, October 5, 1867.

34. *Minutes of the Twenty Ninth Annual Session of the Ohio &c., District Conference, of the African M.E. Church, Convened at the City of Cleveland, O.* (Cleveland, 1859), 5.

35. Regarding the stereotypes about Indigenous people and alcohol, see Peter Mancall, *Deadly Medicine: Indians and Alcohol in Early America* (Ithaca, NY: Cornell University Press, 1995); and Roxanne Dunbar-Ortiz and Dina Gilio-Whitaker, *"All the Real Indians Died Off": And 20 Other Myths about Native Americans* (Boston: Beacon Press, 2016).

36. *Minutes of the Twenty Ninth Annual Session of the Ohio &c., District Conference*, 5.

37. *Minutes of the Twenty Ninth Annual Session*, 16.

38. "Rev. Thos. Dana," *Christian Recorder*, May 11, 1872.

39. Another physical description of him comes from a newspaper in 1884. The article described him as "dark-skinned" and "broad-shouldered," with "long, straight hair" and a "smoothly shaven" face. He wore a "ministerial black suit." "Thomas Sunrise," *Evening Bulletin* (Providence, RI), July 21, 1884.

40. "Thomas S. Dana," *New Jersey, United States, United Methodist Church Records, 1800–1970 (database),* Ancestry.com, dataset uploaded 2016, https://www.ancestry.com; *Advocate of Peace* 7, no. 12 (December 1876): 69; "Thomas Sunrise Dana," *US Passport Applications, 1795–1905* (database), Ancestry.com, dataset uploaded 2007, https://www.ancestry.com; "A Red Man in the Clerical Role," *Virginian-Pilot*, December 9, 1875; "Religious," *Rock Island Argus and Daily Union*, August 9, 1879.

41. He also composed a poem, "The Indian's Lament," about the losses that Native people had suffered; see Thomas Sunrise, "The Indian's Lament" (1850), Harris Broadsides, Brown Digital Repository, Brown University Library, accessed December 9, 2020, https://repository.library.brown.edu/studio/item/bdr:288021/.

42. "Indian, Indian, Indian," *Baltimore Sun*, October 19, 1875; *Brooklyn Daily Eagle*, October 22, 1881; "Wesley Grove Southern M.E. Camp Meeting," *Baltimore Sun*, August 12, 1875; *St. Louis Post-Dispatch*, February 24, 1879; *Quad-City Times*, August 4, 1879; "Lecture by an Indian," *Shippensburg Chronicle*, February 1, 1884.

43. In February 1851, Sunrise lectured at Israel Church in Philadelphia on the "Manners and Customs of the Western Indians." The advertisement in the local newspaper promised that Sunrise would appear in "full Prince dress." In January 1852, Sunrise accepted a speaking engagement at Ebenezer Church in Philadelphia. Again, the local newspaper assured readers that he would appear in "full Indian costume." In May 1852, a newspaper correspondent from Worcester, Massachusetts, noted that when Sunrise lectured in Town Hall on the "manners, customs and mode of reli-

gious worship of the Indians," he was "dressed in his native costume." *Public Ledger* (Philadelphia, PA), February 20, 1851; *Public Ledger (*Philadelphia, PA), January 27, 1852; "A Savage Reformer," *Easton (MD) Star*, May 25, 1852.

44. Dickerson-Cousin, "I Call You Cousins," 80. Eastman's relative Kate Beane explores this dynamic in the riveting documentary *Ohiyesa: The Soul of an Indian* (Vision Maker Media, 2018), film, 57 min.

45. "Something Good," *Quad-City Times*, August 1, 1879; see also Alfred Ronald Conkling, *The Life and Letters of Roscoe Conkling: Orator, Statesman, Advocate* (New York: Charles L. Webster, 1889).

46. "Religious," *Rock Island Argus and Daily Union*, August 9, 1879.

47. "Providence, RI, City Directory," p. 598, *US City Directories, 1822–1995* (database), Ancestry.com, dataset uploaded 2011, https://www.ancestry.com.

48. "Scraps," *Indianapolis News*, October 6, 1888. Variations of this article were published by newspapers in Saint Louis, Missouri; Pittsburgh, Pennsylvania; Little Rock and Galveston, Texas; Saint Paul, Minnesota; Columbus, Ohio; Independence, Kansas; and Oshkosh, Wisconsin.

49. "Sunrise," *Morning Call (*Allentown, PA), October 14, 1888.

50. "Missions, Etc.," *Worcester Daily Spy*, August 2, 1891.

51. Sunrise was unique among his ministerial peers, but there were other Native people who assisted freedom seekers. Roy E. Finkenbine, a professor at the University of Detroit Mercy, is developing a book on this subject, currently titled "Freedom Seekers in Indian Country."

52. Scholars have written a great deal about this tumultuous decade. See, for example, Eric H. Walther, *The Shattering of the Union: America in the 1850s* (New York: SR Books, 2004).

53. "An Indian Lecturer," *Worcester Daily Spy*, August 16, 1888.

54. *Reprint of the First Edition of the Discipline of the African Methodist Episcopal Church*, 100.

55. Smith, *A History of the African Methodist Episcopal Church*, 14.

56. Payne, *History of the African Methodist Episcopal Church*, 87.

57. Dickerson, *The African Methodist Episcopal Church*, 83–85.

58. Samson Occom, *The Collected Writings of Samson Occom, Mohegan*, ed. Joanna Brooks (New York: Oxford University Press, 2006), 97n67.

59. Pamela Newkirk, ed., *Letters from Black America* (New York: Farrar, Straus and Giroux, 2009), 91.

60. Bernd Peyer, ed., *American Indian Nonfiction: An Anthology of Writings, 1760s-1930s* (Norman: University of Oklahoma Press, 2007), 76.

61. Peyer, 78.

62. *Minutes of the Third Annual Conference of the New England District*, 14.

63. *Minutes of the Fourth Annual Conference of the New England District*, 13.

64. Pamela R. Peters, *The Underground Railroad in Floyd County, Indiana* (Jefferson, NC: McFarland, 2001), 33; Thomas Adams Upchurch, *Abolition Movement* (Denver, CO: Greenwood, 2011), xxviii; Wilbur H. Siebert, *The Underground Railroad:*

From Slavery to Freedom (New York: Macmillan, 1898), 37, 82, 133, and 219; "Portland Freedom Trail Self-Guided Walking Map"; Price and Talbot, *Maine's Visible Black History*, 148–49; Mary Ellen Snodgrass, *The Underground Railroad: An Encyclopedia of People, Places, and Operations* (New York: Routledge, 2015), 466. See also Bolster, *Black Jacks*.

65. "Special Notices," *Cincinnati Commercial Tribune*, July 21, 1856.

66. See, for example, Eric R. Jackson and Richard Cooper, *Cincinnati's Underground Railroad* (Charleston, SC: Arcadia, 2014).

67. Mary Ellen Snodgrass, *Civil Disobedience: An Encyclopedic History of Dissidence in the United States* (New York: Routledge, 2009), 39; "Local Intelligence," *Pittsburg Dispatch*, July 30, 1859.

68. "An Indian Lecturer," *Worcester Daily Spy*, August 8, 1888.

69. "An Indian Lecturer," *Worcester Daily Spy*, August 16, 1888.

70. *Minutes of the Fourth Session of the Michigan Annual Conference of the African Methodist Episcopal Church, Held at East Saginaw, Michigan, September 10 to 15, 1890* (Detroit: W. L. Smith, 1890), 7–8; Heidi Bohaker, "'Nindoodemag': The Significance of Algonquin Kinship Networks in the Eastern Great Lakes Region, 1600–1701," *William and Mary Quarterly*, 3rd ser., 63, no. 1 (January 2006): 25; William Whipple Warren, *History of the Ojibway Nation* (Saint Paul: Minnesota Historical Society, 1885), 41–53; "The Indian Camp Meeting," *Saginaw News*, September 1, 1881; "Lo, the Poor Indian," *Saginaw News*, September 2, 1881; "Church Appointments," *Saginaw News*, September 15, 1890; *Minutes of the Sixth Session of the Michigan Annual Conference of the African Methodist Episcopal Church, Held at Jackson, Michigan, September First to Sixth to 15, 1892* (Detroit, 1892), 12; "Local News," *Democratic Expounder* (Marshall, MI), October 20, 1893; *Correspondence, Field Notes, and the Census Roll of All Members or Descendants of Members Who Were on the Roll of the Ottawa and the Chippewa Tribes of Michigan in 1870, and Living on March 4, 1907 (Durant Roll)* (Washington, DC: National Archives, 1996), microfilm, M-2039.

71. *Minutes of the Sixth Session of the Michigan Annual Conference*, 11.

72. For more on Native communities in Michigan, see Charles E. Cleland, *Rites of Conquest: The History and Culture of Michigan's Native Americans* (Ann Arbor: University of Michigan Press, 1992); and Andrew J. Blackbird, *History of the Ottawa and Chippewa Indians of Michigan* (Ypsilanti, MI: Ypsilantian Job Printing House, 1887).

73. Helen Hornbeck Tanner, *Atlas of Great Lakes Indian History* (Norman: University of Oklahoma Press, 1987), 163–68, 179; *1900 Michigan Census, Isabella County, Isabella Township* (dataset), pp. 116–18, *HeritageQuest Online*; *1900 Michigan Census, Isabella County, US Indian Industrial School* (dataset), pp. 143–45, *HeritageQuest Online*; *1880 Michigan Census, Isabella County, Isabella Township* (dataset), pp. 519–30, *HeritageQuest Online*; *The Executive Documents of the House of Representatives for the Second Session of the Fifty-First Congress, 1890–91, with Index, in Thirty-Eight Volumes* (Washington, DC: Government Printing Office, 1891), clxxii–clxxv, 437, 826;

The Executive Documents of the House of Representatives for the Third Session of the Fifty-Third Congress, 1894–95, with Index, in Thirty-Five Volumes (Washington, DC: Government Printing Office, 1895), 383–85; Isaac Alger Fancher and Myrta Wilsey Burwash, *Past and Present of Isabella County, Michigan* (Indianapolis, IN: B. F. Bowen, 1911), 75–79; Jack R. Westbrook, *Isabella County: 1859–2009* (Chicago: Arcadia, 2008), 89; Trafzer, Keller, and Sisquoc, *Boarding School Blues*, 1–34.

74. Missionaries from various denominations had been working among the Ojibwe for centuries. See Christopher Vecsey, *Traditional Ojibwa Religion and Its Historical Changes* (Philadelphia: American Philosophical Society, 1983); and Donald B. Smith, *Sacred Feathers: The Reverend Peter Jones (Kahkewaquonaby) and the Mississauga Indians* (Lincoln: University of Nebraska Press, 1987).

75. *Minutes of the Fourth Session of the Michigan Annual Conference*, 7. The Wesleyan Methodists began their missionary efforts in Upper Canada during the 1820s, and by the late 1860s the denomination had established seventeen Indigenous missions. Hall may have visited any one of these sites and helped the Wesleyans communicate with the residents. *Minutes of the Forty-Fourth Annual Conference of the Wesleyan Methodist Church in Canada* (Toronto, 1867), 106; Neil Semple, *The Lord's Dominion: The History of Canadian Methodism* (Montreal: McGill-Queen's University Press, 1996), 153, 161–63; *The Methodist Magazine, Designed as a Compend of Useful Knowledge and of Religious and Missionary Intelligence, for the Year of Our Lord 1828*, vol. 9 (New York: Azor Hoyt, 1828), 229–30; Wesleyan Methodist Missionary Society, *The Wesleyan Missionary Notices, Relating Principally to the Foreign Missions under the Direction of the Methodist Conference*, vol. 2 (London, 1855), 147–48; Peter Jones, *Life and Journals of Keh-ke-wa-guo-nā-by: (Rev. Peter Jones,) Wesleyan Missionary* (Toronto: Anson Green, 1860), 2, 6–7, 9–17, 245, 419–20.

76. "The Indian Camp Meeting," *Saginaw News*, September 1, 1881; "Lo, the Poor Indian," *Saginaw News*, September 2, 1881. See also David Hempton, *Methodism: Empire of the Spirit* (New Haven, CT: Yale University Press, 2005), 68–74; and Michael D. McNally, *Ojibwe Singers: Hymns, Grief, and a Native Culture in Motion* (Saint Paul: Minnesota Historical Society Press, 2000).

77. Jesse Lee, *A Short History of the Methodists in the United States of America* (Baltimore: Magill and Clime, 1810), 279.

78. Jones, *Life and Journals of Keh-ke-wa-guo-nā-by*, 90.

79. Wright, *The Centennial Encyclopedia*, 318; "Editorial Correspondence," *Christian Recorder*, September 15, 1887; "A.M.E. Conference," *Battle Creek Daily Moon*, August 26, 1887; "A.M.E. Conference," *Battle Creek Daily Moon*, August 27, 1887; "A.M.E. Conference," *Battle Creek Daily Moon*, August 29, 1887; *Minutes of the Fourth Session of the Michigan Annual Conference*, 7–8.

80. *Minutes of the Sixth Session of the Michigan Annual Conference*, 12.

81. *Minutes of the Fourth Session of the Michigan Annual Conference*, 7.

82. *Minutes of the Fourth Session of the Michigan Annual Conference*, 8.

83. *Minutes of the Fourth Session of the Michigan Annual Conference*, 8.

84. "Gathered from All Points of the Compass," *Christian Recorder*, September 19, 1890 (quoted); *Minutes of the Fourth Session of the Michigan Annual Conference*, 7–8, 25.

85. "Saginaw and Vicinity," *Detroit Free Press*, September 13, 1890.

86. "Church Appointments," *Saginaw News*, September 15, 1890; "The AME Conference: Evidences of the Growth and Progress of the Church," *Plaindealer* (Detroit), September 19, 1890.

87. *Minutes of the Fourth Session of the Michigan Annual Conference*, 7–8, 25.

88. "Gathered from All Points of the Compass," *Christian Recorder*, September 19, 1890.

89. *Minutes of the Sixth Session of the Michigan Annual Conference*, 11 (quoted), 12; *Minutes of the Fourth Session of the Michigan Annual Conference*, 7–8.

90. Bohaker, "Nindoodemag," 25–26; George Copway, *The Traditional History and Characteristic Sketches of the Ojibway Nation* (London: Charles Gilpin, 1850), 119–22; Peter Jones, *History of the Ojebway Indians: With Especial Reference to their Conversion to Christianity* (London: A. W. Bennett, 1861), 109; Reuben Gold Thwaites, ed., *Collections of the State Historical Society of Wisconsin*, vol. 17, *The French Regime in Wisconsin II, 1727–1748* (Madison: Historical Society of Wisconsin, 1906), 44, 46.

91. *Minutes of the Fourth Session of the Michigan Annual Conference*, 7–8; *Minutes of the Sixth Session of the Michigan Annual Conference*, 11–12.

92. *Niikaanis* (*nikanis*) was the word for "brother" that Peter Jones used in his translation of the Gospel According to Matthew (12:50, 18:21). See Peter Jones, trans., *The Gospel According to Matthew in the Ojibwa Language* (Boston: Crocker and Brewster, 1839), 44, 65.

93. Jones, *History of the Ojebway Indians*, 120; *Minutes of the Sixth Session of the Michigan Annual Conference*, 12.

94. Richard A. Rhodes, *Eastern Ojibwa-Chippewa-Ottawa Dictionary* (New York: Mouton, 1985), 197. This dictionary includes two dialects of the Ojibwe language, Eastern Ojibwe and Ottawa.

95. *Minutes of the Fourth Session of the Michigan Annual Conference*, 8.

96. This term is an Ojibwe adaptation of "bonjour," the French word for "hello." Rhodes, *Eastern Ojibwa-Chippewa-Ottawa Dictionary*, 494; Smith, *Sacred Feathers*, 22.

97. Smith, *Sacred Feathers*, 41–42; Edward Francis Wilson, *Missionary Work among the Ojebway Indians* (London: Society for Promoting Christian Knowledge, 1886), 34.

98. For a full-length work on this topic, see Carol E. Mull, *The Underground Railroad in Michigan* (Jefferson, NC: McFarland, 2010).

99. Carol McGinnis, *Michigan Genealogy: Sources and Resources* (Baltimore: Genealogical, 2005), 199–201; *Minutes of the Fourth Session of the Michigan Annual Conference*, 5–8.

100. For example, in *Black, White, and Indian*, Claudio Saunt demonstrated how the Graysons, a Creek family that enslaved Black laborers, divided along racial lines.

Some family members intermarried with Black people. Their descendants faced discrimination both within the larger family and within the Creek Nation.

101. James C. Embry, *The Doctrine and Discipline of the African Methodist Episcopal Church* (Philadelphia: Book Concern of the AME Church, 1888), 128.

102. Embry, 130.

103. *Minutes of the Sixth Session of the Michigan Annual Conference*, 11–18; Smith, *A History of the African Methodist Episcopal Church*, 163, 173.

104. Embry, *The Doctrine and Discipline of the African Methodist Episcopal Church*, 127–28, 408–13; Wright, *The Doctrines and Discipline of the AME Church*, 193–94, 401–3.

105. *Minutes of the Sixth Session of the Michigan Annual Conference*, 18.

106. *Minutes of the Fourth and Fifth Sessions of the Indian Mission Annual Conference of the African Methodist Episcopal Church, Held at McAllister, Indian Territory, from October 26th to October 31st, 1882, and at Brazille, Indian Territory, from October 24th to October 29th, 1883* (Terre Haute, IN: C. W. Brown, 1883); Little, *Disciples of Liberty*, 69, 87. Note that although the 1882 and 1883 minutes were published together as a single volume, their pagination is not continuous. Subsequent citations to this text are divided, cited as *Minutes of the Fourth Session of the Indian Mission Annual Conference* and *Minutes of the Fifth Session of the Indian Mission Annual Conference*, respectively.

107. *Minutes of the Sixth Session of the Michigan Annual Conference*, 12.

108. *Minutes of the Sixth Session of the Michigan Annual Conference*, 12.

109. *Minutes of the Sixth Session of the Michigan Annual Conference*, 40.

110. Tanner, *Atlas of Great Lakes Indian History*, 163–68; Westbrook, *Isabella County*, 71; Fancher and Burwash, *Past and Present of Isabella County*, 61–74; *The Executive Documents* [. . .] *1890–91*, 826; *The Executive Documents* [. . .] *1894–95*, 383; *Minutes of the Twenty-Second Session of the Michigan Annual Conference of the Methodist Episcopal Church, Held at Lansing, Mich., Sept. 16–22, 1857* (Lansing, 1857), 10, 15; "Indian Missions," *Christian Recorder*, March 30, 1861; *1900 Michigan Census, Isabella County, Isabella Township*, 116–18; *1900 Michigan Census, Isabella County, US Indian Industrial School*, 143–45; *1880 Michigan Census, Isabella County, Isabella Township*, 519–30.

111. By the 1890s, roughly five hundred Native people were living in Isabella. *The Executive Documents* [. . .] *1894–95*, 383.

112. *Minutes of the Sixth Session of the Michigan Annual Conference*, 12.

113. The 1890 census is not available for Michigan. However, Peter Jackson appears in both the 1880 and 1900 censuses for Isabella, so I surmise that he was also present in the 1890s when John Hall visited. *1900 Michigan Census, Isabella County, Isabella Township*, 116–18; *1900 Michigan Census, Isabella County, US Indian Industrial School*, 143–45; *1880 Michigan Census, Isabella County, Isabella Township*, 519–30.

114. Reuben Gold Thwaites, ed., *Collections of the State Historical Society of Wisconsin*, vol. 16, *The French Regime in Wisconsin I, 1634–1727* (Madison: Historical Society of Wisconsin, 1902), 106.

115. *Minutes of the Sixth Session of the Michigan Annual Conference*, 12.

116. *Minutes of the Ninth Session of the Michigan Conference of the African Methodist Episcopal Church, Convened in Ebenezer A.M.E. Church, 191 Erskine St., Detroit, Mich., September 4th to 9th, 1895* (Detroit: Wilton-Smith, 1895), 42.

117. *Minutes of the Sixth Session of the Michigan Annual Conference*, 12; *Minutes of the Ninth Session of the Michigan Conference*, 42–43.

118. *Minutes of the Sixth Session of the Michigan Annual Conference*, 12.

119. *Minutes of the Fourth Session of the Michigan Annual Conference*, 8.

120. *Minutes of the Sixth Session of the Michigan Annual Conference*, 12.

121. "Brevities," *Saginaw News*, June 15, 1893.

122. Jones, *Life and Journals of Keh-ke-wa-guo-nā-by*; Smith, *Sacred Feathers*; Dickerson, "Canaan in Canada," 64.

123. Hall's postal address was located in Athens, so he was probably living there. *Minutes of the Ninth Session of the Michigan Conference*, 56.

124. "Local News," *Democratic Expounder* (Marshall, MI), October 20, 1893.

125. *Minutes of the Eighth Session of the Michigan Annual Conference of the African Methodist Episcopal Church, Held at Lansing, Michigan, September 5–10, 1894* (Detroit: Wilton-Smith, 1894), 16, 33.

126. Hall had the second highest travel money of all the twenty-three pastors in the conference. *Minutes of the Eighth Session of the Michigan Annual Conference*, 33, table of general statistics.

127. *Minutes of the Ninth Session of the Michigan Conference*, 56, statistical tables A and B, financial tables A and B.

128. *Minutes of the Tenth Session of the Michigan Conference of the African Methodist Episcopal Church, Convened in Bethel A.M.E. Church, Fourth Avenue, Ann Arbor, Mich., from August 26th to 30th, 1896* (Detroit: Wolverine, 1896); *Minutes of the Twenty-Ninth Session of the Michigan Conference, Fifteenth Episcopal District of the African Methodist Episcopal Church, Held in Ebenezer African M.E. Church, Detroit, Michigan, September 1–5, A.D., 1915* (Nashville: AMEC Sunday School Union, 1915), 82–87, Bentley Historical Library (hereafter BHL), University of Michigan; *Minutes of the Thirtieth Annual Session of the Michigan Conference, Fifteenth Episcopal District of the African Methodist Episcopal Church, Held in Arnett Chapel A.M.E. Church, Grand Rapids, Michigan, September 6–10, A.D. 1916* (Nashville: AMEC Sunday School Union, 1916), 82–87, BHL; *Minutes of the Thirty-First Annual Session of the Michigan Conference, Fifteenth Episcopal District of the African Methodist Episcopal Church, Held in Olivet A.M.E. Church, South Bend, Indiana, September 6–9, A.D. 1917* (Nashville: AMEC Sunday School Union, 1917), 62–66, BHL; *Minutes of the Thirty-Second Annual Session of the Michigan Conference, Fifteenth Episcopal District of the African Methodist Episcopal Church, Held in Allen Chapel, A.M.E. Church, Kalamazoo, Michigan, September 12–15, A.D. 1918* (Nashville: AMEC Sunday School Union, 1918), 68–72, BHL; *Minutes of the Thirty-Third Annual Session of the Michigan Conference, Fifteenth Episcopal District of the African Methodist Episcopal Church, Held in Bethel*

A.M.E. Church, Detroit, Michigan, September 10–15, A.D. 1919 (Nashville: AMEC Sunday School Union, 1919), 82–86, BHL.

129. T. Lindsay Baker and Julie P. Baker, ed., *The WPA Oklahoma Slave Narratives* (Norman: University of Oklahoma Press, 1996), 28–30; "Allen Wright," *Native American Applications for Enrollment;* "Notice," *Christian Recorder*, July 5, 1894.

Chapter 3. The African Methodist Migration and the All-Black Town Movement

1. The Methodist system of episcopal governance, in which bishops assign pastors to various churches, is different than the Baptist system, in which congregations choose their own pastors. I am unaware of any comprehensive studies on Black Baptist migration during this period. The different governing structures, however, would have made Black Baptist migration patterns somewhat different than their Methodist counterparts. For African Methodists, migration was systematic and consistent, whereas Baptist migration was less so.

2. "Church News," *Christian Recorder*, March 15, 1877; "Dennis Barrows" (Poteau, LeFlore, OK) *1920 US Federal Census* (database), Ancestry.com, dataset uploaded 2010, https://www.ancestry.com; *Minutes of the Ninth Session of the Arkansas Annual Conference of the African Methodist Episcopal Church, Held at Little Rock, November 9, 10, 11, 12, & 13, 1876* (Little Rock, W. H. Windsor, 1876), 2, 5, 21, Joseph F. Murrow Collection, folder 10, box 3, Oklahoma Historical Society Research Center; James F. A. Sisson, "A Word from the Indian Territory," *Christian Recorder*, October 25, 1877.

3. *Christian Recorder*, June 10, 1880; A. J. Miller, "The Indian Mission Conference," *Christian Recorder*, December 15, 1881; "An Ecclesiastical Magnet," *Freeman*, November 7, 1891; J. F. Dyson, "Indian Mission Conference," *Christian Recorder*, December 7, 1882.

4. Hempton, *Methodism*, 30; Dickerson, *The African Methodist Episcopal Church*, 65–80.

5. Black Presbyterians engaged in similar endeavors concurrent with African Methodists. For more on that topic, see Andrew Murray, *Presbyterians and the Negro: A History* (Philadelphia: Presbyterian Historical Society, 1966).

6. Much has been written about Black migration in the nineteenth and early twentieth centuries. A recent example is Anna-Lisa Cox, *The Bone and Sinew of the Land: America's Forgotten Black Pioneers and the Struggle for Equality* (New York: Hachette Book Group, 2018). This book examines Black farming communities in the Northwest Territory in the first half of the nineteenth century. Cox cites this early westward movement of Black people as an important and understudied example of Black migration.

7. These were the sentiments of bishops Daniel Alexander Payne and Henry McNeal Turner in 1862. Quinn was the living embodiment of this idea in the 1830s. *Minutes of the Baltimore Annual Conference of the African M.E. Church, Held in Washington, D.C., From April 17 to May 2* (Baltimore: Bull and Tuttle, 1862), 21.

8. Christina Dickerson, "New France, 1689–1763: Forgotten Outpost of Black Slavery," *AME Church Review* 124, no. 416 (2009): 21–30; Norman Dwight Harris, *The History of Negro Servitude in Illinois* (Chicago: A. C. McClurg, 1904); Christopher P. Lehman, *Slavery in the Upper Mississippi Valley, 1787–1865: A History of Human Bondage in Illinois, Iowa, Minnesota and Wisconsin* (Jefferson, NC: McFarland, 2011); Carl J. Ekberg, *French Roots in the Illinois Country: The Mississippi Frontier in Colonial Times* (Urbana: University of Illinois Press, 2000).

9. *Minutes of the Baltimore Annual Conference*, 21. See also Cox's *The Bone and Sinew of the Land* for more on Black migration to this region.

10. Wright, *The Centennial Encyclopedia*, 280–81.

11. Sundiata Keita Cha-Jua, *America's First Black Town: Brooklyn, Illinois, 1830–1915* (Urbana: University of Illinois Press, 2000), 31–46; George A. Singleton, *The Romance of African Methodism: A Study of the African Methodist Episcopal Church* (New York: Exposition Press, 1952), 72–73; "Priscilla Baltimore" (Bellefontaine Cemetery, Saint Louis, MO), *US Find a Grave Index, 1600s–Current* (database), Ancestry.com, dataset uploaded 2012, https://www.ancestry.com.

12. Hempton, *Methodism*, 30.

13. Cha-Jua, *America's First Black Town*, 31–46; Singleton, *The Romance of African Methodism*, 72–73; Payne, *History of the African Methodist Episcopal Church*, 170–72; Wright, *The Encyclopedia of the African Methodist Episcopal Church*, 443; "Priscilla Baltimore" (Bellefontaine Cemetery, Saint Louis, Missouri), *US Find a Grave Index, 1600s–Current*.

14. Payne, *History of the African Methodist Episcopal Church*, 170–72.

15. Payne, 170–72; Sarah J. W. Early, *Life and Labors of Rev. Jordan W. Early, One of the Pioneers of African Methodism in the West and South* (Nashville: AMEC Sunday School Union, 1894), 39–40; Coy D. Robbins, *Reclaiming African Heritage at Salem, Indiana* (Bowie, MD: Heritage Books, 1995), 54; Henry Davenport Northrop, Joseph R. Gay, and Irvine Garland Penn, *The College of Life or Practical Self: A Manual of Self-Improvement for the Colored Race* (n.p.: Premier, 1896), 40.

16. Payne, *History of the African Methodist Episcopal Church*, 417–18; Smith, *A History of the African Methodist Episcopal Church*, 59; Wright, *The Centennial Encyclopedia*, 129–30.

17. Wright, *The Encyclopedia of the African Methodist Episcopal Church*, 357, 360, 361, 395; Wright, *The Centennial Encyclopedia*, 15, 290; Smith, *A History of the African Methodist Episcopal Church*, 170; "Proceedings of the First Session of the Kansas Conference of the African M.E. Church," *Christian Recorder*, October 26, 1876; Charles Simpson Butcher, *The Ecumenical Budget of the African Methodist Episcopal Church: Giving the Status of the African Methodist Episcopal Church, Numerically, Financially, Educationally, and a List of the Delegates to the Ecumenical Conference, London, September 4th, 1901* (Philadelphia, 1901), historical table.

18. Circulation numbers for newspapers were sometimes difficult to calculate. In 1867, there were an estimated five thousand subscribers to the *Christian Recorder*.

In 1873 there were an estimated twenty-eight hundred subscribers, and in 1876 there were an estimated four thousand subscribers. Keep in mind that in the nineteenth century individual subscribers often shared their newspapers with family, friends, and church members. Copies might be read aloud to accommodate illiterate populations. So, one subscriber might represent a dozen or more "readers." Eric Gardner, *Black Print Unbound: The Christian Recorder, African American Literature, and Periodical Culture* (New York: Oxford University Press, 2015), 85.

19. "Notes from California," *Christian Recorder*, September 14, 1876.

20. D. E. Johnson, "California Annual Conference," *Christian Recorder*, September 18, 1890.

21. Wright, *The Centennial Encyclopedia*, 194–95.

22. "Rev. John Turner of the Colorado Conference," *Christian Recorder*, May 19, 1887 (quoted); "A Western Man for Bishop," *Christian Recorder*, May 3, 1888.

23. Painter, *Exodusters*, 12, 121, 225–30.

24. Painter, 3–16.

25. Painter, 3–68, 108–17.

26. Painter, 225–26.

27. *Journal of the 17th Session and the 16th Quadrennial Session of the General Conference of the African Methodist Episcopal Church in the United States, Held at St. Louis, Missouri. May 3–25, 1880* (Xenia, OH: Torchlight, 1882), 23.

28. Painter, *Exodusters*, 260 (quoted), 256–61.

29. Zellar, *African Creeks*, 238.

30. O'Dell, "All-Black Towns"; Hamilton, *Black Towns and Profit*, 120–33; Bill Sherman, "94-Year-Old Bixby Pastor on Jim Crow Era," *Tulsa World*, February 12, 2017; Tonya Bolden, *Searching for Sarah Rector: The Richest Black Girl in America* (New York: Abrams, 2014), 34.

31. Hallie S. Jones, "A History of Boley, 1904–1945," in *Stories of Early Oklahoma: A Collection of Interesting Facts, Biographical Sketches and Stories Relating to the History of Oklahoma*, ed. Hazel Ruby Mc-Mahan (Oklahoma City: Oklahoma Historical Society, 1945), n.p.

32. *Souvenir Program of Boley's 30th Anniversary Celebration, September 18 to 23, 1934*, Dill Collection, Okfuskee County Historical Society, Okemah, OK.

33. Hamilton, *Black Towns and Profit*, 120–33; "Thomas Haines" (OK), *1900 US Federal Census* (database), Ancestry.com, dataset uploaded 2004, https://www.ancestry.com; "Thomas Haynes" (Los Angeles, CA), *1930 US Federal Census* (database), Ancestry.com, dataset uploaded 2002, https://www.ancestry.com; "Tommie Haynes" (Creek, Okfuskee, OK), *1920 US Federal Census*; "Tom Haynes" (Creek, Okfuskee, OK), *1930 US Federal Census*; "Tom Haynes," *US World War I Draft Registration Cards, 1917–1918* (database), Ancestry.com, dataset uploaded 2005, https://www.ancestry.com.

34. *Souvenir Program of Boley's 30th Anniversary Celebration*; Jones, "A History of Boley."

35. Jones, "A History of Boley."

36. Larry O'Dell, "Boley," *EOHC*, accessed February 17, 2017.

37. Booker T. Washington, "Boley: A Negro Town in the West," *Outlook*, January 1908, 28–31.

38. Zellar, *African Creeks*, 238.

39. Barbara Krauthamer explains how treaties that the Five Civilized Tribes signed in 1866 paved the way for this policy. See Krauthamer, *Black Slaves, Indian Masters*; and Barbara Krauthamer, "Indian Territory and the Treaties of 1866: A Long History of Emancipation," in *The World the Civil War Made*, ed. Gregory P. Downs and Kate Masur (Chapel Hill: University of North Carolina Press, 2015), 226–48. Clara Sue Kidwell also discussed these dynamics in *The Choctaws in Oklahoma: From Tribe to Nation, 1855–1970* (Norman: University of Oklahoma Press, 2007).

40. Jones, "A History of Boley."

41. Homer Williams, pers. comm., March 23, 2017.

42. "Negroes Making Good at Boley," *Coffeyville Daily Journal*, July 1, 1913.

43. Washington, "Boley," 28–31; "Five Die in a Fire at Boley," *Muskogee Times-Democrat*, May 18, 1912.

44. Jones, "A History of Boley."

45. The Colored Methodist Episcopal Church was founded in 1870. The organization changed its name to the Christian Methodist Episcopal Church in 1954.

46. Jones.

47. Jones.

48. G. B. Richardson, "General Church News: Texas," *Christian Recorder*, April 1, 1897; *Proceedings of the Twenty-Eighth Session of the Indian Mission Annual Conference*, 65, statistical tables; "Negro Conference Ends," *Daily Arkansas Gazette*, October 30, 1917.

49. Jones, "A History of Boley."

50. "African Methodist Session," *El Paso Herald*, December 15, 1905.

51. "Dawson Praised," *Black Dispatch*, February 21, 1920.

52. Wright, *The Encyclopedia of the African Methodist Episcopal Church*, 94.

53. Jones, "A History of Boley" (quoted); *Proceedings of the Twenty-Eighth Session of the Indian Mission Annual Conference*, 65; "Thomas Haines" (OK), *1900 US Federal Census*; "Thomas Haynes" (Los Angeles, CA), *1930 US Federal Census*; "Tommie Haynes" (Creek, Okfuskee, OK), *1920 US Federal Census*; "Tom Haynes" (Creek, Okfuskee, OK), *1930 US Federal Census*; "Tom Haynes," *US World War I Draft Registration Cards, 1917–1918*; "Henry Cavil" (Paden, Okfuskee, OK), *1920 US Federal Census*; "Willie Cavil" (Paden, Okfuskee, OK), *1920 US Federal Census*; "W. H. Jessie" (Red Mound, Seminole, OK), *1920 US Federal Census*; "Mary Jessie" Red Mound, Seminole, OK), *1920 US Federal Census*; "Charles Chiles" (Boley, Okfuskee, OK), *1910 US Federal Census* (database), Ancestry.com, dataset uploaded 2006, https://www.ancestry.com; "Hannah Chiles" (Boley, Okfuskee, OK), *1910 US Federal Census*; "Walter Williams," *US Find a Grave Index, 1600s–Current*.

54. Hamilton, *Black Towns and Profit*, 120–33; Jones, "A History of Boley"; "Thomas Haines" (OK), *1900 US Federal Census*; "Thomas Haynes" (Los Angeles, CA), *1930 US Federal Census*; "Tommie Haynes" (Creek, Okfuskee, OK), *1920 US Federal Census*; "Tom Haynes" (Creek, Okfuskee, OK), *1930 US Federal Census*; "Tom Haynes," *US World War I Draft Registration Cards, 1917–1918*.

55. *Souvenir Program of Boley's 30th Anniversary Celebration*.

56. Wright, *The Encyclopedia of the African Methodist Episcopal Church*, 270.

57. Jones, "A History of Boley."

58. "Chief Sam's Terror and Nemesis Here," *Black Dispatch*, March 22, 1918 (quoted); "Boley, Okla. Gets New Postmaster," *Black Dispatch*, April 20, 1922.

59. Wright, *The Encyclopedia of the African Methodist Episcopal Church*, 290.

60. The jurisdiction continued to exist, but it was renamed several times after Oklahoma statehood.

61. *Proceedings of the Twenty-Eighth Session of the Indian Mission Annual Conference*, 11.

62. "Boley News," *Black Dispatch*, March 4, 1921.

63. "Boley News," *Black Dispatch*, April 20, 1922.

64. Homer Williams, pers. comm., March 23, 2017.

65. Larry O'Dell, "Rentiesville," *EOHC*, accessed February 17, 2017; "William Rentie" (Rentiesville Ward 4, McIntosh, OK), *1910 US Federal Census*.

66. *Proceedings of the Twenty-Eighth Session of the Indian Mission Annual Conference*, 54, church statistical table; "Susie Love," *Native American Applications for Enrollment*.

67. Wright, *The Encyclopedia of the African Methodist Episcopal Church*, 84.

68. John Hope Franklin, *Mirror to America: The Autobiography of John Hope Franklin* (New York: Farrar, Straus and Giroux, 2005), 11. For more on Buck Colbert Franklin, see also John Hope Franklin and John Whittington Franklin, eds., *My Life and an Era: The Autobiography of Buck Colbert Franklin* (Baton Rouge: Louisiana State University Press, 1997).

69. Benjamin P. Bowser, Louis Kushnick, Paul Grant, eds., *Against the Odds: Scholars Who Challenged Racism in the Twentieth Century* (Boston: University of Massachusetts Press, 2002), 63.

70. "David Franklin," *Native American Applications for Enrollment*; "Andrew Franklin," *Native American Applications for Enrollment*; Franklin, *Mirror to America*, 9–12.

71. Wright, *The Centennial Encyclopedia*, 77.

72. Franklin, *Mirror to America*, 11.

73. Franklin, *Mirror to America*, 11–12; Wright, *The Centennial Encyclopedia*, 77.

74. Franklin, *Mirror to America*, 21–22.

75. Franklin, *Mirror to America*, 12–26.

76. *Proceedings of the Twenty-Eighth Session of the Indian Mission Annual Conference*, 53–65.

77. Larry O'Dell, "Vernon," *EOHC*, accessed May 26, 2017.

78. "William T. Vernon," *US Passport Applications, 1795–1925*; Wright, *The Centennial Encyclopedia*, 281–82.

79. David A. Chang, *The Color of the Land: Race, Nation, and the Politics of Landownership in Oklahoma, 1832–1929* (Chapel Hill: University of North Carolina Press, 2010), 160–61.

80. "That Washington Trip," *Muskogee Cimiter*, November 1, 1907.

81. "Republican Politics Takes New Life in Washington," *New York Age*, October 31, 1907; Chang, *The Color of the Land*, 160–61.

82. "That Washington Trip," *Muskogee Cimiter*, November 1, 1907.

83. Larry O'Dell, "Taft," *EOHC*, accessed December 22, 2018; Bolden, *Searching for Sarah Rector*, 34.

84. "Flipper Chapel A.M.E. Turns 100," *Muskogee Phoenix*, November 20, 2009.

85. M. Kaye Tatro, "Curtis Act (1898)," *EOHC*, accessed February 9, 2017; John W. Flenner, "Protest against Vernon, the Negro," *Muskogee Times-Democrat*, June 9, 1911.

86. John W. Flenner, "Negro Gets Big Gov't Job Here," *Muskogee Times-Democrat*, June 8, 1911.

87. Flenner (quoted); "Don't Want Vernon," *Wichita Beacon*, June 8, 1911.

88. "Taft's Latest Insult to Oklahoma," *Muskogee Times-Democrat*, June 9, 1911.

89. "The Indians Don't Like It," *Muskogee Times-Democrat*, June 10, 1911 (quoted); Pugh A. Edwards, "Notice," *Christian Recorder*, July 5, 1894.

90. "Vernon Assigned," *Muskogee Times-Democrat*, June 30, 1911.

91. "Prof. Vernon Here," *Lawrence Daily Journal-World*, April 11, 1912.

92. "W.T. Vernon Heads College," *Vicksburg Evening Post*, June 28, 1912; Wright, *The Centennial Encyclopedia*, 281–82.

93. O'Dell, "Vernon"; "Boley Man in Town," *Tulsa Star*, June 13, 1913; J. E. W. Clarke, "Helena, Mont.," *Kansas City Sun*, May 11, 1918; "Vernon Business Men Visit Tulsa," *Tulsa Star*, February 28, 1920; "A Vernon Letter," *Indian Journal*, November 26, 1936. See also "Black Towns in Oklahoma: Vernon, A Pastor Learns to Forgive," YouTube video, 4:13, uploaded March 29, 2015 by the Struggle and Hope project, https://www.youtube.com/watch?v=DUt8adwHy2k.

94. Scott Ellsworth, *Death in a Promised Land: The Tulsa Race Riot of 1921* (Baton Rouge: Louisiana State University Press, 1982), 12; Lonnie Johnson, pers. comm., June 16, 2015.

Chapter 4. "Ham Began . . . to Evangelize Japheth"

1. Wadkins, "Brief Sketch of Bethel A.M.E. Church," 64; John T. Jenifer, *The First Decade of African Methodism in Arkansas and in the Indian Territory* (Boston: D. F. Jones, 1882), 15; Jenifer, *Centennial Retrospect History*, 103–4; "Dennis Barrows" (Poteau, Le Flore, OK), *1920 US Federal Census*; Lonnie Johnson, pers. comm., June 16, 2015.

2. Bishop Daniel Alexander Payne was instrumental in establishing educational requirements for AME clergy. The two years of study that John Hall went through to

be ordained a deacon was a requirement that Payne helped institute. See Campbell, *Songs of Zion*, 37–39.

3. Wesley J. Gaines, *African Methodism in the South; or, Twenty-five Years of Freedom* (Atlanta: Franklin, 1890), 13.

4. The Cherokee spoke an Iroquoian language. The other four tribes spoke a Muskogean language. Daniel Littlefield, *The Chickasaw Freedmen: A People without a Country* (Westport, CT: Greenwood Press, 1980), 3–4; Andrew K. Frank, "Five Civilized Tribes," *EOHC*, accessed September 14, 2015; William L. Anderson, "Sequoyah," *EOHC*, accessed January 26, 2016.

5. Christina Snyder explains the complexity of captive-taking among Native people in *Slavery in Indian Country: The Changing Face of Captivity in Early America* (Cambridge, MA: Harvard University Press, 2010).

6. Arrell M. Gibson, *The Chickasaws* (Norman: University of Oklahoma Press, 1971), 140–41; Littlefield, *The Chickasaw Freedmen*, 5–10; Krauthamer, *Black Slaves, Indian Masters*, 2–5, 17, 39; Naylor, *African Cherokees in Indian Territory*, 9–12. Many scholars have discussed the system of African slavery among the Five Civilized Tribes. See also Perdue, *Slavery and the Evolution of Cherokee Society*; Miles, *Ties That Bind*; Miles, *The House on Diamond Hill*.

7. Gibson, *The Chickasaws*, 140–41; Littlefield, *The Chickasaw Freedmen*, 5–10; Krauthamer, *Black Slaves, Indian Masters*, 2–5, 17, 39; Naylor, *African Cherokees in Indian Territory*, 9–12.

8. "Annie Keel" (Township 2, Choctaw Nation, Indian Territory), *1900 US Federal Census*. Annie Keel's son, Charley, contended that she was born in Mississippi. See "Charley Keel" (Wilson, Atoka, OK), *1920 US Federal Census*.

9. "Jacob Keel," *Native American Applications for Enrollment*; Lonnie Johnson, pers. comm., June 16, 2015; Gibson, *The Chickasaws*, 104–5; Krauthamer, *Black Slaves, Indian Masters*, 2; Littlefield, *The Chickasaw Freedmen*, 15.

10. Gibson, *The Chickasaws*, 179–82.

11. Littlefield, *The Chickasaw Freedmen*, 11.

12. Jon D. May, "Boggy Depot," *EOHC*, accessed September 12, 2015.

13. "Edmond Flint," interview 12361, *Indian-Pioneer Papers Collection*, Western History Digital Collections, University of Oklahoma, accessed November 26, 2020, https://digital.libraries.ou.edu/whc/pioneer/.

14. "Jacob Keel," *Native American Applications for Enrollment*; Lonnie Johnson, pers. comm., June 16, 2015.

15. "Edmond Flint," interview 12361, *Indian-Pioneer Papers Collection.*

16. Baker and Baker, *The WPA Oklahoma Slave Narratives*, 246.

17. Baker and Baker, 108–9.

18. Baker and Baker, 109.

19. Baker and Baker, 109 (quoted), 109–10.

20. Baker and Baker, 111 (quoted), 111–12.

21. "Annie Keel" (Township 2, Choctaw Nation, Indian Territory), *1900 US Federal Census*; "Jacob Keel," *Native American Applications for Enrollment*; "Jacob Keel," *En-*

rollment Cards for the Five Civilized Tribes; "Charley Keel," *Enrollment Cards for the Five Civilized Tribes*; "Betsie (Keel) Brown," *Enrollment Cards for the Five Civilized Tribes*; "Daniel Keel," *Enrollment Cards for the Five Civilized Tribes*; "Lucy Ann (Keel) McDermott," *Enrollment Cards for the Five Civilized Tribes*; Littlefield, *The Chickasaw Freedmen*, 15.

22. Baker and Baker, *The WPA Oklahoma Slave Narratives*, 246–48.

23. "Annie Keel" (Township 2, Choctaw Nation, Indian Territory), *1900 US Federal Census*; "Jacob Keel," *Native American Applications for Enrollment*; "Jacob Keel," *Enrollment Cards for the Five Civilized Tribes*; "Charley Keel," *Enrollment Cards for the Five Civilized Tribes*; "Betsie (Keel) Brown," *Enrollment Cards for the Five Civilized Tribes*; "Daniel Keel," *Enrollment Cards for the Five Civilized Tribes*; "Lucy Ann (Keel) McDermott," *Enrollment Cards for the Five Civilized Tribes*; Littlefield, *The Chickasaw Freedmen*, 15.

24. Baker and Baker, *The WPA Oklahoma Slave Narratives*, 248 (quoted), 251–52.

25. "Edmond Flint," interview 12361, *Indian-Pioneer Papers Collection.*

26. Littlefield, *The Chickasaw Freedmen*, 19.

27. Murray R. Wickett, *Contested Territory: Whites, Native Americans, and African Americans in Oklahoma, 1865–1907* (Baton Rouge: Louisiana State University Press, 2000), 6.

28. Littlefield, *The Chickasaw Freedmen*, 18–19.

29. Gibson, *The Chickasaws*, 265.

30. "Booker Keel," *US Confederate Service Records, 1861–1865* (database), Ancestry.com, dataset uploaded 2007, https://www.ancestry.com; "Booker Keel," *Civil War Service Records (CMSR)—Confederate—Confederate Government (CSA)* (database), Fold3, dataset uploaded 2008, https://www.fold3.com/; "Jacob Keel," *Native American Applications for Enrollment.*

31. Baker and Baker, *The WPA Oklahoma Slave Narratives*, 112–17, 173.

32. "Rev. John Turner of the Colorado Conference," *Christian Recorder*, May 19, 1887.

33. Baker and Baker, *The WPA Oklahoma Slave Narratives*, 112–17, 173–78.

34. Baker and Baker, 112–17.

35. Kevin Mulroy, *The Seminole Freedmen: A History* (Norman: University of Oklahoma Press, 2007), 205.

36. Naylor, *African Cherokees in Indian Territory*, 153–54, 160, 294n37; Linda Reese, "Freedmen," *EOHC*, accessed May 21, 2021; Zellar, *African Creeks*, 77, 97–99; Mulroy, *The Seminole Freedmen*, 200–205.

37. Charles J. Kappler, ed., *Indian Affairs: Laws and Treaties*, vol. 2, *Treaties* (Washington, DC: Government Printing Office, 1904), 919–20.

38. Kappler, *Indian Affairs*, 919; Krauthamer, *Black Slaves, Indian Masters*, 114–31; Littlefield, *The Chickasaw Freedmen*, 21; Jon D. May, "Leased District," *EOHC*, accessed May 21, 2021.

39. Krauthamer, *Black Slaves, Indian Masters*, 140–41; Reese, "Freedmen."

40. Testimony of Lemon Butler, in *Report of Committees of the House of Representatives for the Third Session of the Forty-Second Congress, 1872–1873* (Washington, DC: Government Printing Office, 1873), 463.

41. "Edmond Flint," interview 0000, *Indian-Pioneer Papers Collection*.

42. Wadkins, "Brief Sketch of Bethel A.M.E. Church," 64.

43. Littlefield, *The Chickasaw Freedmen*, 80 (quoted), 80–82; Krauthamer, *Black Slaves, Indian Masters*, 127–28.

44. "List of Appointments," *Christian Recorder*, October 9, 1869.

45. Reginald F. Hildebrand, "Richard Harvey Cain, African Methodism & the Gospel of Freedom in South Carolina," *AME Church Review* 117, no. 381 (January/March 2001): 43.

46. Bridget "Biddy" Mason was a contemporary of Keel. Like her, Mason played a crucial role in building an AME church in the West. Around 1872, she provided the financial support to establish First AME Church in Los Angeles, California. See Jean Kinney Williams, *Bridget "Biddy" Mason: From Slave to Businesswoman* (Minneapolis, MN: Compass Point Books, 2006).

47. Lonnie Johnson, pers. comm., June 16, 2015; Janet Duitsman Cornelius, *Slave Missions and the Black Church in the Antebellum South* (Columbia: University of South Carolina Press, 1999), 9–12.

48. Lonnie Johnson, pers. comm., June 16, 2015.

49. Jenifer, *Centennial Retrospect History*, 102; Lonnie Johnson, pers. comm., June 16, 2015; Wadkins, "Brief Sketch of Bethel A.M.E. Church," 64.

50. Stewart began preaching in the 1850s and helped establish the churches in what would become the Presbytery of Kiamichi in the Choctaw Nation.

51. By 1876, the MECS's Indian Mission Conference, which was established in 1844, included twenty-five churches with over four thousand Native and almost three hundred Black members. By 1890, several thousand Black Baptists were in Indian Territory. In 1890, Presbyterians reported twenty-two churches in the Choctaw and Chickasaw Nations and over six hundred members, while the Catholic Church had about fifteen churches sprinkled throughout Indian Territory. Matthew Simpson, *Cyclopedia of Methodism* (Philadelphia: Louis H. Everts, 1883), 472; Smith, *Capture These Indians for the Lord*, 19, 48; *Annual Report of the Commissioner of Indian Affairs to the Secretary of the Interior for the Year 1880* (Washington, DC: Government Printing Office, 1880), 279; *Annual Report of the Commissioner of Indian Affairs to the Secretary of the Interior for the Year 1883* (Washington, DC: Government Printing Office, 1883), 240–41; *Annual Report of the Commissioner of Indian Affairs to the Secretary of the Interior for the Year 1890* (Washington, DC: Government Printing Office, 1890), 94–95; Henry King Carroll, *Report on Statistics of Churches in the United States at the Eleventh Census: 1890* (Washington, DC: Government Printing Office, 1894), 683–85; Andrea M. Martin, "Joseph Murrow," *EOHC*, accessed February 1, 2016; D. C. Gideon, *Indian Territory, Descriptive, Biographical and Genealogical* (New York: Lewis, 1901), 235–38; Reginald F. Hildebrand, *The Times Were Strange and Stirring:*

Methodist Preachers and the Crisis of Emancipation (Durham, NC: Duke University Press, 1995), 3–27. See also Robert Elliott Flickinger, *The Choctaw Freedmen and the Story of Oak Hill Industrial Academy* (Fonda, IA: Journal and Times Press, 1914).

52. Thomas Donaldson, *Eleventh Census of the United States, Extra Census Bulletin, Indians, the Five Civilized Tribes of Indian Territory: Cherokee Nation, Creek Nation, Seminole Nation, Choctaw Nation, and Chickasaw Nation* (Washington, DC: Government Printing Office, 1893), 25; Charles Henry Phillips, *The History of the Colored Methodist Episcopal Church in America: Comprising Its Organization, Subsequent Development, and Present Status* (Jackson, TN: CME Church, 1898), 95; Simpson, *Cyclopedia of Methodism*, 472; Smith, *Capture These Indians for the Lord*, 19, 48; *Annual Report of the Commissioner of Indian Affairs* [. . .] *for the Year 1880*, 279; *Annual Report of the Commissioner of Indian Affairs* [. . .] *for the Year 1883*, 240–41; *Annual Report of the Commissioner of Indian Affairs* [. . .] *for the Year 1890*, 94–95; Carroll, *Report on Statistics of Churches*, 683–85; Martin, "Joseph Murrow"; Gideon, *Indian Territory*, 235–38; Hildebrand, *The Times Were Strange and Stirring*, 3–27.

53. For more on the historical significance of the *Christian Recorder*, see Julius H. Bailey, *Race Patriotism: Protest and Print Culture in the A.M.E. Church* (Knoxville: University of Tennessee Press, 2012).

54. Smith, *A History of the African Methodist Episcopal Church*, 103–4, 341–42, 348; *The Fifteenth Quadrennial Session of the General Conference of the African Methodist Episcopal Church. Place of Session, Nashville, TN, May 6, 1872* (Philadelphia: African Methodist Episcopal Church, 1872), 48–50.

55. W. E. B. Du Bois, *The Souls of Black Folk* (Rockville, MD: Arc Manor, 2008), 130.

56. Cha-Jua, *America's First Black Town*, 31–46; Williams, *Bridget "Biddy" Mason*, 89–90.

57. The AME Church began to ordain women as local ministers in 1948. The denomination allowed for the full ordination of women, as both local and itinerant ministers, in 1960.

58. Dennis C. Dickerson, "Rocky Mountain Evangelists: AME Women in Ministry, 1905–1906," in Dickerson, *Religion, Race and Region*, 113–18.

59. Allen Wright, a Black Choctaw, testified before the Dawes Commission in 1899, 1905, and 1907. He identified Chief Allen Wright as the man who owned him and his parents, Easter and Henry Wright. Frances Banks, also a Black Choctaw, claimed that the Wright family owned her grandfather, Wallace Willis. Willis later became famous for composing Negro spirituals like "Swing Low, Sweet Chariot" and "Steal Away to Jesus." See "Allen Wright," *Native American Applications for Enrollment*; Baker and Baker, *The WPA Oklahoma Slave Narratives*, 28–30.

60. See Krauthamer, *Black Slaves, Indian Masters*, 122; and Littlefield, *The Chickasaw Freedmen*, 55–56; who both cited his testimony from 1872.

61. *Minutes of the Tenth General Conference of the African Methodist Episcopal Church, Held in the City of New York, from May 3d to May 20th* (Philadelphia: Wm.

S. Young, 1852); Wright, *The Encyclopedia of the African Methodist Episcopal Church*, 451.

62. John Bartlett Meserve, "Chief Allen Wright," *Chronicles of Oklahoma* 19, no. 4 (December 1941): 317.

63. Meserve, 314–21.

64. Testimony of Allen Wright, in *Report of Committees of the House of Representatives for the Third Session of the Forty-Second Congress, 1872–1873*, 563–65.

65. James F. A. Sisson, "Word from Indian Territory," *Christian Recorder*, July 22, 1877 (quoted); James F. A. Sisson, "Our Work," *Christian Recorder*, February 12, 1874.

66. Krauthamer, *Black Slaves, Indian Masters*, 114.

67. Testimony of Allen Wright, *Report of Committees of the House of Representatives for the Third Session of the Forty-Second Congress, 1872–1873*, 563–65.

68. During the 1870s, Arkansas Annual Conference meetings typically took place in November. See Jenifer, *The First Decade of African Methodism in Arkansas and in the Indian Territory*, 1–14.

69. Jenifer, *Centennial Retrospect History*, 102; Lonnie Johnson, pers. comm., June 16, 2015; Wadkins, "Brief Sketch of Bethel A.M.E. Church," 64.

70. This land included the Cherokee Outlet from the Cherokee, on which the Cherokee permitted the federal government to place other tribes. This land also included the Leased District from the Choctaw and Chickasaw, and significant portions of land from the Creek and Seminole. William D. Pennington, "Reconstruction Treaties," *EOHC*, accessed May 21, 2021.

71. Arrell Morgan Gibson, *Oklahoma, a History of Five Centuries*, 2nd ed. (Norman: University of Oklahoma Press, 1981), 143; Jimmie Lewis Franklin, *Blacks in Oklahoma* (Norman: University of Oklahoma Press, 1980), 4–6; *Journal of the Twenty-First Quadrennial Session of the General Conference of the African M. E. Church, Held in the Auditorium, Columbus, Ohio, May 7–25, 1900* (Philadelphia: Book Concern of the AME Church, 1900), historical table.

72. *The Fifteenth Quadrennial Session of the General Conference of the African Methodist Episcopal Church*, 44–45.

73. Lonnie Johnson, pers. comm., June 16, 2015; Wadkins, "Brief Sketch of Bethel A.M.E. Church," 64.

74. *Minutes of the Ninth Session of the Arkansas Annual Conference*, 21.

75. James F. A. Sisson, "Word from Indian Territory," *Christian Recorder*, July 12, 1877.

76. John T. Jenifer, "African Methodism on 'The Little Rock,'" *Christian Recorder*, January 24, 1878.

77. "Brevities," *Christian Recorder*, March 7, 1878.

78. Those churches not mentioned were located in places that I cannot identify.

79. A. T. Gillett, "Word from the Indian Territory," *Christian Recorder*, August 22, 1878; *Minutes of the Eleventh Session of the Arkansas Annual Conference of the African Methodist Episcopal Church, Held at Bethel Church, Little Rock, Arkansas, March 10,*

1879 (Atlanta: Jas. P. Harrison, 1879), 21, statistical table, Joseph F. Murrow Collection, folder 10, box 3, Oklahoma Historical Society Research Center.

80. This might have been the same Red River Mission cited elsewhere as part of the Choctaw Nation or a different site altogether.

81. James F. A. Sisson, "Notes from the Indian Territory," *Christian Recorder*, November 1, 1877; John T. Jenifer, "African Methodism on 'The Little Rock,'" *Christian Recorder*, January 24, 1878; A. T. Gillett, "Word from the Indian Territory," *Christian Recorder*, August 22, 1878; James F. A. Sisson, "The Indian Conference," *Christian Recorder*, January 6, 1881; James F. A. Sisson, "At Home," *Christian Recorder*, November 17, 1881.

82. *Minutes of the Eleventh Session of the Arkansas Annual Conference*, 13.

83. Smith, *A History of the African Methodist Episcopal Church*, 32, 194.

84. Wadkins, "Brief Sketch of Bethel A.M.E. Church," 64; Jenifer, *Centennial Retrospect History*, 103.

85. Jenifer, *The First Decade of African Methodism in Arkansas and in the Indian Territory*, 15; Jenifer, *Centennial Retrospect History*, 103; "Charley Chapman," *Enrollment Cards for the Five Civilized Tribes*; "Nelson Johnson," *Native American Applications for Enrollment*; "Isaac Kemp," *Native American Applications for Enrollment*; "Watson Brown," *Native American Applications for Enrollment*.

86. Jenifer, *Centennial Retrospect History*, 103–4.

87. Jenifer, 103–4.

88. Jenifer, 104.

89. Jenifer, 104.

90. Jenifer, *The First Decade of African Methodism in Arkansas and in the Indian Territory*, 17.

Chapter 5. "Blazing Out the Way"

1. James F. A. Sisson, "Word from Indian Territory," *Christian Recorder*, July 12, 1877.

2. *Minutes of the Ninth Session of the Arkansas Annual Conference*, 21, 26.

3. Zellar, *African Creeks*, 26–32.

4. Kent Carter, *The Dawes Commission and the Allotment of the Five Civilized Tribes, 1893–1914* (Orem, UT: Ancestry.com, 1999), 53; Zellar, *African Creeks*, 43, 95, 100–101, 109; "Peter Stidham," *Enrollment Cards for the Five Civilized Tribes*; "James Ross," *Native American Applications for Enrollment*; "Peter Stidham," *US Find a Grave Index, 1600s–Current*.

5. "Peter Stidham," *Enrollment Cards for the Five Civilized Tribes*; "James Ross," *Native American Applications for Enrollment*; "Peter Stidham," *US Find a Grave Index, 1600s–Current*; *Minutes of the Ninth Session of the Arkansas Annual Conference*, 6; *Minutes of the Eleventh Session of the Arkansas Annual Conference*, 20.

6. A. T. Gillett, "A Word from the Indian Territory," *Christian Recorder*, August 22, 1878.

7. Baker and Baker, *The WPA Oklahoma Slave Narratives*, 84; Zellar, *African Creeks*, 168.

8. Zellar, *African Creeks*, 168.

9. Zellar, 164 (quoted), 163–64, 167–69.

10. *Minutes of the Fifth Session of the Indian Mission Annual Conference*, 4; "Peter Stidham," *Enrollment Cards for the Five Civilized Tribes*; "James Ross," *Native American Applications for Enrollment*; "Peter Stidham," *US Find a Grave Index, 1600s–Current*.

11. For a detailed treatment of this family, see Saunt, *Black, White, and Indian*.

12. Zellar, *African Creeks*, 41–77.

13. Zellar, *African Creeks*, 97–99, 219; "Victoria Sherman," *Dawes Packets* (database), Fold3, dataset uploaded 2008, https://www.fold3.com/; "George Johnson," *Dawes Packets*. I discovered the following documents in the database *Oklahoma, Historical Indian Archives Index, 1856–1933* (Ancestry.com, dataset uploaded 2014, https://www.ancestry.com), and then I received the full documents from the Oklahoma Historical Society in Oklahoma City: *Pay Roll . . . Members, Nat'l Council, Oct Term '77*, document 32,563; *Pay Roll, House of Warriors, October 18, 1887*, document 32,920; *North Fork Colored Town, September 6, 1887*, document 32,901; *An Act, December 5, 1901*, document 33,900.

14. During the Green Peach War, Grayson supported the Loyal Party against Samuel Checote. He and at least a dozen others were charged with treason and whipped. Zellar, *African Creeks*, 139–42; *Report of the Secretary of the Interior*, vol. 2 (Washington, DC: Government Printing Office, 1883), 685–86.

15. "Alice Watson," *Native American Applications for Enrollment*.

16. *Minutes of the Eleventh Session of the Arkansas Annual Conference*, 20–21; Jenifer, *Centennial Retrospect History*, 103–4.

17. Jenifer, *Centennial Retrospect History*, 103–4; Zellar, *African Creeks*, 167; C. N. Hopkins, *Christian Recorder*, March 5, 1885; *Minutes of the Fourth Session of the Indian Mission Annual Conference*, 25; *Minutes of the Fifth Session of the Indian Mission Annual Conference*, 16–18, 30.

18. Zellar, *African Creeks*, 97–98; "Victoria Sherman," *Dawes Packets*; "George Johnson," *Dawes Packets*; "Ardine Vann," *Dawes Packets*.

19. *Minutes of the Fourth Session of the Indian Mission Annual Conference*, 10 (quoted), 6–15.

20. C. N. Hopkins, *Christian Recorder*, March 5, 1885.

21. "Johnson Lee," *Enrollment Cards for the Five Civilized Tribes*; "Richard Carr" (Township 13, Creek Nation, Indian Territory), *1900 US Federal Census*.

22. *Creek Schools Neighborhood, October 1, 1885*, document 38,167, Oklahoma Historical Society, Oklahoma City. I discovered this document in the database *Oklahoma, Historical Indian Archives Index, 1856–1933* on Ancestry.com and then received the full document from the historical society.

23. "John A. Broadnax" (Great Bend, Barton, KS), *1930 US Federal Census*; "A.F. & A Masons," *Oklahoma Times Journal*, January 5, 1894; *Springfield Missouri Republi-*

can, November 15, 1908; John A. Broadnax, *Christian Recorder*, April 26, 1894; John A. Broadnax, "Letter from the Creek Nation," *Christian Recorder*, March 20, 1884; "Church News," *Christian Recorder*, January 8, 1885.

24. C. N. Hopkins, "The Indian Mission," *Christian Recorder*, March 5, 1885.

25. Zellar, *African Creeks*, 45–46, 99, 170.

26. Ellen N. Rentie, "A Pleasant Evening," *Indian Journal*, March 12, 1885.

27. "Muskogee Announces Her Local Committees," *Nashville Globe*, May 2, 1913.

28. *Indian Journal*, July 16, 1885.

29. C. N. Hopkins, "The Indian Mission," *Christian Recorder*, March 5, 1885; *Cherokee Advocate*, February 5, 1886; *Cherokee Advocate*, March 6, 1886.

30. Zellar, *African Creeks*, 167.

31. "Isaac Kemp," *Dawes Packets*; Jenifer, *The First Decade of African Methodism in Arkansas and in the Indian Territory*, 15; "Nelson Johnson," *Native American Applications for Enrollment*; "Watson Brown," *Native American Applications for Enrollment*; "Charley Chapman," *Enrollment Cards for the Five Civilized Tribes*.

32. George Duffin periodically worked with the Methodist Episcopal Church (MEC), but he identified himself as an African Methodist; see "Appointments of the Kansas Conference," *Atchison Daily Champion*, March 17, 1881; "Ministers in Council," *Topeka Daily Capital*, March 11, 1882; "Second Day," *Fort Scott Daily Monitor*, March 9, 1888. See also "George B. Duffin," *Native American Applications for Enrollment*; "Sarah Moss," *Native American Applications for Enrollment*; "List of Appointments of South Kansas M.E. Conference," *Leavenworth Weekly Times*, March 26, 1874; "Emancipation Celebration," *Chetopa Advance*, July 29, 1880; *Coffeyville Daily Journal*, October 14, 1902; *Minutes of the Fifth Session of the Indian Mission Annual Conference*, 19; "Fanny Evans," *Native American Applications for Enrollment*; "Fannie Evans," *Oklahoma and Indian Territory, United States, Land Allotment Jackets for Five Civilized Tribes, 1884–1934* (database; hereafter *Land Allotment Jackets*), Ancestry.com, dataset uploaded 2014, https://www.ancestry.com; "Malinda Evans," *Native American Applications for Enrollment*; "William Evans," *Native American Applications for Enrollment*; "Mary Walker," *Native American Applications for Enrollment*; "Malinda Evans," *Enrollment Cards for the Five Civilized Tribes*; "Henry Harlin," *Native American Applications for Enrollment*; *Minutes of the Fourth Session of the Indian Mission Annual Conference*, 1–14; *Minutes of the Fifth Session of the Indian Mission Annual Conference*, 17, 30.

33. "Lacey Barrows," *Native American Applications for Enrollment*.

34. "Watson Brown" (Township 2, Choctaw Nation, Indian Territory), *1900 US Federal Census*; "Watson Brown," *Native American Applications for Enrollment*; *Minutes of the Eleventh Session of the Arkansas Annual Conference*, 15; Jenifer, *The First Decade of African Methodism in Arkansas and in the Indian Territory*, 15.

35. "Henry Harlin," *Native American Applications for Enrollment*.

36. E. Malcolm Argyle, "Multum in Parvo in Oklahoma," *Christian Recorder*, March 2, 1893; J. A. Broadnax, *Christian Recorder*, April 26, 1894; "A.F. & A Masons," *Oklahoma Times Journal*, January 5, 1894; "Rev John A Broadnax," "Pittsburg, KS,

City Directory, 1914," *US City Directories, 1822–1995*; "Grand Master at a Local Colored Masonic Meeting," *Leavenworth Times*, April 27, 1921; "Rev John A Broadnax," "Omaha, NE, City Directory, 1918," *US City Directories, 1822–1995*; "Rev John A Broadnax," "Marysville, Yuba City, CA, 1936," *US City Directories, 1822–1995*; "Rev John A Broadnax," *California, United States, Death Index, 1905–1939* (database), Ancestry.com, dataset uploaded 2013, https://www.ancestry.com.

37. Chang, *The Color of the Land*, 152.

38. Intermarriage between Black Indians and African Americans also raised legal questions about citizenship and property rights. See Fay A. Yarbrough, *Race and the Cherokee Nation: Sovereignty in the Nineteenth Century* (Philadelphia: University of Pennsylvania Press, 2008), 74–92, 93–111.

39. "Church News," *Christian Recorder*, March 15, 1877; "Dennis Barrows" (Poteau, Le Flore, OK), *1920 US Federal Census*; *Minutes of the Ninth Session of the Arkansas Annual Conference*, 2, 5, 21; James F. A. Sisson, "A Word from the Indian Territory," *Christian Recorder*, October 25, 1877.

40. James F. A. Sisson, "A Word from the Indian Territory," *Christian Recorder*, October 25, 1877 (quoted); Brad Agnew, "Cherokee Male and Female Seminaries," *EOHC*, accessed October 8, 2015; *Cherokee Advocate*, January 1, 1878.

41. "Annie Barrows," *Enrollment Cards for the Five Civilized Tribes*; "Lacey (Barrows) Cahill," *Enrollment Cards for the Five Civilized Tribes*; "Lacey Barrows," *Native American Applications for Enrollment*; "Mrs. Alice Barrows Is Dead at Age of 73," *Suburbanite Economist*, October 22, 1941; "Mildred (Barrows) Johnson," *US Social Security Applications and Claims Index, 1936–2007* (database), Ancestry.com, dataset uploaded 2015, https://www.ancestry.com; *Minutes of the Fourth Session of the Indian Mission Annual Conference*, 3, 12, 25; *Minutes of the Fifth Session of the Indian Mission Annual Conference*, 25; *The Miscellaneous Documents of the Senate of the United States for the Third Session of the Fifty-Third Congress, 1894–1895*, vol. 1, no. 24 (Washington, DC: Government Printing Office, 1895), 15–23.

42. "Jacob Young" (Fort Gibson, Cherokee Nation, Indian Territory), *1900 US Federal Census*; "Jacob Young (Jr.)," *Native American Applications for Enrollment*; "Polly Young," *Native American Applications for Enrollment*; "Peggy Young," *Enrollment Cards for the Five Civilized Tribes*; "Jacob Young," *US Burial Registers, Military Posts and National Cemeteries, 1862–1960* (database), Ancestry.com, dataset uploaded 2012, https://www.ancestry.com; J. A. Broadnax, "Muskogee District," *Christian Recorder*, November 5, 1891; Debra J. Sheffer, *The Buffalo Soldiers: Their Epic Story and Major Campaigns* (Denver, CO: Praeger, 2015), 39–40.

43. R. R. Wright Jr., comp., *Who's Who in the General Conference* (Philadelphia: Book Concern of the AME Church, 1912), 94–95; "James F. Morris" (McAlester Ward 2, Pittsburg, OK), *1910 US Federal Census*; "James F. Morris" (Chickasha, Grady, OK), *1930 US Federal Census*; "James F. Morris" (Tulsa, OK), *1940 US Federal Census* (database), Ancestry.com, dataset uploaded 2012, https://www.ancestry.com; "Francis A. Morris" (McAlester Ward 2, Pittsburg, OK), *1910 US Federal*

Census; "Frances Morris," *Oklahoma and Indian Territory, United States, Dawes Census Cards for Five Civilized Tribes, 1898–1914* (database), Ancestry.com, dataset uploaded 2014, https://www.ancestry.com; "James Morris," *Native American Applications for Enrollment*; "Want Act Permitting Enrollment of Children," *Guthrie Daily Leader*, May 25, 1905; *Report of the Select Committee to Investigate Matters Connected with Affairs in the Indian Territory*, vol. 1 (Washington, DC: Government Printing Office, 1907), 962–65.

44. *Flipper-Key-Davis University Annual Catalog*, 17–18; Wright, *The Encyclopedia of the African Methodist Episcopal Church*, 102; "Appointments of the Arkansas Conference," *Christian Recorder*, December 22, 1881; *New York Daily Tribune*, October 9, 1897; *Proceedings of the Twenty-Eighth Session of the Indian Mission Annual Conference*, 7; James F. A. Sisson, "From the Indian Territory," *Christian Recorder*, August 9, 1883; *Indian Journal*, June 28, 1883; *Minutes of the Fifth Session of the Indian Mission Annual Conference*, 16; "Personal," *Christian Recorder*, September 2, 1886; "Personal," *Christian Recorder*, September 29, 1887; *Christian Recorder*, November 18, 1897; Smith, *A History of the African Methodist Episcopal Church*, 216; "GAL Dykes" (Campbell, Lawrence, AR), *1940 US Federal Census*.

45. The AME Church founded this school in 1870. In the 1880s, the denomination moved the school to Columbia, South Carolina, and renamed it Allen University. F. Erik Brooks and Glenn L. Starks, *Historically Black Colleges and Universities: An Encyclopedia* (Denver, CO: Greenwood, 2011), 53.

46. "An Ecclesiastical Magnet," *Freeman* (Indianapolis, IN), November 7, 1891; "A Loan Association," *New York Freeman*, April 24, 1886; "Arkansas," *Christian Recorder*, February 26, 1891.

47. *Christian Recorder*, June 10, 1880; A. J. Miller, "The Indian Mission Conference," *Christian Recorder*, December 15, 1881; "An Ecclesiastical Magnet," *Freeman* (Indianapolis, IN), November 7, 1891; J. F. Dyson, "Indian Mission Conference," *Christian Recorder*, December 7, 1882.

48. Zellar, *African Creeks*, 118–23.

49. "Personal," *Christian Recorder*, May 18, 1882.

50. A. J. Miller, "The Indian Territory," *Christian Recorder*, July 26, 1883.

51. *Proceedings of the Twenty-Eighth Session of the Indian Mission Annual Conference*, 8–9; *Proceedings of the Eleventh Annual Session of the Oklahoma Annual Conference of the African Methodist Episcopal Church, Held in Bethel AME Church, Elreno, Okla., Oct. 31st to Nov. 5th, 1906* (Nashville: AME Sunday School Union, 1906), 3.

52. "Milton W. Austin" (Fort Gibson Ward 2, Muskogee, OK), *1910 US Federal Census*; "James E. Toombs" (Oklahoma City, OK), *1930 US Federal Census*; "Addie R. Toombs" (Oklahoma City, OK), *1930 US Federal Census*; *Proceedings of the Twenty-Eighth Session of the Indian Mission Annual Conference*, 8–9, 54.

53. Theophilus Gould Steward, *Fifty Years in the Gospel Ministry* (Philadelphia: Book Concern of the AME Church, 1921), 70.

54. William F. Reed, *The Descendants of Thomas Durfee of Portsmouth, R.I.*, vol. 1 (Washington, DC: Gibson Bros., 1902), 82–83; "With Sorrow," *Christian Recorder*,

April 5, 1888; *1860 Massachusetts Census, Bristol County, 2nd WD New Bedford* (dataset), *HeritageQuest Online*; *1880 Massachusetts Census, Middlesex County, 2nd WD Newton* (dataset), *HeritageQuest Online*; *1900 Massachusetts Census, Suffolk County, 22nd WD Boston* (dataset), *HeritageQuest Online*.

55. "Letter from Hannibal," *Christian Recorder*, March 16, 1867.

56. Steward, *Fifty Years in the Gospel Ministry*, 70; Smith, *A History of the African Methodist Episcopal Church*, 51–65; "Convention of the AME Church in Eastern Virginia," *Christian Recorder*, January 14, 1865; James F. A. Sisson, "Letter from Portsmouth, VA," *Christian Recorder*, September 3, 1864; "49th Session of the Baltimore Annual Conference of the African Methodist Episcopal Church," *Christian Recorder*, May 5, 1866; James F. A. Sisson, "Correction of a 'Recorder' Statement," *Christian Recorder*, April 7, 1887.

57. In 1844, the Methodist Episcopal Church split over the issue of slavery. It became two separate organizations, the Methodist Episcopal Church and the Methodist Episcopal Church, South. The denomination reunified in 1939.

58. Hildebrand, *The Times Were Strange and Stirring*, 3–27, 75–100; Clarence E. Walker, *A Rock in a Weary Land: The African Methodist Episcopal Church during the Civil War and Reconstruction* (Baton Rouge: Louisiana State University Press, 1982); William B. Gravely, *Gilbert Haven: Methodist Abolitionist* (New York: Abingdon Press, 1973), 194–99.

59. Steward, *Fifty Years in the Gospel Ministry*, 70.

60. Levi Jenkins Coppin, *Unwritten History* (Philadelphia: Book Concern of the AME Church, 1919), 144, 145.

61. Coppin, 145, 146.

62. "Brutal Treatment of the Agent of the A.M.E.P.H. and F.M.S.," *Christian Recorder*, July 14, 1866.

63. "Brutal Treatment of the Agent of the A.M.E.P.H. and F.M.S."; Coppin, *Unwritten History*, 146–47.

64. "Brutal Treatment of the Agent of the A.M.E.P.H. and F.M.S." (quoted); Eric Foner, *Reconstruction: America's Unfinished Revolution* (New York: Perennial Classics, 2002), 119–23; Sarah Bullard, ed., *The Ku Klux Klan: A History of Racism and Violence*, 5th ed., (Montgomery, AL: Southern Poverty Law Center, 1997), 6–15; Walker, *A Rock in a Weary Land*, 67–68.

65. "Convention of the AME Church in Eastern Virginia," *Christian Recorder*, January 14, 1865; James F. A. Sisson, "Letter from Portsmouth, VA," *Christian Recorder*, September 3, 1864; Smith, *A History of the African Methodist Episcopal Church*, 51–65; "49th Session of the Baltimore Annual Conference of the African Methodist Episcopal Church," *Christian Recorder*, May 5, 1866; James F. A. Sisson, "Correction of a 'Recorder' Statement," *Christian Recorder*, April 7, 1887.

66. Samuel Bennet, "Letter from Harrisburg," *Christian Recorder*, February 10, 1866.

67. Enoch Gilchrist, "From Williamsport, PENNA.," *Christian Recorder*, March 3, 1866.

68. *US Freedman's Bank Records, 1865–1871* (database), Ancestry.com, dataset uploaded 2005, https://www.ancestry.com; Jessie Carney Smith, ed., *Encyclopedia of African American Business*, vol. 1 (Westport, CT: Greenwood Press, 2006), 41–44.

69. John T. Simon, ed., *The Papers of Ulysses S. Grant*, vol. 23, *February 1–December 31, 1872* (Carbondale: Southern Illinois University Press, 2000), 408 (quoted), 408–9.

70. Jenifer, *Centennial Retrospect History*, 103 (quoted); "Synopsis of Proceedings of the Arkansas Conference," *Christian Recorder*, December 7, 1872; "Appointments of the Arkansas Conference," *Christian Recorder*, December 14, 1872; Wright, *The Centennial Encyclopedia*, 10; *The Fifteenth Quadrennial Session of the General Conference of the African Methodist Episcopal Church*, 81; Jenifer, *The First Decade of African Methodism in Arkansas and in the Indian Territory*, 8.

71. A. T. Gillett, "Word from the Indian Territory," *Christian Recorder*, August 22, 1878; Jenifer, *The First Decade of African Methodism in Arkansas and in the Indian Territory*, 17.

72. "Personal," *Christian Recorder*, April 21, 1881.

73. "The Late Baltimore African Conference," *Independent (New York)*, June 12, 1884.

74. "Obituary," *Christian Recorder*, April 5, 1888.

75. "The Mississippi Conference," *Christian Recorder*, December 30, 1886; "Obituary," *Christian Recorder*, April 5, 1888; "With Sorrow," *Christian Recorder*, April 5, 1888.

76. James F. A. Sisson, "At Home," *Christian Recorder*, November 17, 1881.

77. James F. A. Sisson, "The Indian Conference," *Christian Recorder*, January 6, 1881.

78. "Church News," *Christian Recorder*, March 31, 1881.

79. Alice Felts, "Our Missionary to the Indians," *Christian Recorder*, March 25, 1880.

80. James F. A. Sisson, "At Home," *Christian Recorder*, November 17, 1881.

81. Dennis Barrows, "An Apostolic Letter," *Christian Recorder*, April 5, 1877.

82. "Lacey Barrows," *Native American Applications for Enrollment*.

83. "Lacey Barrows."

84. Wright, *The Doctrines and Discipline of the AME Church*, 227–30.

85. J. B. Young, "The Fort Gibson District," *Christian Recorder*, May 20, 1886.

86. *Department of Education, African Methodist Episcopal Church, Twelfth Quadrennial Report* (Waco, TX: n.p., 1932), 77; *Journal of the 19th Session and 18th Quadrennial Session of the General Conference of the African Methodist Episcopal Church, in the World, Held in Bethel Church, Indianapolis, Ind, May 7, 1888* (Philadelphia: James C. Embry, 1888), 148; *Journal of the 20th Session and 19th Quadrennial Session of the General Conference of the African Methodist Episcopal Church, in the World, Held in Bethel Church, Philadelphia, Pennsylvania, May 2, 1892* (Philadelphia: James C. Embry, 1892), 211.

87. "An Ecclesiastical Magnet," *Freeman*, November 7, 1891.

88. "A Few Words from the Indian Territory," *Christian Recorder*, July 15, 1880.

89. "An Ecclesiastical Magnet," *Freeman* (Indianapolis, IN), November 7, 1891; "With Sorrow," *Christian Recorder*, April 5, 1888.

90. "Obituary," *Christian Recorder*, April 5, 1888.

91. J. F. Dixon, "From Atoka, Indian Territory," *Christian Recorder*, June 24, 1880.

Chapter 6. Conferences, Churches, Schools, and Publications

1. J. A. Broadnax, "From the Indian Territory," *Christian Recorder*, September 16, 1886; "Notice," *Christian Recorder*, July 5, 1894; "Sisson Industrial Institute," November 15, 1902, document 38,809, Oklahoma Historical Society, Oklahoma City. I discovered this last document in the database *Oklahoma, Historical Indian Archives Index, 1856–1933* on Ancestry.com and then received the full document from the historical society.

2. A. T. Gillett, "Word from the Indian Territory," *Christian Recorder*, August 22, 1878.

3. Smith, *A History of the African Methodist Episcopal Church*, 135; Dennis Barrows, "Word from the Indian Territory," *Christian Recorder*, September 19, 1878; Wright, *The Centennial Encyclopedia*, 230–31; Stephen Ward Angell, *Bishop Henry McNeal Turner and African-American Religion in the South* (Knoxville: University of Tennessee Press, 1992), 53, 91, 94.

4. Dennis Barrows, "Word from the Indian Territory," *Christian Recorder*, August 30, 1877.

5. A. T. Gillett, "A Word from the Indian Territory," *Christian Recorder*, August 22, 1878.

6. Smith, *A History of the African Methodist Episcopal Church*, 135; Dennis Barrows, "Word from the Indian Territory," *Christian Recorder*, September 19, 1878; Wright, *The Centennial Encyclopedia*, 230–31; Angell, *Bishop Henry McNeal Turner*, 53, 91, and 94.

7. Angell, *Bishop Henry McNeal Turner*, 157; *Journal of the 18th Session and 17th Quadrennial Session of the General Conference of the African Methodist Episcopal Church* (Philadelphia, 1884), 2; A. J. Miller, "A Few Words from the Indian Territory," *Christian Recorder*, July 15, 1880; H. M. Turner to Hiram Price, March 17, 1882, Letters Received, Records of the Bureau of Indian Affairs, Record Group 75, National Archives, Washington, DC; H. M. Turner to Hiram Price, March 25, 1882, Letters Received, Records of the Bureau of Indian Affairs, Record Group 75, National Archives, Washington, DC; *Minutes of the Fifth Session of the Indian Mission Annual Conference*, 21.

8. A. J. Miller, "The Indian Mission Conference," *Christian Recorder*, December 15, 1881.

9. *Minutes of the Fifth Session of the Indian Mission Annual Conference*, 7.

10. A. J. Miller, "The Indian Mission Conference," *Christian Recorder*, December 15, 1881.

11. "The General Conference," *Christian Recorder*, May 27, 1880.

12. Mrs. Alice Felts, "Our Missionaries to the Indians," *Christian Recorder*, March 25, 1880.

13. Wright, *The Centennial Encyclopedia*, 366; Smith, *A History of the African Methodist Episcopal Church*, 343–45; Benjamin W. Arnett, *The Budget* (Xenia, OH: Torchlight, 1881), 9–11.

14. *Minutes of the Eleventh Session of the Arkansas Annual Conference*, statistical table.

15. *Journal of the 18th Session and 17th Quadrennial Session*, financial secretary's report, 74; *Proceedings of the Twenty-Eighth Session of the Indian Mission Annual Conference*, financial table.

16. *Minutes of the Fifth Session of the Indian Mission Annual Conference*, dollar money list; "Isom Flint," *Native American Applications for Enrollment*; "Jane Ward," *Enrollment Cards for the Five Civilized Tribes*; "Eliza Flint," *Oklahoma and Indian Territory, United States, Indian Censuses and Rolls, 1851–1959* (database), Ancestry.com, dataset uploaded 2014, https://www.ancestry.com.

17. Dr. Margaret Joan Cousin, a lifelong African Methodist and the wife of Bishop Philip R. Cousin Sr. (retired), frequently uses this phrase to describe AME meetings.

18. Angell, *Bishop Henry McNeal Turner*, 157; *Journal of the 18th Session and 17th Quadrennial Session*, 2.

19. *Minutes of the Fifth Session of the Indian Mission Annual Conference*, 13.

20. Wright, *The Centennial Encyclopedia*, 305.

21. Dennis C. Dickerson, "African Methodism and Wesleyan Hymnody: Bishop Henry M. Turner in Georgia, 1896–1908," in *A Liberated Past: Explorations in AME Church History* (Nashville: AMEC Sunday School Union, 2003), 53–54.

22. Dickerson, 53–64.

23. *Minutes of the Fourth Session of the Indian Mission Annual Conference*; *Minutes of the Fifth Session of the Indian Mission Annual Conference.*

24. T. M. D. Ward, "On the Road," *Christian Recorder*, December 24, 1891.

25. In 1944, the Women's Parent Mite Missionary Society and the Women's Home and Foreign Missionary Society merged to form the Women's Missionary Society of the AME Church.

26. Evelyn Brooks Higginbotham, *Righteous Discontent: The Women's Movement in the Black Baptist Church, 1880–1920* (Cambridge, MA: Harvard University Press, 1993), 1–18, 155–59.

27. Smith, *A History of the African Methodist Episcopal Church*, 203; "The Indian Mission and Oklahoma Annual Conferences," *Christian Recorder*, December 2, 1897.

28. *Proceedings of the Twenty-Eighth Session of the Indian Mission Annual Conference*, financial tables.

29. C. R. Tucker, "Women's Column," *Christian Recorder*, September 22, 1898.

30. "Local Intelligence," *Pittsburg Dispatch*, July 30, 1859. See chapter 2 for the 1859 event.

31. R. B. Brookins, "Convention," *Christian Recorder*, August 10, 1899.

32. "Frances Walker," *Native American Applications for Enrollment*; "Frances Walker," *Enrollment Cards for the Five Civilized Tribes*; "Smith Elliott Walker," *Enrollment Cards for the Five Civilized Tribes*; "The Indian Mission and Oklahoma Annual Conferences," *Christian Recorder*, December 2, 1897.

33. "Personals," *Christian Recorder*, February 10, 1898.

34. *Twenty-Eighth Session of the Indian Mission Annual Conference*, 28–29, 43–44, 53; "James E. Toombs" (Oklahoma City, OK), *1930 US Federal Census*; "Matthew D. Brookins" (Kingfisher, OK), *1930 US Federal Census*; Wright, *The Centennial Encyclopedia*, "Mrs. M.L. Harding Brookins," 44.

35. *Twenty-Eighth Session of the Indian Mission Annual Conference*, 43 (quoted), 55, financial tables; Berry, *A Century of Missions*, 293; "Annie Osborne" (Township 2, Choctaw Nation, Indian Territory), *1900 US Federal Census*; "Annie Osborne" (Moore, Muskogee, OK), *1930 US Federal Census*; "Vivian W. Osborne," *Enrollment Cards for the Five Civilized Tribes*.

36. The McAlester congregation pooled their funds to erect Turner Chapel, named in honor of Bishop Turner. The members who contributed both money and labor included three trustees: Ellis Jones, Lewis Lyons, and Alfred Eubanks. The contributing members also included six stewards: Thomas Reed, W. M. Porter, W. M. Edwards, Frank Briggs, Richard Wilson, and J. F. Dyson. *Minutes of the Fourth Session of the Indian Mission Annual Conference*, 1–16.

37. W. B. Morrison, "The Saga of Skullyville," *Chronicles of Oklahoma* 16, no. 2 (June 1938): 234–40; G. E. Hartshorne, "Skullyville and Its People in 1889," *Chronicles of Oklahoma* 28, no. 1 (Spring 1950): 85–88; John Wesley Morris, Ghost Towns of Oklahoma (Norman: University of Oklahoma Press, 1978), 177–78.

38. *Minutes of the Fifth Session of the Indian Mission Annual Conference*, 18, 30; "The Fast-Day in the Choctaw Nation," *Christian Recorder*, March 25, 1875; "Thomas Blackwater," *Native American Applications for Enrollment*; "Thomas Blackwater," *US Colored Troops Military Service Records, 1863–1865* (database), Ancestry.com, dataset uploaded 2007, https://www.ancestry.com; "Demus Colbert," *US Find a Grave Index, 1600s–Current*; "Demos Colbert" (Wilson, Atoka, OK), *1910 US Federal Census*; "Nicodemus Colbert," *Enrollment Cards for the Five Civilized Tribes*; "Nicodemus Colbert," *Native American Applications for Enrollment*; "L.A. Burk," interview 5,211, IPPC; "Ben Thompson," *Native American Applications for Enrollment*; "Silla Clark," *Native American Applications for Enrollment*; "Nicodemus Colbert," *Native American Applications for Enrollment*.

39. Lonnie Johnson, pers. comm., June 16, 2015 (quoted); May, "Boggy Depot"; Jenifer, *The First Decade of African Methodism in Arkansas and in the Indian Territory*, 15; *Minutes of the Eleventh Session of the Arkansas Annual Conference*, 15, 21; *Christian Recorder*, June 10, 1880; A. J. Miller, "Oklahoma District Conference," *Christian Recorder*, January 20, 1881; A. E. Hubbard, "Atoka District, Indian," *Christian Recorder*, May 21, 1891.

40. "Joe Flax," interview 7,564, IPPC.

41. "Ruth Anderson," *Enrollment Cards for the Five Civilized Tribes*; "Ruthy Anderson" (Township 2, Choctaw Nation, Indian Territory), *1900 US Federal Census.*

42. "Joe Flax," interview 7,564, IPPC.

43. B. W. Williams, "The Atoka District Conference," *Christian Recorder*, April 4, 1889.

44. Lonnie Johnson, pers. comm., June 16, 2015; Homer Noley, *First White Frost: Native Americans and United Methodism* (Nashville: Abingdon Press, 1991), 37.

45. *Minutes of the Fifth Session of the Indian Mission Annual Conference*, dollar money list; *Twenty-Eighth Session of the Indian Mission Annual Conference*, dollar money list; "Isom Flint," *Native American Applications for Enrollment*; "Jane Ward," *Enrollment Cards for the Five Civilized Tribes*; "Eliza Flint," *Oklahoma and Indian Territory, United States, Indian Censuses and Rolls, 1851–1959*; "Joe Flax," interview 7,564, IPPC.

46. *Minutes of the Ninth Session of the Arkansas Annual Conference*, 21; A. T. Gillett, "Word from the Indian Territory," August 22, 1878; *Indian Journal*, June 21, 1883; *Indian Journal*, June 28, 1883; *Flipper-Key-Davis University Annual Catalog*, 16; "Notes and News of and for the Colored People of Muskogee," *Muskogee Phoenix*, October 27, 1898.

47. Christina Dickerson, "The African Methodist Episcopal Church in the Indian and Oklahoma Territories, 1893–1907," *AME Church Review* 123, no. 406 (2007): 29–31; *Proceedings of the Twenty-Eighth Session of the Indian Mission Annual Conference*, statistical records.

48. "Local News," *Indian Journal*, February 2, 1887.

49. "Alex Sango," *Enrollment Cards for the Five Civilized Tribes*; "Nellie McGee," *Enrollment Cards for the Five Civilized Tribes*; Zellar, *African Creeks*, 106, 237; Anna Eddings, "Opothleyahola," *EOHC*, accessed June 16, 2016; "Booker T. Washington: Royally Received in Muskogee," *Muskogee Cimeter*, November 23, 1905; Booker T. Washington, *The Negro in Business* (Boston: Hertel, Jenkins, 1907), 210–11.

50. "Purely Personal," *Muskogee Phoenix*, June 11, 1896.

51. "A.M.E. Conference," *Muskogee Daily Phoenix*, October 23, 1903.

52. "The Conservator Commended," *Sedalia Weekly Conservator*, August 19, 1904.

53. "Piano Recital," *Muskogee Cimeter*, July 20, 1905.

54. *Muskogee Cimeter*, February 15, 1907.

55. J. A. Broadnax, "Letter from Muskogee," *Christian Recorder*, April 23, 1885; J. W. Edwards, "Indian Mission News," *Christian Recorder*, February 3, 1887; *Muskogee Cimeter*, January 13, 1917.

56. *Minutes of the Fifth Session of the Indian Mission Annual Conference*, 18, 30.

57. Broadnax noted that Bethel-on-the-Point was a two-hour ride from Fort Gibson. Assuming that his horse was walking rather than galloping, Broadnax would have traveled about ten miles in those two hours. That distance would place Bethel-on-the-Point around Muskogee. J. A. Broadnax, "From the Indian Territory," *Christian Recorder*, September 16, 1886; Zellar, *African Creeks*, 83.

58. J. A. Broadnax, "From the Indian Territory," *Christian Recorder*, September 16, 1886.

59. Both terms are problematic as they imply that Indigenous identity depended on blood quantum and/or physical appearance. The term "mixed blood" is equally fraught. See Theda Purdue's disagreement with Claudio Saunt in her book *"Mixed Blood" Indians: Racial Construction in the Early South* (Athens: University of Georgia Press, 2003).

60. J. A. Broadnax, "Muskogee District," *Christian Recorder*, November 5, 1891; J. A. Broadnax, "Oklahoma," *Christian Recorder*, April 26, 1894.

61. Fort Gibson Genealogical and Historical Society, "Fort Gibson (Town)," *EOHC*, accessed June 10, 2016; Brad Agnew, "Fort Gibson (Fort)," *EOHC*, accessed June 10, 2016.

62. Dennis Barrows, "Word from the Indian Territory," *Christian Recorder*, August 30, 1877; James F. A. Sisson, "Word from the Indian Territory," *Christian Recorder*, October 25, 1877.

63. *Minutes of the Ninth Session of the Arkansas Annual Conference*, 21; *Minutes of the Eleventh Session of the Arkansas Annual Conference*, 21.

64. *Minutes of the Fourth Session of the Indian Mission Annual Conference*, 22; "Church News," *Christian Recorder*, June 8, 1882.

65. "An Appeal," *Christian Recorder*, January 25, 1883.

66. "Fort Gibson P.E. District," *Christian Recorder*, March 12, 1891.

67. "Col. Kerens and Freedmen," *Saint Louis Post-Dispatch*, January 8, 1897; "Money for the Cherokee Freedmen," *Evening Herald* (Ottawa, KS), January 22, 1897; "Told in a Few Lines," *Estherville Daily News*, March 11, 1897.

68. E. C. King, *Christian Recorder*, September 9, 1897 (quoted); "Serious Trouble Feared," *Austin Weekly Statesman*, July 1, 1897.

69. Harriet Stewart was born in 1873. She was the daughter of "Parson" Charles W. Stewart, who was born in Alabama around 1823. He was originally called Charles Homer, after his Choctaw master John Homer. In 1833, Homer brought Stewart with him to Indian Territory. Homer later sold Stewart to a white shopkeeper in Doaksville named Charles Stewart. His new name became Charles W. Stewart, after this new master. In 1856, he began holding "religious meetings." Around 1860, Charles Stewart sold him to his final master, a Choctaw named Samuel Folsom. Around 1870, the Presbyterian Church licensed him to preach. He ministered to freedmen throughout the Choctaw Nation. He died in 1896. In 1892, Harriet Stewart and her stepsister attended the Mary Allen Seminary in Crockett, Texas. Stewart became a teacher and later operated her own farm in Hugo, Oklahoma. Robert Elliott Flickinger, *The Choctaw Freedmen and the Story of the Oak Hill Industrial Academy* (Fonda, IA: Journal and Times Press, 1914), 297–98, 743–56.

70. "Notice," *Christian Recorder*, July 5, 1894.

71. "Territory News," *Muskogee Phoenix*, May 28, 1896.

72. Krauthamer, *Black Slaves, Indian Masters*, 140–41.

73. Clara Sue Kidwell, *The Choctaws in Oklahoma: From Tribe to Nation, 1855–1970* (Norman: University of Oklahoma Press, 2007), 143–44; "Views of Green McCurtain," *Talihina News*, July 12, 1894, Green McCurtain Collection, box 20, folder 5, Western History Collections, University of Oklahoma, Norman; "Editorial on Green McCurtain," *Caddo Banner*, February 23, 1894, Green McCurtain Collection, box 20, folder 5, Western History Collections, University of Oklahoma, Norman; P. A. Edwards, *Christian Recorder*, February 11, 1897; "What the Choctaw People Saved by Defeating the 'Court Citizens,' 1904," Green McCurtain Collection, box 27, folder 20, Western History Collections, University of Oklahoma Libraries, Norman.

74. Jon D. May, "Skullyville," *EOHC*, accessed May 24, 2016; *Minutes of the Fifth Session of the Indian Mission Annual Conference*, 30; *Proceedings of the Twenty-Eighth Session of the Indian Mission Annual Conference*, 61.

75. Probably in the early 1900s, Bethel in Atoka was rebuilt on land owned by Judge Joseph G. Ralls and Mrs. Eva A. Ralls. In 1956, the land was formally donated to the trustees of the church with the understanding that they would only use it for church purposes and never sell it. This historic church still exists today, but it ceased to be operational around 2000. Wadkins, "Brief Sketch of Bethel A.M.E. Church," 64; "Warranty Deed," State of Oklahoma, Atoka County, Record Book, book 196, p. 257; Pat Gilliland, "Faithful Fight to Save Atoka AME Church," *News OK*, July 11, 1998.

76. Jenifer, *The First Decade of African Methodism in Arkansas and in the Indian Territory*, 15; Lonnie Johnson, pers. comm., June 16, 2015; *Minutes of the Eleventh Session of the Arkansas Annual Conference*, 15, 21; May, "Boggy Depot"; *Christian Recorder*, June 10, 1880; A. J. Miller, "Oklahoma District Conference," *Christian Recorder*, January 20, 1881; A. E. Hubbard, "Atoka District, Indian," *Christian Recorder*, May 21, 1891; *Proceedings of the Twenty-Eighth Session of the Indian Mission Annual Conference*, 53–65.

77. Chang, *The Color of the Land*, 152.

78. Chang, 152–59; Jenifer, *The First Decade of African Methodism in Arkansas and in the Indian Territory*, 15; Lonnie Johnson, pers. comm., June 16, 2015; *Minutes of the Eleventh Session of the Arkansas Annual Conference*, 15, 21; May, "Boggy Depot"; *Christian Recorder*, June 10, 1880; A. J. Miller, "Oklahoma District Conference," *Christian Recorder*, January 20, 1881; A. E. Hubbard, "Atoka District, Indian," *Christian Recorder*, May 21, 1891; *Proceedings of the Twenty-Eighth Session of the Indian Mission Annual Conference*, 53–65.

79. H. A. Guess was Lonnie Johnson's great-uncle. Guess's sister, Ozora, was Johnson's paternal grandmother.

80. "Augustus Guess" (McLennan, TX), *1880 US Federal Census* (database), Ancestry.com, dataset uploaded 2010, https://www.ancestry.com; "Ozora Guess" (McLennan, TX), *1880 US Federal Census*; "W. E. Guess" (McLennan, TX), *1880 US Federal Census*; "Bettie Guess" (McLennan, TX), *1880 US Federal Census*; "Allen's Day '96," *Christian Recorder*, April 2, 1896; "Henry Augustus Guess," *Oklahoma, United States, County Marriage Records, 1890–1995* (database), Ancestry.com, dataset uploaded 2016, https://www.ancestry.com; "Law Class Graduates," Evening Star (Washington, DC),

May 26, 1903; Proceedings of the *Twenty-Eighth Session of the Indian Mission Annual Conference*, 54.

81. Berry, *A Century of Missions*, 293; *Proceedings of the Twenty-Eighth Session of the Indian Mission Annual Conference*, 54; "Mamie E. Thompson" (McAlester Ward 2, Pittsburg, OK), *1910 US Federal Census*; "Mayme E. Thompson" (Ada Ward 2, Pontotoc, OK), *1920 US Federal Census*.

82. "Virginia Larry" (Hartshorne, Pittsburg, OK), *1920 US Federal Census*; "Robert Larry" (Hartshorne, Pittsburg, OK), *1920 US Federal Census*; "Ozella Slaughter" (Aberdeen, Monroe, MS), *1900 US Federal Census*; "Henry Slaughter" (Aberdeen, Monroe, MS), *1900 US Federal Census*; *Proceedings of the Twenty-Eighth Session of the Indian Mission Annual Conference*, 53–65.

83. "James Osbron," *Native American Applications for Enrollment*; "Ruth Anderson," *Enrollment Cards for the Five Civilized Tribes*; "Ruthy Anderson" (Township 2, Choctaw Nation, Indian Territory), *1900 US Federal Census*; "Sunny Grayson," *Enrollment Cards for the Five Civilized Tribes*; "Rentie Sango," *Enrollment Cards for the Five Civilized Tribes*; "Mollie Sango" (Agency, Muskogee, OK), 1930 US Federal Census.

84. "Joe, Joanna, Melvina, Joy Gould, and Larena Clayton" (Township 2, Choctaw Nation, Indian Territory), *1900 US Federal Census*.

85. *Proceedings of the Twenty-Eighth Session of the Indian Mission Annual Conference*, 63; "Thunie Green" (Township 10, Cherokee Nation, Indian Territory), *1900 US Federal Census*; "Nathan Melton," *Native American Applications for Enrollment*; "William McClure," *Native American Applications for Enrollment*; "Jerry Humphreys," *Native American Applications for Enrollment*; "Hattie Humphreys" (Redland, Sequoyah, OK), *1920 US Federal Census*; "Susan Campbell," *Native American Applications for Enrollment*; "Pearl Legrand" (Township 15, Creek Nation, Indian Territory), 1900 US Federal Census.

86. "James Truelove," *Native American Applications for Enrollment*; "Lizzie Tanner," *Enrollment Cards for the Five Civilized Tribes*.

87. Chang, *The Color of the Land*, 152–59.

88. *Annual Report of the Commissioner of Indian Affairs to the Secretary of the Interior for the Year 1877* (Washington, DC: Government Printing Office, 1877), 111 (quoted); "Schools in the Indian Territory," *Christian Recorder*, September 12, 1878.

89. *Christian Recorder*, June 14, 1877.

90. James F. A. Sisson, "School Examination," *Christian Recorder*, August 29, 1878.

91. *Journal of the 17th Session and the 16th Quadrennial Session*, 167.

92. A. J. Miller to Bishop H. M. Turner, November 22, 1880, document 1,579, Records of the Bureau of Indian Affairs, Record Group 75, National Archives, Washington, DC.

93. C. H. Hopkins, "Another Demand," *Christian Recorder*, May 12, 1881.

94. "Church News," *Christian Recorder*, August 4, 1881.

95. A. J. Miller to Bishop H. M. Turner, November 22, 1880, document 1,579, Records of the Bureau of Indian Affairs, Record Group 75, National Archives, Washington, DC; see also Littlefield, *The Chickasaw Freedmen*, 128–39.

96. J. A. Ball to H. M. Turner, November 20, 1880, Records of the Bureau of Indian Affairs, Record Group 75, National Archives, Washington, DC.

97. H. M. Turner to Carl Schurz, November 29, 1880, Records of the Bureau of Indian Affairs, Record Group 75, National Archives, Washington, DC (quoted); H. M. Turner to Hiram Price, received March 20, 1882, document 5,395, Records of the Bureau of Indian Affairs, Record Group 75, National Archives, Washington, DC; H. M. Turner to Commissioner of Indian Affairs, received July 20, 1881, document 12,553, Records of the Bureau of Indian Affairs, Record Group 75, National Archives, Washington, DC; Littlefield, *The Chickasaw Freedmen*, 128.

98. H. M. Turner to Commissioner of Indian Affairs, received August 3, 1881, document 13,442, Records of the Bureau of Indian Affairs, Record Group 75, National Archives, Washington, DC.

99. H. L. Morehouse to Hiram Price, received September 20, 1881, document 16,776, Records of the Bureau of Indian Affairs, Record Group 75, National Archives, Washington, DC; H. M. Turner to Commissioner of Indian Affairs, received January 3, 1882, document 112, Records of the Bureau of Indian Affairs, Record Group 75, National Archives, Washington, DC.

100. H. M. Turner to Commissioner of Indian Affairs, received January 3, 1882, document 112, Records of the Bureau of Indian Affairs, Record Group 75, National Archives, Washington, DC (quoted); H. M. Turner to Hiram Price, received January 26, 1882, document 1,721, Records of the Bureau of Indian Affairs, Record Group 75, National Archives, Washington, DC; H. M. Turner to Hiram Price, received March 20, 1882, document 5,395, Records of the Bureau of Indian Affairs, Record Group 75, National Archives, Washington, DC.

101. H. M. Turner to Hiram Price, received March 20, 1882, document 5,395, Records of the Bureau of Indian Affairs, Record Group 75, National Archives, Washington, DC.

102. H. M. Turner to Hiram Price, received March 20, 1882.

103. H. M. Turner to Hiram Price, received March 20, 1882; H. M. Turner to Hiram Price, received March 27, 1882, document 5,775, Records of the Bureau of Indian Affairs, Record Group 75, National Archives, Washington, DC.

104. Treasury Department, Second Comptroller's Office, received May 29, 1882, document 9,879, Records of the Bureau of Indian Affairs, Record Group 75, National Archives, Washington, DC.

105. *Minutes of the Fifth Session of the Indian Mission Annual Conference*, 21.

106. H. M. Turner to Hiram Price, received September 19, 1882, document 17,160, Records of the Bureau of Indian Affairs, Record Group 75, National Archives, Washington, DC.

107. "Report of E. Whittlesey on the Indian Territory," Washington, DC, December 15, 1882, in *Fourteenth Annual Report of the Board of Indian Commissioners for the Year 1882* (Washington, DC: Government Printing Office, 1883), 29.

108. "Report of E. Whittlesey on the Indian Territory," 30.

109. *Minutes of the Fifth Session of the Indian Mission Annual Conference*, 26.

110. "From South to West," *Christian Recorder*, August 6, 1891.

111. *Journal of the 20th Session and 19th Quadrennial Session*, 211.

112. "From All Parts of the Compass," *Christian Recorder*, September 21, 1893.

113. "General Communications," *Christian Recorder*, May 7, 1896.

114. *Journal of the 20th Quadrennial Session of the General Conference of the African Methodist Episcopal Church, Held in St. Stephens A.M.E. Church, Wilmington, N.C., May 4th, to 22nd, 1896* (Philadelphia: AME, 1896), 153, "Our Schools, 1896"; "General Church News," *Christian Recorder*, June 10, 1897; "General Church News," *Christian Recorder*, August 19, 1897.

115. James F. A. Sisson, "Education," *Christian Recorder*, September 3, 1885.

116. Smith, *A History of the African Methodist Episcopal Church*, 347–69.

117. James M. Townsend was then the secretary of missions.

118. "Obituary," *Christian Recorder*, April 5, 1888; *Department of Education, African Methodist Episcopal Church, Twelfth Quadrennial Report*, 77; *Journal of the 19th Session and 18th Quadrennial Session*, 148; *Journal of the 20th Session and 19th Quadrennial Session*, 211.

119. *Flipper-Key-Davis University Annual Catalog*, 17–18; Wright, *The Encyclopedia of the African Methodist Episcopal Church*, 102; "Appointments of the Arkansas Conference," *Christian Recorder*, December 22, 1881; *New York Daily Tribune*, October 9, 1897.

120. *Journal of the 20th Quadrennial Session*, "The Quadrennial Address of the Bishops of the A.M.E. Church" (1896), 80.

121. "Sisson Institute, Industrial and Training School, Dawes Commission," March 20, 1899, Oklahoma Historical Society, Oklahoma City; *Flipper-Key-Davis University Annual Catalog*, 17–18.

122. "The Sisson Industrial School," *Christian Work: Illustrated Family Newspaper* 63 (November 1897): 841; see also *Indian Chieftain*, January 26, 1899.

123. "Brevity," *Churchman: An Illustrated Weekly News-Magazine* 79, no. 17 (April 1899): 618.

124. "Sisson Institute, Industrial and Training School, Dawes Commission," March 20, 1899, Oklahoma Historical Society, Oklahoma City.

125. Charles J. Kappler, ed., *Indian Affairs: Laws and Treaties*, vol. 1, *Laws* (Washington: Government Printing Office, 1904), "Acts of Fifty-Fifth Congress—Second Session, 1898," chap. 517.

126. "Sisson Industrial Institute," November 15, 1902, document 38,809, Oklahoma Historical Society, Oklahoma City.

127. For more on the Creek Nation's efforts in education, see Rowan Steineker, "'Fully Equal to That of Any Children': Experimental Creek Education in the Antebellum Era," *History of Education Quarterly* 56, no. 2 (May 2016): 273–300.

128. *Flipper-Key-Davis University Annual Catalog*, 15; Kappler, *Indian Affairs: Laws and Treaties*, vol. 1, "Acts of Fifty-Sixth Congress—Second Session, 1901," chap. 676; Larry O'Dell, "Tullahassee," *EOHC*, accessed February 26, 2016; *Department of Education, African Methodist Episcopal Church, Twelfth Quadrennial Report*, 77.

129. O'Dell, "Tullahassee."

130. Wright, *The Encyclopedia of the African Methodist Episcopal Church*, 87; Wright, *The Centennial Encyclopedia*, 90.

131. *Flipper-Key-Davis University Annual Catalog*, 15.

132. "Notice of Sheriff's Sale," *Boynton Index*, June 11, 1915; *Department of Education, African Methodist Episcopal Church, Twelfth Quadrennial Report*, 77; *Flipper-Key-Davis University Annual Catalog*, 6–58.

133. *Flipper-Key-Davis University Annual Catalog*, 55; "Rosella Grayson," *Native American Applications for Enrollment*; "Robert Grayson," *Land Allotment Jackets*; "Pearlie Murrell," *Native American Applications for Enrollment*; "Fred Murrell," *Enrollment Cards for the Five Civilized Tribes*.

134. *Proceedings of the Twenty-Eighth Session of the Indian Mission Annual Conference*, 53; "Ruth Larry" (Harts Home Ward 2, Pittsburg, OK), *1910 US Federal Census*; O'Dell, "Tullahassee."

135. *Flipper-Key-Davis University Annual Catalog*, 13.

136. Isaiah R. McGee, "The Origin and Historical Development of Prominent Professional Black Choirs" (PhD diss., Florida State University, 2007), 48–49; "Flipp-Key-Davis University Closes Its Most Successful Year," *Black Dispatch* (Oklahoma City), June 11, 1920; Lula Mitchell, "Muskogee, Okla.," *Black Dispatch* (Oklahoma City), March 11, 1921.

137. Wright, *The Encyclopedia of the African Methodist Episcopal Church*, 94.

138. "Flipp-Key-Davis University Closes Its Most Successful Year," *Black Dispatch* (Oklahoma City), June 11, 1920; "Beatrice Rentie," *Native American Applications for Enrollment in Five Civilized Tribes*; "Mozell Lee Rentie," *Enrollment Cards for the Five Civilized Tribes*.

139. "Flipp-Key-Davis University Closes Its Most Successful Year," *Black Dispatch* (Oklahoma City), June 11, 1920.

140. Probably due to financial problems, the school closed in 1935. O'Dell, "Tullahassee."

141. Wright, *The Encyclopedia of the African Methodist Episcopal Church*, 89; *Department of Education, African Methodist Episcopal Church, Twelfth Quadrennial Report*, 77.

142. James P. Pate, "Cherokee Advocate," *EOHC*, accessed December 15, 2020; Linda D. Wilson, "Indian Journal," *EOHC*, accessed December 15, 2020.

143. Wright, *The Centennial Encyclopedia*, 220–21; Foner and Branham, *Lift Every Voice*, 577.

144. James F. A. Sisson, "Word from Indian Territory," *Christian Recorder*, July 12, 1877.

145. James F. A. Sisson, "Notes from the Indian Territory," *Christian Recorder*, November 1, 1877.

146. *Minutes of the Fourth Session of the Indian Mission Annual Conference*, 24; A. T. Gillett, "Word from the Indian Territory," *Christian Recorder*, August 22, 1878.

147. Pate, "Cherokee Advocate."

148. "Methodist Church Services," *Cherokee Advocate*, October 3, 1877.

149. *Cherokee Advocate*, January 1, 1878.

150. Pate, "Cherokee Advocate"; Quintard Taylor, *In Search of the Racial Frontier: African Americans in the American West, 1528–1990* (New York: W. W. Norton, 1998), 118; Andrew Denson, *Demanding the Cherokee Nation: Indian Autonomy and American Culture, 1830–1900* (Lincoln: University of Nebraska Press, 2004), 173.

151. Thomas Burnell Colbert, "Boudinot, Elias Cornelius," *EOHC*, accessed June 20, 2016; see also James W. Parins, *Elias Cornelius Boudinot: A Life on the Cherokee Border* (Lincoln: University of Nebraska Press, 2006).

152. *Cherokee Advocate*, February 5, 1886.

153. Wilson, "Indian Journal."

154. *Indian Journal*, June 26, 1879; see also "Heck Robins," *Enrollment Cards for the Five Civilized Tribes*; "Heck Robins" (Euchee, Creek, OK), *1910 US Federal Census*.

155. *Indian Journal*, November 6, 1879; *Indian Journal*, March 25, 1880; *Indian Journal*, June 30, 1881.

156. *Indian Journal*, November 6, 1879; *Indian Journal*, October 23, 1884; *Indian Journal*, October 30, 1884.

157. *Indian Journal*, April 14, 1881 (quoted). The newspaper misrepresented Bishop Turner as a Senator. He was actually in the Georgia House of Representatives, not the Georgia Senate; *Indian Journal*, June 28, 1883; "A Pleasant Evening," *Indian Journal*, March 12, 1885; *Reports of Committees of the Senate of the United States for the Third Session of the Forty-Fifth Congress, 1878–1879* (Washington, DC: Government Printing Office, 1879), 695–96.

158. *Indian Journal*, October 23, 1884; *Indian Journal*, October 30, 1884.

159. James F. A. Sisson, *Indian Journal*, August 2, 1883.

160. "A New Paper," *Muskogee Phoenix*, July 20, 1893; Jonita Mullins, *Muskogee Phoenix*, "African-American Publishers Served Community," February 8, 2015.

161. *Minutes of the Fourth Session of the Indian Mission Annual Conference*, 3–12; *Minutes of the Fifth Session of the Indian Mission Annual Conference*, 3–16.

162. Other AME historians wrote regionally based histories of the denomination. W. H. Mixon documented AME history in Alabama. I. F. Butts, Wesley J. Gaines, and C. S. Long did the same for Virginia, Georgia, and Florida, respectively.

163. *Christian Recorder*, August 10, 1882; Jenifer, *Centennial Retrospect History*, 103–4; Wright, *The Centennial Encyclopedia*, 10, 129–30.

164. Richard Allen, *The Life, Experience, and Gospel Labours of the Rt. Rev. Richard Allen* (Philadelphia: Martin and Boden, 1833); Thomas W. Henry, *Autobiography of Rev. Thomas W. Henry, of the AME Church* (Baltimore, 1872); Payne, *Recollections of Seventy Years*; Payne, *History of the African Methodist Episcopal Church*.

165. Other books on AME history written by African Methodists include Early, *Life and Labors of Rev. Jordan W. Early*; Handy, *Scraps of African Methodist Episcopal Church History*; Israel L. Butt, *History of African Methodism in Virginia, or Four Decades in the Old Dominion* (Hampton, VA: Hampton University Press, 1908); William H. Heard, *From Slavery to the Bishopric in the AME Church, an Autobiography* (Philadelphia: Book Concern of the AME Church, 1928).

166. Wright, *The Centennial Encyclopedia*, 130.

167. Wright, 129–30; Jenifer, *The First Decade of African Methodism in Arkansas and in the Indian Territory*, 5.

168. *Minutes of the Ninth Session of the Arkansas Annual Conference*, 19–20.

169. J. T. Jenifer, "African Methodism on 'The Little Rock,'" *Christian Recorder*, January 24, 1878.

170. *Minutes of the Eleventh Session of the Arkansas Annual Conference*, 13.

171. Wright, *The Centennial Encyclopedia*, 129–30; Smith, *A History of the African Methodist Episcopal Church*, 137–38; A. W. Wayman, "An Open Letter to Bishop Turner," *Christian Recorder*, December 29, 1881.

172. "Personal," *Christian Recorder*, July 27, 1882.

173. J. T. Jenifer, *Christian Recorder*, January 18, 1883. A copy of this rare book is held at the Boston University Theology Library.

174. Jenifer, *The First Decade of African Methodism in Arkansas and in the Indian Territory*, 14–15 (quoted), 14–18.

175. Jenifer, 18, 19.

Chapter 7. "All the Rights . . . of Citizens"

1. Kent Carter's book *The Dawes Commission and the Allotment of the Five Civilized Tribes* offers the most extensive treatment of the Dawes Commission but makes no mention of the AME Church. Neither Gary Zellar's *African Creeks* nor Celia Naylor's *African Cherokees in Indian Territory* nor Barbara Krauthamer's *Black Slaves, Indian Masters* fully discusses the role of the AME denomination in the fight for Black Indian tribal citizenship.

2. Carter, *The Dawes Commission*, 1; see also Debo, *And Still the Waters Run*.

3. Elizabeth Cooke, ed., *Modern Studies in Property Law*, vol. 4 (Portland: Hart, 2007), 306.

4. Carter, *The Dawes Commission*, 2.

5. Carter, 3 and 5 (quoted), 1–6; Kappler, *Indian Affairs: Laws and Treaties*, vol. 1, "Acts of Fifty-Sixth Congress—Second Session, 1893," chap. 209; *Indian Chieftain*, January 25, 1894.

6. Carter, *The Dawes Commission*, 9–38.

7. Carter, 9–38, 87, 151.

8. Carter, 52–53, 109.

9. Carter, 53, 119.

10. Carter, 41, 64, 99, 122; David A. Chang, "From Indian Territory to White Man's Country: Race, Nation, and the Politics of Land Ownership in Eastern Oklahoma, 1889–1940" (PhD diss., University of Wisconsin-Madison, 2002), 98.

11. Cornelius King, "The Wrongs of the American Indian Cry Out for Justice," *Times* (Philadelphia), February 3, 1901.

12. "Cornelius King," *Georgia, United States, Marriage Records from Select Counties, 1828–1978* (database), Ancestry.com, dataset uploaded 2013, https://www.ancestry

.com; Gregory D. Coleman, *We're Heaven Bound! Portrait of a Black Sacred Drama* (Athens: University of Georgia Press, 1992), 52.

13. There is some discrepancy regarding the location of Cornelius's birth. In a news article from 1905, Cornelius claimed that he was born in Indian Territory. In his application for Eastern Cherokee citizenship and in the 1930 US census, he contended that he was born in Mississippi. Most likely, he was born in Mississippi but spent time in Indian Territory during his youth. "Cornelius King," *US Records Related to Enrollment of Eastern Cherokee by Guion Miller, 1908–1910* (database), Ancestry.com, dataset uploaded 2014, https://www.ancestry.com; "Atlanta Appointee Talks," *Atlanta Constitution*, September 2, 1905; "Cornelius King" (Atlanta, Fulton, GA), *1930 US Federal Census*.

14. Edward R. Carter, *The Black Side: A Partial History of the Business, Religious and Educational Side of the Negro in Atlanta, GA* (Atlanta, 1894), 157–61; Stephen Birmingham, *Certain People: America's Black Elite* (Boston: Little, Brown, 1977), 235; "Cornelius King" (Atlanta, Fulton, GA), *1930 US Federal Census*; "The Wrongs of the American Indian Cry Out for Justice," *Times* (Philadelphia), February 3, 1901.

15. Birmingham, *Certain People*, 235; *Minutes of the Fifth Session of the Indian Mission Annual Conference*, 7; *Christian Recorder*, December 29, 1887; Carter, *The Black Side*, 157–61; M. A. Mason, *Christian Recorder*, July 25, 1889; "The Wrongs of the American Indian Cry Out for Justice," *Times* (Philadelphia), February 3, 1901; "Cornelius King," *Georgia, United States, Marriage Records from Select Counties, 1828–1978*.

16. Carter, *The Black Side*, 157–61; Birmingham, *Certain People*, 235; "Cornelius King" (Atlanta, Fulton, GA), *1930 US Federal Census*; "Rev. R. H. Singleton Warmly Received in Atlanta," *Savannah Tribune*, December 16, 1916; Coleman, *We're Heaven Bound!*, 52; *Big Bethel AME Church 150th Anniversary Book* (n.p.: n.p., [1997]), 7–8.

17. "Atlanta Appointee Talks," *Atlanta Constitution*, September 2, 1905.

18. "The Wrongs of the American Indian Cry Out for Justice," *Times* (Philadelphia), February 3, 1901.

19. Birmingham, *Certain People*, 235; Carter, *The Black Side*, 161; *Evening Star* (Washington, DC), January 16, 1894; "Mr. Cornelius King," *Cleveland Gazette*, January 27, 1894; "Caught a Plum," *Freeman* (Indianapolis, IN), February 10, 1894; "Atlanta Appointee Talks," *Atlanta Constitution*, September 2, 1905; "Bishop Turner's Letter in Behalf of Hoke Smith," *Atlanta Constitution*, September 2, 1905; "Negro Office Holders All Right, Hoke Says," *Atlanta Constitution*, September 6, 1905.

20. Carter, *The Black Side*, 161 (quoted); Birmingham, *Certain People*, 235; "Mr. Cornelius King," *Cleveland Gazette*, January 27, 1894; "Caught a Plum," *Freeman* (Indianapolis, IN), February 10, 1894; "Atlanta Appointee Talks," *Atlanta Constitution*, September 2, 1905; "Bishop Turner's Letter in Behalf of Hoke Smith," *Atlanta Constitution*, September 2, 1905; "Negro Office Holders All Right, Hoke Says," *Atlanta Constitution*, September 6, 1905.

21. "Atlanta Appointee Talks," *Atlanta Constitution*, September 2, 1905.

22. Carter, *The Dawes Commission*, 11.

23. Carter, 11.

24. Carter, 7.

25. "Statement of the Choctaw Freedmen, Setting Forth Their Wrongs, Grievances, Claims, and Wants, August, 1894," in *The Miscellaneous Documents of the Senate of the United States for the Third Session of the Fifty-Third Congress, 1894–1895*, vol. 1, no. 24, p. 15; Carter, *The Dawes Commission*, 7.

26. *Muskogee Phoenix*, April 5, 1894.

27. Carter, *The Dawes Commission*, 2–4; *Indian Chieftain*, January 25, 1894; *Muskogee Phoenix*, April 5, 1894.

28. "The Wrongs of the American Indian Cry Out for Justice," *Times* (Philadelphia), February 3, 1901.

29. "Cornelius King," *US Records Related to Enrollment of Eastern Cherokee by Guion Miller*.

30. "Cornelius King," *Georgia, United States, Death Index, 1919–1998* (database), Ancestry.com, dataset uploaded 2001, https://www.ancestry.com; "Nina C. King," *Georgia, United States, Death Index, 1919–1998*.

31. Birmingham, *Certain People*, 235 (quoted), 236–38; Patrice Shelton Lassiter, *Generations of Black Life in Kennesaw and Marietta, Georgia* (Charleston, SC: Arcadia, 1999), 8, 32–33; Tananarive Due and Patricia Stephens Due, *Freedom in the Family: A Mother-Daughter Memoir of the Fight for Civil Rights* (New York: Ballantine Books, 2003).

32. Carter, *The Dawes Commission*, 33–38.

33. "Lacey (Barrows) Cahill," *Enrollment Cards for the Five Civilized Tribes*; "Lacey Barrows," *Native American Applications for Enrollment*; "Mrs. Alice Barrows Is Dead at Age of 73," *Suburbanite Economist* (Chicago), October 22, 1941; "Mildred (Barrows) Johnson," *US Social Security Applications and Claims Index, 1936–2007*; Wright, *Who's Who in the General Conference*, 94–95; "Want Act Permitting Enrollment of Children," *Guthrie Daily Leader*, May 25, 1905; *Report of the Select Committee to Investigate Matters Connected with Affairs in the Indian Territory*, vol. 1, 962–65; Carter, *The Dawes Commission*, 71.

34. "Statement of the Choctaw Freedmen," 15; "Charles A. Stroud," *Native American Applications for Enrollment*; *Proceedings of the Twenty-Eighth Session of the Indian Mission Annual Conference*, 55; "Lucinda McKinney," *Native American Applications for Enrollment*; "Wesley McKinney," *Native American Applications for Enrollment*; "Wesley McKinney," *Enrollment Cards for the Five Civilized Tribes*.

35. "Statement of the Choctaw Freedmen," 15; Carter, *The Dawes Commission*, 7.

36. "Statement of the Choctaw Freedmen," 16.

37. "Statement of the Choctaw Freedmen," 17.

38. "Statement of the Choctaw Freedmen," 21–22.

39. Jenifer, *The First Decade of African Methodism in Arkansas and in the Indian Territory*, 15; "Statement of the Chickasaw Freedmen, Setting Forth Their Wrongs,

Grievances, Claims, and Wants, 1894," in *The Miscellaneous Documents of the Senate of the United States for the Third Session of the Fifty-Third Congress, 1894–1895*, vol. 1, no. 24, pp. 25–43; "Isaac Kemp," *Native American Applications for Enrollment*; "Isaac Kemp" (Thomas, Johnston, OK), *1910 US Federal Census*.

40. E. Malcolm Argyle, "Multum in Parvo in Oklahoma," *Christian Recorder*, March 2, 1893; J. A. Broadnax, *Christian Recorder*, April 26, 1894.

41. Carter, *The Dawes Commission*, 7, 71.

42. Kappler, *Indian Affairs: Laws and Treaties*, vol. 1, "Acts of Fifty-Fifth Congress, Second Session, 1898," 98. See also Krauthamer, *Black Slaves, Indian Masters*, 147–52.

43. Wright, *Who's Who in the General Conference*, 94–95; "Want Act Permitting Enrollment of Children," *Guthrie Daily Leader*, May 25, 1905; *Report of the Select Committee to Investigate Matters Connected with Affairs in the Indian Territory*, vol. 1, 962–65; Carter, *The Dawes Commission*, 71.

44. "Ethel Pierson," *Native American Applications for Enrollment*; "Wesley McKinney," *Native American Applications for Enrollment*; "Charity Glover," *Native American Applications for Enrollment*; *Proceedings of the Twenty-Eighth Session of the Indian Mission Annual Conference*, 55; Pat Spearman, "Alderson," *EOHC*, accessed January 4, 2016; "Lucinda McKinney," *Native American Applications for Enrollment*.

45. "Prepare to Fight," *Guthrie Daily Leader*, May 25, 1905.

46. *Report of the Select Committee to Investigate Matters Connected with Affairs in the Indian Territory*, vol. 1, 884, 962–65.

47. *Report of the Select Committee*, vol. 1, 963.

48. *Report of the Select Committee*, vol. 1, 964–65 (quoted), 962–65.

49. *Report of the Select Committee*, vol. 1, 966–67.

50. "Lacey Barrows," *Native American Applications for Enrollment* (quoted); "Lacey (Barrows) Cahill," *Enrollment Cards for the Five Civilized Tribes*; "Mrs. Alice Barrows Is Dead at Age of 73," *Suburbanite Economist* (Chicago), October 22, 1941; "Mildred (Barrows) Johnson," *US Social Security Applications and Claims Index, 1936–2007*.

51. He declared that he had already chosen a plot of land and made improvements on it. Charles A. Welch, however, claimed this same land as well as the lands of Annie's brother William on behalf of his son, Maxey Welch. The case went before Tams Bixby, the commissioner of Indian affairs. Bixby decided in favor of the Barrows children in 1906. "Annie Barrows," *Land Allotment Jackets*.

52. "James Wesley Morris," *Native American Applications for Enrollment*.

53. "Susie Love," *Native American Applications for Enrollment*; Albert Alexander Sears, *Christian Recorder*, May 4, 1899.

54. "Susie Love," *Native American Applications for Enrollment*.

55. Several other Black Indians cited Sears's memorandum book for their citizenship cases, some even presenting pages directly from the book. Not all these cases were successful. See "Sarah Jefferson," *Native American Applications for Enrollment*; "William Malvern," *Native American Applications for Enrollment*. See also "Sally (Love) Nash," *Oklahoma and Indian Territory, Indian and Pioneer Historical Collec-*

tion, 1937 (database), Ancestry.com, dataset uploaded 2014, https://www.ancestry.com.

56. "Susie Love," *Native American Applications for Enrollment.*

57. *Proceedings of the Twenty-Eighth Session of the Indian Mission Annual Conference*, 54; "Susie Love," *Land Allotment Jackets.*

58. "Mary Canard," *Native American Applications for Enrollment.*

59. James was Susie Love's half-brother.

60. "Earl Love," *Native American Applications for Enrollment.*

61. "Pink Thompson," *Native American Applications for Enrollment*; *Proceedings of the Twenty-Eighth Session of the Indian Mission Annual Conference*, 60; "Pink Thompson," *Land Allotment Jackets*; "Minerva McChristian," *Native American Applications for Enrollment*; "Mary Gross," *Native American Applications for Enrollment.*

62. Native American Applications for Enrollment, "Pink Thompson."; *Proceedings of the Twenty-Eighth Session of the Indian Mission Annual Conference*, 60; "Pink Thompson," *Land Allotment Jackets*; "Minerva McChristian," *Native American Applications for Enrollment*; "Mary Gross," *Native American Applications for Enrollment*; "Minerva McChristian," *Native American Applications for Enrollment*; "Mary Hall," *Native American Applications for Enrollment.*

63. Charlotte Grayson is the maternal grandmother of Dr. Lonnie Johnson Sr.

64. Letitia Wallace, "Indian Territory," *Christian Recorder*, February 25, 1897; "Letters from the Field," *Christian Recorder*, August 21, 1902; "Charlotte Grayson" (Ash Flat, Coal, OK), *1910 US Federal Census*; "Roosevelt Grayson," *Dawes Packets*; Lonnie Johnson, pers. comm., June 16, 2015.

65. "Morris Battiest," *Native American Applications for Enrollment.*

66. "Ben Brown," *Dawes Packets.*

67. "Simon Keel," *Native American Applications for Enrollment* (quoted); "Robert Keel," *Native American Applications for Enrollment* (quoted); "Annie Keel," *Enrollment Cards for the Five Civilized Tribes*; "Annie Keel," *Land Allotment Jackets*; "Betsie Brown," *Land Allotment Jackets*; "Charley Keel," *Enrollment Cards for the Five Civilized Tribes*; "Simon Keel," *Enrollment Cards for the Five Civilized Tribes*; "William Keel," *Enrollment Cards for the Five Civilized Tribes.*

68. "Simon Keel," *Land Allotment Jackets.*

69. "Robert Keel," *Land Allotment Jackets.*

70. *Report of the Select Committee to Investigate Matters Connected with Affairs in the Indian Territory*, vol. 1, 884, 962–65; Littlefield, *The Chickasaw Freedmen*, 219–24; Debo, *And Still the Waters Run*, 126–58; "Simon Keel" (Wilson, Atoka, OK), *1910 US Federal Census*; "Simon Keel" (Wilson, Atoka, OK), *1930 US Federal Census.*

Index

CHRISTINA DICKERSON-COUSIN is an assistant professor of history at Quinnipiac University.

The University of Illinois Press
is a founding member of the
Association of University Presses.

University of Illinois Press
1325 South Oak Street
Champaign, IL 61820-6903
www.press.uillinois.edu